COLLOQUIAL
ITALIAN

THE COLLOQUIAL SERIES

*Colloquial Albanian
*Colloquial Arabic (Levantine)
*Colloquial Arabic of the Gulf and Saudi Arabia
*Colloquial Arabic of Egypt
*Colloquial Chinese
*Colloquial Czech
 Colloquial Dutch
*Colloquial English
*Colloquial French
 Colloquial German
 Colloquial Greek
*Colloquial Hungarian
*Colloquial Italian
*Colloquial Japanese
*Colloquial Persian
*Colloquial Polish
 Colloquial Portuguese
*Colloquial Romanian
 Colloquial Russian
*Colloquial Serbo-Croat
 Colloquial Spanish
*Colloquial Swedish
 Colloquial Turkish

*Accompanying cassette available

COLLOQUIAL
ITALIAN

Flavio Andreis

London and New York

First published in 1982
by Routledge & Kegan Paul
Reprinted in 1989 and 1991
by Routledge
11 New Fetter Lane, London EC4P 4EE

Published simultaneously in the USA and Canada
by Routledge
a division of Routledge, Chapman and Hall, Inc.
29 West 35th Street, New York, NY 10001

Set in 9/11 pt Times by
Input Typesetting Ltd, London
and printed in Great Britain
By Cox & Wyman Ltd
Reading, Berkshire

Library of Congress Cataloguing in Publication Data

Andreis, Flavio

Colloquial Italian.
(Colloquial series)
1. Italian language–Conversion and phrase books.
2. Italian language–Spoken Italian.   I. Title.
PC1121.A56   458.3'421   81–22747

ISBN 0–415–03946–0 (paperback)   AACR2
ISBN 0–415–03891–X (cassette)
ISBN 0–415–03892–8 (book and cassette course pack)

To Charles C. Russell

CONTENTS

PREFACE

This book is intended for use by anyone who wants to start learning Italian. It is not traditionally structured throughout nor does it always follow standard terminology. Its free treatment of terms and rules may be frowned upon by some grammarians and linguists. Its main purpose is to make Italian simple, clear and easy for the learner, as the author is aware that many who wish to learn a language often have difficulty in finding time in which to do so and prefer their study to be uncluttered by complicated grammatical rules.

Learning a language is much more than knowing how the language works. It means being able to use it, i.e. to understand, to speak, to read and to write it, in a variety of everyday situations. It means being able to build up an interest and a feeling for the language.

It is hoped that, after having completed this book, the student visiting Italy should be able to manage well enough in ordinary situations, such as ordering a meal or arranging accommodation, showing pleasure or expressing dissatisfaction, understanding an opera or reading a notice-board.

Then the student will be in a position to acquire wider and deeper skills, by listening, looking, talking, reading and writing. No one need become a professional pianist in order to enjoy playing the piano. Similarly, the student of Italian should not worry if his or her standard is not that of a native speaker. Being able to communicate and to widen an appreciation of a different culture and a different way of life should in itself prove an enriching experience.

A casette has been produced to accompany this book so that you can hear Italian spoken by native speakers. All material recorded on the cassette is marked by a ■ in the text.

ACKNOWLEDGMENTS

I am indebted to Mr John Martell, an historian with a special interest in the Italian language and culture, for suggestions I greatly valued.

I am also indebted to the publishers of the Milan daily newspaper *Il Corriere della Sera* for permission to quote articles. The article 'Milano celebra la festa di S. Ambrogio. Sandro Pertini alla "Prima" della Scala' was signed by Glauco Licata. The article 'Come si vive nel Mezzogiorno. Chi non fugge si rinchiude nel paese dei fantasmi', of which an extract is quoted, was signed by Adriano Baglivo.

I am grateful to my wife, Tiziana, for the assistance and encouragement she gave during the compilation of the book.

The Publishers would like to thank Ms Caterina Paone for providing the Key to the Exercises.

INTRODUCTION
The Italian Language

The Italian language stems from Latin, just like French or Spanish. Therefore any knowledge of Latin, French, Spanish, or even Portuguese, Catalan, Provençal or Romanian you may have will be useful. There are enormous similarities in structure and vocabulary. But a warning is necessary. Do not carry your trust too far, as they are all different languages.

A language entails a whole set of ideas, customs and grammatical rules. In a word, language and culture are very closely knit. So sharpen your ears and open your eyes. Read – not only books but also papers of all kinds, advertisements, names of shops, and anything written in Italian. Watch films. Talk to Italians. Look at the country and the people. Your awareness of the grammatical structure and of the meanings will be reinforced. Try to say aloud the Italian that you see or hear or read.

Many people think of Italy as a country of the arts, music, opera and the Renaissance. Others add to those the Roman Empire, the Middle Ages, Roman Catholicism, the prosperous and powerful city-states of Florence, Venice and the others, the *Divine Comedy* of Dante, Machiavellian princes who patronized the arts, the discoverers and navigators such as Marco Polo, Christopher Columbus, Amerigo Vespucci and the Cabot brothers, the Risorgimento and Garibaldi, and eventually Mussolini, Fascism and the rebirth of Italy since the Second World War. Perhaps a smaller percentage may think of Italy as a place of scientific and technical achievements, of Galileo, Volta, Galvani, Marconi, Fermi, of some of the longest railway tunnels in the world and of the fastest cars like Ferrari, Maserati, Alfa Romeo and Lamborghini.

Italian is the official language of the Republic of Italy and one of the three official languages of Switzerland. It is the mother tongue or the second language of minorities elsewhere. But various dialects are also spoken in Italy. A large number of Italians still use their local dialect when they speak at home or to local people, while restricting the standard language for use in school or at work and with people from other parts of the country. In this respect Italy is different from Britain or the USA, as a double language standard is to be found with many Italians. This is due to the weaker centralizing influence in Italy, as compared with the well-established political, economic and linguistic standardizing influence of London in Britain or Paris in France. In a way Italy's linguistic development is similar to that of Germany, as both countries were for centuries collections of states, each with a definite local culture and dialect, though recognizing a common language for the whole nation. In Italy more than one city can claim to have some of the prerogatives of a capital city. Rome can claim its ancient and religious importance and, since 1870, its status as the capital city of unified Italy. Florence was the cradle of the Italian language and the main cultural centre in the Middle Ages and the Renaissance. Milan is the leading economic centre. Naples was the capital of a kingdom covering half of Italy for centuries and for a long time the largest city. Turin developed into the capital city of the kingdom which undertook the unification of the country and was also Italy's first capital city. Venice was for centuries the capital of one of the longest established republics in Europe. Trieste was the fourth most important city in the Austro-Hungarian Empire and its maritime and business centre. Palermo was also the capital of an independent kingdom lasting for centuries, and so were various other cities in other parts of Italy. This fact also accounts for the amazing variety of architecture and history of the Italian regions and cities, even though in some cases they are situated very close to each other.

The single most important recent development has been the massive migration of people, particularly from the south and east to the north-west and from the countryside to the towns, due especially to the post-war industrial growth. This has been accompanied by many social changes, easier access to schooling, the spread of literacy standards, the extension of the media and greater affluence, in turn encouraging, together with the mixture of people from various parts of the peninsula, a greater use of the standard language or at least a dilution of the dialects through the introduction of supposedly more refined words, expressions and pronunciation. The final result of this 'melting-pot' is possibly best observed in the larger cities, especially those of the north-west. There is a prevailing northern blend of accents in the media, of which the radio, television and films – particularly dubbed films – are foremost, while the bulk of the language structure and vocabulary remains predominantly Tuscan in origin. The most 'neutral' speakers in the media, then, could be considered the model of standard language to be followed, as they in fact are in Italy, whether consciously or unconsciously.

In spite of the advances of the standard language, you could be sitting at a café in Italy and not be able to recognize the language spoken by the people next to you. Such situations are not rare in Italy, though amazing at times for the eager student. At times speaking dialect is a way of feeling closer to your own community at all levels of society and particularly now that there is a reaction to the decline of dialects and local accents.

The dialects cling more tenaciously in certain areas than in others. This is due to a variety of reasons: the more different the dialect sounds from the standard language, the more frequently people give it up; the stronger the historical importance, the prouder people are of their dialect; the less mixed or less educated people are in an area, the easier it will be to communicate in dialect all the time. The three regions around Venice and those south of Rome are perhaps more conservative in this respect. This means also that local accents are stronger when people speak Italian, because of their habit of speaking most of the time in dialect.

The various dialects should actually be called languages, because such they are, all stemming from Latin and most possessing records and literature of their own. Some examples of this literature, in fact, rival those in the standard language and are normally studied in academic courses, such as the Venetian Goldoni, the Milanese Porta, the Roman Belli and Trilussa and the Neapolitan Pascarella.

There are also places in Italy where dialects and languages having their main centres outside Italy are spoken and officially recognized, such as German in South Tyrol, French in the Valley of Aosta and Slovene in the Trieste and Gorizia areas. Greek, Albanian, Provençal, Croat and Catalan minorities are also to be found.

A large number of English terms of Latin origin naturally possess an equivalent in a language such as Italian. It will give some idea of their number to point out such of these words as have occurred in the previous sentence:

(English)	(Italian)
large	*largo*
number	*nùmero*
term	*tèrmine*
origin	*orìgine*
naturally	*naturalmente*
possess	*possedere*
equivalent	*equivalente*
language	*linguàggio*, *lìngua*
Italian	*italiano*

Fewer similarities would be found in the grammatical structure, though it should be noticed that Italians may have closer familiarity with long words of Latin origin than English speakers, who in fact tend to be more familiar with and actually prefer to use shorter terms, usually of Anglo-Saxon origin, especially in informal situations.

Recognizing a word or even a full expression in writing is not the same, however, as remembering that word or phrase when occasion arises to use it. Repetition, imitation, reading, memorizing are simple and efficacious techniques to master a language, both in its appropriate usage in the proper situation and in its accurate and fluent pronunciation and intonation.

Associations of ideas, comparisons and contrast can be of much help in creating a linguistic habit. Thus the student could notice that most English words ending in '-tion' end in *-zione* in Italian and are feminine, e.g.

collezione	*creazione*	*persecuzione*	*dissoluzione*
registrazione	*azione*	*reazione*	*soluzione*
definizione	*associazione*	*emozione*	*popolazione*
stazione		*perfezione*	*devozione*

The English noun ending in 'ty' is frequently found in Italian as *-tà*. In this case the word stress falls on this final syllable and the word does not change in the plural and is always feminine, e.g.

generosità	*realtà*	*università*	*tranquillità*
novità	*creatività*	*attività*	*avidità*
quantità	*qualità*	*facoltà*	*parità*

Various nouns end in 'ment' or 'ent' in English, with equivalent endings in *-mento* or *-ento* in Italian. These are all masculine:

intento	*fermento*	*ornamento*	*sentimento*
sacramento	*esperimento*	*testamento*	*accento*
appuntamento (appointment)			

Various adjectives and nouns end in 'ant' or 'ent' in English and in *-ante* or *-ente* in Italian, e.g.

presente	*recente*	*emigrante*	*distante*
assente	*precedente*	*importante*	*studente*
presidente			

For those who remember Latin it may be of interest to point out that Italian nouns were formed from the accusative case of the Latin original, that 'l' following another consonant became *i* in Italian, that 'ct' and 'pt' became *tt*, and that doubling resulted from assimilation of two, or contraction of more, originally different letters, e.g.

(Latin)	(Italian)	(English)
florem	*fiore*	flower
plenum	*pieno*	full, replenished
clamare	*chiamare*	to call
clavem	*chiave*	key
oculum	*òcchio*	eye
factum	*fatto*	fact
acceptare	*accettare*	to accept
activitatem	*attività*	activity
civitatem	*città*	city

Italians are often described to be willing gesticulators. In fact, gestures, though not a part of speech, are very important in communication – and in misunderstanding! The student of this book should not overlook them, but try to interpret them correctly and avoid imitating them or producing one's own unless he or she is perfectly sure of not being misunderstood or misjudged. It is beyond the scope of this book to deal with gestures, but the author refers the student to specialist publications on the subject.

Before examining pronunciation in more detail, a few remarks should perhaps be made on the Italian way of speaking, i.e. the actual organs of speech and the muscles of the face. The English jaw is more drooping, while the facial and tongue muscles are more relaxed, whereas the English throat muscles are more constricted, with the tip of the tongue usually held, in repose, in the middle of the mouth, in roughly the sound of 'er'. The facial muscles of the Italians are more tense, whereas their throat muscles are relaxed. The jaw is held firmly closed and the tongue in repose is raised somewhat in the front of the mouth. Thus, while the English speakers would tend to precede an initial vowel sound with a 'catch in the throat', or, when hesitating, to say 'er . . . er', Italians would tend to say *eh . . . eh* (open *e*).

Italian sounds are usually well rounded and frontal, with neatly pronounced syllables, one carrying the stress, though not so markedly as in English, and the others being unstressed, but not so weakened or indistinct as they might be in English. Just take the English word 'preferable' and the Italian one *preferíbile*. In the former the syllable 'pre' is very heavily stressed while the rest is rather jammed together. The latter word has a word stress on *ri*, but the other syllables are clearly pronounced. This feature of Italian accounts for the predictability of Italian spelling, once you know a few easy rules, in contrast with the unpredictability of English, and also for the preference amongst Italians for dividing words into syllables, i.e. *pre-fe-ri-bi-le*, rather than spelling them. Syllables end in a vowel, or in a consonant, when two or doubles are found, e.g. *for-te* (strong), *bel-lo* (beautiful). But *s* remains attached to the following consonant: *re-spi-ra-re* (to breathe).

Some have observed that Italians are not such quick speakers as the English, because their words are often longer and need clear pronunciation throughout. Stressing the syllable division of a word is also used as a way of emphasis, demanding attention and confirmation, driving something in, or as a rhetorical device of orators. The result can be unpleasantly monotonous, as was the case with notorious demagogues of the recent past.

The pitch and quality of the voice may vary remarkably according to the various regions of Italy. Other regional features concern the tendency to disregard double consonants and the z sounds in northern Italy. Conversely, double consonants tend to overflow in southern Italy.

It is interesting to note that almost all Italian words end in the vowels *a*, *o*, *e*, *i*. Very few words end in consonants, though endings in *l*, *n* and *r* are not uncommon. In poetical texts, consonant endings in *l*, *n* and *r*, resulting from the omission of the final vowels or syllables, are frequent.

What shall one do and where shall one go in order to carry on the study of Italian? As mentioned before, cities possess a wider proportion of accurate speakers. Educated people are often preferable. Radio and television, especially news and commentaries, are best for accuracy. So usually are films and theatrical performances of a non-local type.

Italian, like any other language, is a living thing. Therefore, it is not always the same everywhere. It has varied in time. Thus you should not expect to find classical literature easily accessible without training, but you will find it more intelligible than old English, French, German or Spanish literature, because Italian has varied much less and is firmly grounded on the fourteenth-century Tuscan authors, such as Dante, Petrarch and Boccaccio. The language also varies in space and according to the people and the situations. So do not expect to be able to understand or express yourself appropriately in any given situation and style under all circumstances. To be able to master all kinds of varieties of a language takes time, practice and patience.

Although spelling is not as essential in Italian as division into syllables, we might as well start to consider the Italian alphabet, with its twenty-one letters as pronounced in isolation. Then we shall briefly examine how these letters combine in spelling to keep the alphabetical sound or represent new ones.

■ SPELLING AND PRONUNCIATION

The Italian alphabet has twenty-one letters. Some of them have more than one sound, according to their position in a word, or may combine with other letters to represent certain sounds:

(letter)	(pronunciation)	(English example)	(Italian example)
a	*a* /ah/	f*a*ther	*pane* (bread)
b	*bi* /bee/	em*b*ark	*bene* (well)
c	*ci* /tchee/	*ch*est	*cena* (dinner)
d	*di* /dee/	a*d*dict	*dente* (tooth)
e	*e* /eh/	*e*nter	*entrata* (entrance)
f	*effe* /'ef-feh/	*f*ame	*fame* (hunger)
g	*gi* /dgee/	*g*entle	*gentile* (kind)
h	*acca* /'ahk-kah/	*h*our	*ho* (I have)
i	*i* /ee/	mach*i*ne	*cintura* (belt)
l	*elle* /'el-leh/	*l*ate	*latte* (milk)
m	*emme* /'em-meh/	*m*ale	*male* (evil)
n	*enne* /'en-neh/	*n*et	*nato* (born)
o	*o* /aw/	*o*rder	*òrdine* (order)
p	*pi* /pee/	*o*pen	*ponte* (bridge)
q	*cu* /koo/	*q*uick	*quinto* (fifth)
r	*erre* /'er-reh/	B*r*uce (in Scots)	*brutto* (ugly)
s	*esse* /'es-seh/	*s*un	*suono* (sound)
t	*ti* /tee/	a*t*om	*tonno* (tunny fish)
u	*u* /oo/	br*u*te	*bruto* (brute)
v	*vu* /voo/	en*v*y	*voto* (vote)
z	*zeta* /'dzeh-tah/	*z*one, a*dz*e	*zàino* (rucksack)

The following letters also occur in some words:

j	*i lunga* /ee'loongah/	*y*ield	*Jugoslàvia* (Yugoslavia)
k	*kappa* /'kahp-pah/	*k*ey	*Kènia* (Kenya)
y	*ìpsilon* /'eepsilon/	*y*oga	*yoga* (yoga)
w	*vu dòppia* / voo'dop-pyah/	*W*agner	*watt* (watt), *Walter* (Walter)

The letters of the alphabet are usually treated as feminine and do not vary in the plural, e.g.

la s or *la esse* (the s), *le s* or *le esse* (the s's).

Capital letters are called *le lèttere maiùscole*, e.g.

H, *l'acca maiùscola*.

Small letters are *le lettere minùscole*, e.g.

m, *l'emme minùscola* (small m).

Italian spelling, as suggested earlier, is fairly consistent, as sounds have changed little in the history of the language. But not all letters of the alphabet have only one possible sound. At times the sounds are predictable, as they are about the same as they would be in English in the same positions. E.g. *c* is pronounced /k/ as in English, and not /tch/ as in the alphabet, when it is followed by *a, o, u, l, n, r, t*, such as the words *cane* (dog), *corno* (horn), *acuto* (acute), *clero* (clergy), *acme* (acme), *acro* (acre), *tècnico* (technical). Similarly, there is a correspondence of sounds with *g*, as in *gatto* (cat), *gonna* (skirt), *grido* (cry, shout). But if *c* is followed by *e* or *i*, then it is pronounced as in the alphabet, i.e. /tch/. Similarly, *g* followed by *e* or *i* is always pronounced /dg/, e.g. *cena* (dinner), *cielo* (sky, heaven), *gelo* (frost), *giro* (drive, ride, tour).

Some English sounds and clusters of letters are not found in Italian, as is the case with 'th', which occurs in a couple of Italian words, such as *the* /teh/ (tea), and is pronounced /t/; *h* is always soundless in Italian and is only used for spelling reasons in the clusters shown below and in the following other cases: *ho* /aw/ (I have), *hai* /áhi (you have), *ha* /ah/ (he, she, it has), *hanno* /'ahn-no/ (they have), *ah!* (ha, oh!), *ahi!* (ouch!), *ehi!* (hey!), *oh!* (oh!), *eh!* (hey!, I see), *ahimè!* (alas!).

Now notice the pronunciation of the following clusters of letters:

che /keh/, as in '*ch*emistry', e.g. *perchè* (why, because);
chi /keeh/, as in '*chi*mera', e.g. *chiave* (key);
sche /skeh/, as in '*sche*me', e.g. *schema* (scheme, draft);
schi /skee/, as in '*schi*zophrenia', e.g. *schizofrenia*;

as contrasted with:

ce /tcheh/, *ci* /tchee/, *cia* /tchah/, *cio* /tchaw/, *ciu* /tchoo/, as in 'chest', 'chin', 'charge', 'chore', 'atchoo', e.g. *cera* (wax), *cinema* (cinema), *arància* (orange), *bàcio* (kiss), *ciuffo* (forelock, tuft of hair);
ge /dgeh/, *gi* /dgee/, *gia* /dgah/, *gio* /dgaw/, *giu* /dgoo/, as in English 'gentleman', 'giant', 'jungle', 'jaw', 'june', e.g. *gente* (sing.,

people), *gigante* (giant), *giungla* (jungle), *giòvane* (young, youth), *giugno* (june);
sce /sheh/, *sci* /shee/, *scia* /shah/, *scio* /shaw/, *sciu* /shoo/, as in English 'shed', 'sheen', 'shark', 'shawl', 'shoe', e.g. *scena* (scene, stage), *uscita* (exit), *àscia* (axe), *fàscio* (sheaf), *sciupare* (to waste).

Special care should be taken in pronouncing doubled consonants (*le consonanti dòppie*, or *le dòppie*). They are to be said separately with a slight pause in between, or in such a way that the first consonant is not completed but rather lengthened. Doubles of this kind are the following:

bb, *cc*, *dd*, *ff*, *gg*, *ll*, *mm*, *nn*, *pp*, *rr*, *ss*, *tt*, *vv*, *zz*, *cq* (standing for double *q*).

Similar occurrences are to be found in English compound nouns such as: nigh*t*-*t*able, ca*r*-*r*ace, joint-sto*ck*-*c*ompany, pe*n*-*n*ib, etc. In these cases it can be observed that in normal speed speech the final consonant of the first word is not completed but carried on to the next which is completed. Therefore treat Italian nouns with a double consonant as if they were two separate words in a compound noun.

The sound *r* consists in a light trill, that is in brief tapping of the tongue against the upper teeth ridge. It should not be too emphatic, but rather similar to the English r in the words 've*r*y', 'tho*r*ough', 'fa*r* away', 'greate*r* and greater', or like Scots r or Shakespearean or stage r (but possibly not so marked). Some Italians, especially in the north, pronounce r as in French or German. Double *r* is not so easy to say. Besides rolling your tongue a little stronger you should remember the pause. So pronounce the two parts of the word as if they were two separate words.

There are two *z* sounds, one as in the alphabet, /dz/, usually at the beginning of words, and a voiceless one, /tz/.

Double *z* may be found either voiced (/dz/) or voiceless (/tz/). The student should learn word by word, as no rule applies.

There are two sounds for *s*. /s/ at the beginning (and at the end) of words and after and before a consonant, e.g. *sono* (I am), *àutobus* (bus), *basta* (that's enough). /z/ is found between vowels and before *l*, *m* and *n*, e.g. *casa* (house), *slittare* (to sleigh, to slip, to skid), *smòrfia* (grimace), *snello* (slender).

Double *s* always sounds voiceless (/ss/).

Special care must also be taken by English native speakers in pronouncing *t* and *d*. These are dental in Italian, that is they are articulated by pointing the tip of the tongue against the teeth ridge, not against the palate as in English. They never vary in pronunciation and never have any of the various English features, like the explosive quality to be found before a stressed syllable or the peculiar English *tr*, *ture*, *tu*, *ti*-like sounds. Pronounce *t* and *r* separately, and so do with other clusters.

B and *p* also do not have in Italian the explosive quality that they have in English before stressed consonants. Therefore they may sound to the student more similar to each other than in English.

Q is always found followed by *u*, which must be pronounced. Thus *qui*, *qua*, *que*, *quo* are always pronounced /kwee/, /kwah/, /kweh/, /kwaw/.

Similarly, *gui*, *gua*, *gue*, *guo* are always pronounced /gwee/, /gwah/, /gweh/, /gwaw/.

Both consonants of *ps* must be pronounced, e.g. *psicologia* /pseekawlo'dgeea/ (psychology), *psichiatria* /pseekya'treea/ (psychiatry), *psiche* (psyche) /pseekeh/.

The two vowels *e* and *o* can be pronounced either open or closed. It is usually not essential to know which is the correct sound, except for *è* (open, stressed *e*) meaning 'he, she, it is' and *e* (close *e*) meaning 'and'.

Two clusters of letters will raise some difficulties because of their peculiar sounds:

gli, vaguely resembling the 'li' in the English word 'million', is a palatal lateral sound. In order to pronounce it correctly, the student should try to raise the tongue to touch the hard palate, while the tip of the tongue touches the upper teeth ridge; air is let out of both sides of the tongue, with a slight hissing sound. E.g. *gli altri* (the others), *figlio* (son). In a very few words the two consonants are pronounced separately (g-l). E.g. *glicine* (wistaria), *glicerina* (glycerol), *glicemia* (glycemia), *glifo* (glyph, link-block).

gn, a palatal nasal consonant, is pronounced by raising the front of the tongue against the front part of the palate. As air is let out through the nose, the tip of the tongue touches the lower teeth ridge. This sound is also to be found in French, Spanish, Portuguese, Russian and the other Latin and Slavonic languages, e.g.

pugno (fist, fistful) /pooŋaw/, *montagna* (mountain) /mawn'taŋa/.

In Italian words are often stressed on the first before last syllable, e.g. *generale* (general), *accompagnamento* (accompaniment).

Several Italian words are stressed on the final vowel. This must be written with an accent on top of it. These words come from originally longer words which were cut short or truncated, e.g. *verità* (truth), *virtù* (virtue). A few short words have a stress to distinguish them from others having the same spelling, e.g. *là* (there) versus *la* (the), *dà* (he, she, it gives) versus *da* (from), *tè* (tea) versus *te* (you), *lì* (there) versus *li* (them).

Various words are stressed on the second before last syllable. A few more are stressed on the third syllable before the last. These are especially the third persons plural of verb tenses, e.g. *ĕvitano* (they avoid), *ăncorano* (they anchor).

Throughout this book a little cross will be placed on top of a stressed vowel when the stress is on the second or third syllable before the last. This device is intended only for the convenience of the student and must not be considered part of the Italian spelling system.

The author refers the student to the text *The Pronunciation of Italian, A Practical Introduction* (Bell & Hyman, London, 1979) by Marguerite Chapallaz, for a complete study of the Italian sound system.

Capital letters are used in Italian mostly as in English. But the names of the days of the week, months, seasons, nationality and *io* (I) are normally written with small letters, e.g.: *lunedì* (Monday), *aprile* (April), *l'autunno* (autumn), *inglese* (English). Titles before nouns are also sometimes written with small letters, while *Lei*, and *Loro*, i.e. the formal forms for 'you', are often capitalized.

The Italian punctuation marks include:

> *punto* (full stop, period), *caporiga* (period, new line)
> *vĭrgola* (comma)
> *punto e vĭrgola* (semi-colon)
> *due punti* (colon)
> *punto di domanda* or *punto interrogativo* (question mark)
> *punto esclamativo* (exclamation mark)
> *puntini di sospensione* (dots)
> *lineetta* (dash)

\-   *trattino* (hyphen)

" " or « » *virgolette* (inverted commas), *tra virgolette* (between
         inverted commas), *aperte le virgolette* (open inverted
         comma, quote), *chiuse le virgolette* (closed inverted
         commas, unquote), *cito* (I quote), *citazione* (quotation)

( )   *parèntesi* or *parèntesi rotonde* (brackets), *aperta parèntesi*
         (open brackets), *chiusa parèntesi* (closed brackets), *tra*
         parèntesi (between brackets)

[ ]   *parèntesi quadre* (square brackets)

*   *asterisco* (asterisk)

{ }   *graffa* or *parèntesi graffa* (braces)

+	*più* (plus)	:	*diviso (per)* (divided by)
=	*uguale* (equal)	×	*per*, *volte*, *moltiplicato per*
−	*meno* (minus)		(by, times, multiplied by)
'	*apòstrofo* (apostrophe)	%	*per cento* (per cent)
`	*accento* (accent)	/	*sbarra* (stroke)

_____*sottolineatura* (underlining), *sottolineare* (to underline)

LESSON 1

■ AL BAR, PRESENTAZIONI E SALUTI

AT THE CAFÉ. INTRODUCTIONS AND GREETINGS

Buon giorno, signore. Prego, desìdera?

Good morning, sir. What would you like?

Mi dà un cappuccino e una brioche, per favore?

Could you give me a white coffee and a croissant, please?

Ecco, signore.

Here you are, sir.

Gràzie.

Thank you.

Prego.

Not at all.

(He is spotted by Mr Rossi)

Oh, Dottor Conti, buon giorno, come sta?

Oh, Dr Conti, good morning, how are you?

Salve, Signor Rossi, come va?

Hello, Mr Rossi, how are you getting on?

Bene, gràzie. Questa è la Signorina Marisa Bianchi, la mia fidanzata.

Well, thank you. This is Miss Marisa Bianchi, my fiancée.

Molto lieto, signorina.

Very pleased (to meet you), madam.

Piacere.

Pleased to meet you.

E questa è la sua sorellina Carla.

And this is her little sister Carla.

Ciao, Carla.

Hello, Carla.

Buon giorno, dottore.

Good morning, doctor.

Prego! Un caffè, qualcosa da bere? O un gelato?

Please (sit down). (Would you like) a coffee, something to drink? Or ice-cream?

No, gràzie. Arrivederci, dottore.

No, thank you. Good-bye, doctor.

Cameriere, quant'è, per favore?	Waiter, how much is it, please?
Ottocentocinquanta lire, signore.	Eight hundred and fifty lire, sir.
Ecco il resto.	Here's your change.
Tenga pure il resto.	Do keep the change.
Molte grăzie, signore.	Many thanks, sir.

Prego? and *desĭdera?* (short for *che cosa desĭdera?* 'what do you wish?') are used to ask 'can I help you?', 'what would you like?' or 'what can I do for you?', in cafés, restaurants, shops, hotels, as well as when entertaining guests. Both or either one of the two can be used.

Mi dà? (could you give me?) or *vorrei* (I'd like) are commonly used in polite requests.

Brioche is pronounced as in French: /bree'osh/.

A *bar* or *caffè* is a place where you can get spirits at any time of the day until midnight or later, but also other types of drink, especially coffee which is a favourite drink with Italians, and small snacks or pastry.

People usually say *buon giorno* (good day) from early morning until late in the afternoon. Later they say *buona sera* (good evening) and *buona notte* (good night).

Cappuccino is one of the various types of Italian coffee. It consists of black coffee with some creamy milk on top. Other types of coffee are: *caffè* (black coffee), sometimes called *caffè nero* (black coffee), usually served in tiny cups and brewed very strong; *caffè ristretto* (very strong black coffee); *caffè macchiato* (coffee with a tiny bit of milk); *caffelatte* (coffee-and-milk) served in a large cup; *caffè corretto* (black coffee with brandy or other spirit); *caffè espresso* or simply *espresso*, which is made very strong by special machines called *măcchine da caffè espresso* and used in *bar* by blowing highly pressurized steam through thinly ground coffee beans.

Ecco means 'here is, here are, there is, there are, here you are, there you are'.

Ciao (hello, good-bye) can only be said to close acquaintances, relatives and children. Otherwise, *salve* or, more formally, *buon giorno* or *buona sera* are to be used. *Arrivederci* or, more formally, *arrivederLa* (see you again, good-bye) can be used with anyone.

Tenga pure (do keep, please keep) is a polite form to offer *una mància* (a tip), which is often given when service is not included in the price (*servìzio non compreso*, service not included).

La mia fidanzata (my fiancée), *la mia sorellina* (my little sister): possessives are usually preceded by an article in Italian.

Come sta? (how are you?) or, more casual, *come va?* (how are you getting on?) are commonly used in conversation.

Prego means 'please, if you please, please do', or is the polite answer to *gràzie* (thank you) meaning 'not at all, don't mention it, you're welcome'. *Prego?* can mean 'I beg your pardon?' or 'What would you like, what can I do for you?'

Per favore, per piacere or *per cortesia* just mean 'Please'.

È is the third person singular of the present tense indicative of the verb *èssere* (to be).

TITLES: SIGNORE, SIGNORA, SIGNORINA AND OTHER TITLES

Signore means 'sir' or 'gentleman', *Signor* 'Mr'; *signora* 'madam' (for a married woman) or 'lady', *Signora* 'Mrs'; *signorina* 'madam' (for an unmarried woman) or 'young lady', *Signorina* 'Miss'. They are preceded by articles, unless a person is addressed directly, e.g.

Il Signor Conti è al bar (Mr Conti is at the café)
Il signore è dottore (The gentleman is a doctor)
Buon giorno, signore (Good morning, sir)
Prego, signora (Please, madam)
Come va, Signora Bianchi? (How are you, Mrs Bianchi?)

Until the seventeenth century, the usual title forms were *messere* (gentleman, sir), *Messer* or *Ser* (Mr), *madonna, donna* or *monna* (lady, young lady), which were capitalized when preceding names and used without articles (Mrs, Miss). The student will come across these titles especially when reading older literature. Thus, Dante, the author of the medieval poem *The Divine Comedy*, was referred to or addressed as *Messer Dante* or *Ser Dante* or *messere*, and the girl he idealized was known as *Madonna Beatrice*. The only surviving reminders of this old usage are the present way of referring to the Virgin Mary as *la Madonna* and the wives of Presidents of the

Republic and other noble or distinguished ladies as *Donna* So-and-So.

Dottore (doctor), or *Dottor, Dott., Dr* if followed by a name, is the title that is often bestowed to any university graduate in Italy, not only to medics. All teachers of secondary schools, as well as of universities, are normally given the title of *professore* (professor), *Professor* or *Prof.* followed by the name, and *professoressa* (lady professor), *Professoressa* or *Prof.ssa* when followed by a name. Similarly, other titles include *ingegnere* (graduate engineer), *Ingegner* or *Ing.* when followed by a name; *ragioniere* (accountant), *Ragionier* or *Rag.* when followed by a name; *ragioniera* (lady accountant), *Ragioniera* or *Rag.ra* when followed by a name; *geòmetra* (surveyor), *Geòmetra* or *Geom.* when followed by a name; *avvocato* (lawyer, solicitor), *Avvocato* or *Avv.* when followed by a name; *avvocatessa* (lady lawyer, solicitor), *Avvocatessa* or *Avv.ssa* when followed by a name; *reverendo* (reverend), *Reverendo* or *Rev.* when followed by a name; *cavaliere, commendatore* (honorary titles), *Cavaliere* or *Cav.* and *Commendatore* or *Comm.* when followed by a name. The use of the articles with all these titles follows the same rules as for *signore*, e.g.

Questo è l'Ingegner Bruni e la signorina è la Dott.ssa Rossi (This is Mr Bruni, engineer, and the young lady is Dr Rossi).

You can also have two, and even three, titles, e.g. *signore, signora, signorina* followed by another title or other titles, as a way of great respect, especially when addressing letters. E.g.:

La Sig.na Rag.ra Verdi (Miss Verdi, accountant)
Buona sera, signor dottore (Good evening, doctor, sir)
Al Signor Avvocato Fabbri (To Mr Fabbri, solicitor)

Il Signore and *la Signora* also mean respectively 'the lord, the owner' and 'the lady, the landlady', or someone who looks or behaves as a distinguished, refined or wealthy person. *Il Signore* also means 'the Lord God', i.e. *Dio* (God) or *il Signore Iddio* (the Lord God).

SURNAMES

Italian surnames often end in *-i*, e.g. *Bianchi, Rossi, Verdi, Fabbri, Ferrari, Leoni*.

Others end in another vowel, such as *o*, *a* and *e*, while *u* is common in Sardinia.

Several surnames end in *-is* and are, or are not, preceded by *de*. These are old Latinized forms, e.g. *de Laurentiis, de Sanctis*.

Other surnames, especially in south Italy, are preceded by *di* or *de*, e.g. *di Filippo, di Cicco, di Stefano, de Gregorio*.

The final vowel is often dropped in surnames of the Venetian area after *-n*, *-l* and *-r*, e.g. *Merlin, Camon, Martin*.

CHRISTIAN NAMES

These often end in *-o*, sometimes in *-e*, and less commonly in *-a* or a consonant, for males, e.g.

Andrea (Andrew)
Vittore or *Vittòrio* (Victor)
Daniele (Daniel)
Gabriele (Gabriel)
Giovanni (John)
Gianni, Gian, Vanni (Johnny, Jack)
Carlo (Charles)
Carletto (Charlie, Chuck)
Filippo (Philip)
Franco (Frank)
Francesco (Francis)
Ludovico (Ludovic)
Giuseppe (Joseph)
Loris

Federico (Frederick)
Vincenzo (Vincent)
Alberto (Albert)
Roberto (Robert)
Salvatore (common in Sicily)
Cristòforo (Christopher)
Antònio (Anthony)
Tònio, Toni (Tony)
Lorenzo, Renzo (Lawrence)
Luigi (Lewis, Louis)
Luigino (Louie)
Beppe, Peppe, Bepi (Joe)
Stèfano (Stephen)
Màrio

Names of women often end in *-a*, only a few in other vowels or in a consonant,

Anna
Roberta
Carmela

Lìdia (Lydia)
Luisa, Luigina (Louise)
Laura

Federica
Ada
Alice
Mariarosa (Rosemary)
Rosamaria (Rosemary)
Rosa, Rosina (Rose)
Daniela
Irma
Gina
Clara, Claretta
Paola, Paolina (Paula, Pauline)
Piera, Pierina (Petra)
Rita

Donatella, Donata
Cristina (Christina)
Maria, Mariuccia (Mary)
Bàrbara
Tiziana
Stella
Àngela, Angelina
Lina
Sofia (Sophia)
Emìlia (Emily)
Fiorella
Margherita (Margaret)
Patrìzia (Patricia, Pat)
Linda

Exercise 1

The following are introduction phrases. Give the appropriate follow-up:

(a) *Ecco Marisa, la mia sorellina.*
(b) *Questo è il Professor Puccini.*
(c) *Questa è la mia fidanzata, Anna Verdi.*

Exercise 2

In the following sentences, write the titles between brackets with or without article and with or without final *e*, as appropriate:

(a) *Buona sera, (ingegnere) Martelli.*
(b) *Qualcosa da bere, (signora) Giusti?*
(c) *(signorina) è la mia fidanzata.*
(d) *Gràzie e arrivederci, (dottore).*
(e) *(signore) Conti è dottore.*

Exercise 3

Give an appropriate follow-up phrase to the following sentences:

(a) *Qualcosa da bere?*
(b) *Ecco cappuccino e brioche, signore.*

(c) *Ciao, Carla.*
(d) *Ecco il resto.*
(e) *Salve, Signor Bianchi. Prego?*

Exercise 4

Give a suitable phrase that could precede the following sentences:

(a) ....
Piacere, signorina
(b) ....
Molto bene, grazie.
(c) ....
Un caffè, per favore.
(d) ....
Tenga pure il resto.
(e) ....
Ciao, Marisa, bene, gràzie.

Exercise 5

Fill the gaps with the missing words:

(a) *Vorrei una brioche, ... favore.* (b) *Qualcosa . . . . . bere?*
(c) *Tenga . . . . il resto.*
(d) *Cameriere, ... è?*
(e) *. . . . . mia fidanzata è la Signorina Bianchi.*

Exercise 6

Fill the gaps with appropriate words:

(a) *Buon* ....*sta?*
(b) *Vorrei* .... *prego.*
(c) *Salve* ....*sta?*
(d) *No,* .... *signore.*
(e) *Questa* .... *Carla.*

LESSON 2

■ AL RISTORANTE

Buona sera, signori.

Buona sera. Ha un tàvolo libero?
Quanti sono?
Siamo in quattro.
Prego, signori, ecco qui.

Ecco il menù. Come primo abbiamo cannelloni, tagliatelle, spaghetti al sugo o al pomodoro o alla carbonara, risotto con i funghi, oppure minestrone di fagioli, pasta in brodo. . . . Come piatto del giorno ci sono i ravioli alla panna. Bene, ravioli per tutti, allora.

Per secondo c'è arrosto di vitello, rosbif, costata di manzo, bistecca alla fiorentina, oppure pesce. . . . Allora, costata per due, una trota lessa e una sògliola, con contorno di patate fritte e insalata mista per tutti e quattro. Poi formàggio locale, frutta fresca, dolce, caffè e un litro di bianco secco della casa.

AT THE RESTAURANT

Good evening, ladies and gentlemen.
Good evening. Have you got a free table?
How many of you are there?
There are four of us.
Please. Here you are, ladies and gentlemen.
Here's the menu. As a first course, we've got cannelloni, noodles, spaghetti with meat or tomato sauce or with ham and egg sauce, rice with mushrooms, or minestrone with beans, pasta in chicken soup. . . . As dish of the day there is ravioli with cream. Well, ravioli for everybody, then.

As main dish there's roast veal, roast beef, beef-steak, Florentine-style steak, or fish. . . .
Then, beef-steak for two, one boiled trout and one sole, with fried potatoes and mixed salad for the four of us. Then local cheese, fresh fruit, sweet, and a litre of dry white house wine.

Cameriere, il conto, per favore. Abbiamo fretta.

Waiter, the bill, please. We are in a hurry.

NOUNS AND ARTICLES

All nouns are either masculine or feminine. The gender is often not natural, but merely grammatical. This means that things may be either masculine or feminine, as well as people and animals, irrespective of the fact that in nature things are neither masculine nor feminine and animals and people are. The gender of nouns must be learnt gradually. So nouns ending in *-ine* and *-ione* are always feminine. Nouns ending in *-a* are often feminine while those ending in *-o* are mostly masculine. Nouns ending in *-e* may be either. More indications on the gender of nouns are to be found in the Introduction.

So far in this lesson we have met the following nouns:

la lezione (lesson), f.	pl. *le lezioni*
il ristorante (restaurant), m.	pl. *i ristoranti*
il signore (gentleman), m.	pl. *i. signori*
il tàvolo (table), m.	pl. *i tàvoli*
il menù (menu), m.	pl. *i menù*
il cannellone (stuffed pasta noodle), m.	pl. *i cannelloni*
la tagliatella (noodle), f.	pl. *le tagliatelle*
lo spaghetto (spaghetti), m.	pl. *gli spaghetti*
il sugo (sauce), m.	pl. *i sughi*
il pomodoro (tomato), m.	pl. *i pomodori*
la carbonara (pasta with ham and egg), f.	pl. *le carbonare*
il risotto (rice dish), m.	pl. *i risotti*
il fungo (mushroom), m.	pl. *i funghi*
il minestrone (minestrone soup), m.	pl. *i minestroni*
il fagiolo (bean), m.	pl. *i fagioli*
la pasta (pasta; cake), f.	pl. *le paste*
il brodo (chicken or meat soup), m.	pl. *i brodi*
il piatto (plate, dish), m.	pl. *i piatti*

il giorno (day), m.	pl. *i giorni*
il raviolo (kind of stuffed noodle), m.	pl. *i ravioli*
la panna (cream), f.	pl. *le panne*
l'arrosto (roast), m.	pl. *gli arrosti*
il vitello (veal; calf), m.	pl. *i vitelli*
il rosbif (roast-beef), m.	pl. *i rosbif*
la costata (steak), f.	pl. *le costate*
il manzo (beef), m.	pl. *i manzi*
la bistecca (steak), f.	pl. *le bistecche*
il pesce (fish), m.	pl. *i pesci*
la trota (trout), f.	pl. *le trote*
la sògliola (sole), f.	pl. *le sògliole*
il contorno (side-dish), m.	pl. *i contorni*
la patata (potato), f.	pl. *le patate*
l'insalata (lettuce; salad), f.	pl. *le insalate*
il formaggio (cheese), m.	pl. *i formaggi*
il frutto (fruit), m.	pl. *i frutti or la frutta*
la frutta (fruit), f.	
il dolce (sweet), m.	pl. *i dolci*
il caffè (coffee; café), m.	pl. *i caffè*
il litro (litre), m.	pl. *i litri*
la casa (house), f.	pl. *le case*
il cameriere (waiter), m.	pl. *i camerieri*
il conto (bill), m.	pl. *i conti*
il favore (favour), m.	pl. *i favori*
la fretta (hurry, haste), f.	(no plural)
la lira (Italian currency), f.	pl. le lire

As can be seen from this list, plurals often end in -*i*. But feminine nouns ending in -*a* in the singular form their plurals in -*e*. Nouns ending in a stressed vowel, i.e. -*à*, -*è*, -*ò*, -*ì* and -*ù*, like *caffè*, do not change in the plural. Also nouns ending in a consonant do not change in the plural, like *rosbif* or *àutobus* (bus), as well as those ending in -*ie*, like *la spècie* (species), and those resulting from the shortening of a long noun, like *il cìnema*, short for *cinematògrafo* (cinema), and *la ràdio*, which is short for *radiofonia* (radio, wireless).

Nouns ending in -*ca*, -*ga* and -*go* add -*h*- in the plural, e.g.

l'amica (woman friend), f.	pl. *le amiche*
il gerarca (political boss), m.	pl. *i gerarchi*
la marca (brand; excise stamp), f.	pl. *le marche*
la paga (pay, wages, salary), f.	pl. *le paghe*
il diàlogo (dialogue), m.	pl. *i diàloghi*

But some nouns ending in -*co* do not add -*h*-, e.g.

il greco (Greek), m.	pl. *i greci*
l'amico (male friend), m.	pl. *gli amici*
il nemico (enemy), m.	pl. *i nemici*

One-syllable nouns do not change in the plural, e.g.

il re (king), m.	pl. *i re*
il the or *il tè* (tea), m.	pl. *i the* or *i tè*

A few nouns have unusual plurals:

la mano (hand), f.	pl. *le mani*
l'ala (wing), f.	pl. *le ali*
il bue (ox), m.	pl. *i buoi*
l'uomo (man), m.	pl. *gli uòmini*
il dio (the god), m.	pl. *gli dei*

A group of masculine nouns become feminine in the plural, often ending in -*a*, e.g.

il dito (finger), m.	pl. *le dita*, f.
il bràccio (arm), m.	pl. *le bràccia*, f.
l'orècchio (ear), m.	pl. *le orècchie*, f.
il cìglio (eyelid), m.	pl. *le cìglia*, f.
il sopraccìglio (brow), m.	pl. *le sopraccìglia*, f.
il filo (thread), m.	pl. *le fila* (threads of a plot), f. but *i fili* (threads)
il muro (wall), m.	pl. *le mura* (town walls), f., but *i muri* (walls).
l'uovo (egg), m.	pl. *le uova*, f.

Compound nouns consisting of the word *capo* (head, chief) and another noun only change the word *capo* into *capi*, e.g.

il capoufficio (office manager)	pl. *i capiufficio*

il capostazione (station master)	pl. *i capistazione*
il capotreno (chief train conductor)	pl. *i capitreno*
il caporeparto (head of store department)	pl. *i capireparto*
il caposquadra (foreman)	pl. *i capisquadra*

Compound nouns consisting of verb and noun do not change in the plural, e.g.

il portalèttere (postman)	pl. *i portalèttere*
l'affittacàmere (landlord), m.	pl. *gli affittacàmere*
la lavastovìglie (dish-washer)	pl. *le lavastovìglie*
il giradischi (record-player)	pl. *i giradischi*
il parafùlmine (lighting conductor)	pl. *i parafùlmine*
il dormivèglia (doze)	pl. *i dormivèglia*
il parabrezza (windscreen)	pl. *i parabrezza*

Similarly, compound nouns formed by a preposition and a noun do not change in the plural, e.g.

il senzatetto (the homeless)	pl. *i senzatetto*
il fuoribordo (outboard engine motorboat)	pl. *i fuoribordo*
il fuorilegge (outlaw)	pl. *i fuorilegge*

The student will already have noticed the different forms of definite articles. In the masculine singular, *il*, changing into *l'* before vowel and into *lo* before *s* followed by a consonant, or *z*, or *ps*, or *gn*. In the masculine plural, *i*, changing to *gli* if the following word starts with vowel, *s*+consonant, *z, ps*, or *gn*, e.g.

il nome (name)	pl. *i nomi*
l'animale (animal)	pl. *gli animali*
lo zio (uncle)	pl. *gli zii*
lo studio (study; studio)	pl. *gli studi*
lo psicanalista (psychoanalyst)	pl. *gli psicanalisti*
lo gnocco (potato noodle)	pl. *gli gnocchi*

In the feminine singular, *la* changes into *l'* before vowel. *Le* is the plural, e.g.

la lìngua (language; tongue)	pl. *le lìngue*
l'arància (orange)	pl. *le arance*

The demonstrative adjectives *questo* (this) and *quello* (that), the prepositional articles, i.e. combinations of prepositions and articles, and the adjectives *bello* (beautiful), *grande* (great, big) and *Santo* (Saint) follow about the same pattern of changes as the definite articles:

Masc. sing.	Masc. sing + vowel	Masc. sing. followed by s+cons., z, ps and gn	Masc. pl.	Masc. pl. followed by vowel, s+cons., z, ps and gn
il (the)	*l'*	*lo*	*i*	*gli*
al (to the)	*all'*	*allo*	*ai*	*agli*
dal (from the)	*dall'*	*dallo*	*dai*	*dagli*
del (of the)	*dell'*	*dello*	*dei*	*degli*
nel (in the)	*nell'*	*nello*	*nei*	*negli*
sul (on the)	*sull'*	*sullo*	*sui*	*sugli*
questo (this)	*quest'* (*questo*)	*questo*	*questi*	*questi*
quel (that)	*quell'*	*quello*	*quei*	*quegli* (*quelli*)
bel (beautiful)	*bell'*	*bello*	*bei*	*begli* (*belli*)
gran (great)	*grand'* (*grande*)	*grande*	*grandi*	*grandi*
San (Saint)	*Sant'* (*Santo*)	*Santo*	*Santi*	*Santi*

Feminine singular	Feminine sing. followed by vowel	Feminine plural
la	*l'*	*le*
alla	*all'*	*alle*
dalla	*dall'*	*dalle*

della	*dell'*	*delle*
nella	*nell'*	*nelle*
sulla	*sull'*	*sulle*
questa	*quest'* or *questa*	*queste*
quella	*quell'* or *quella*	*quelle*
bella	*bell'* or *bella*	*belle*
grande	*grand'* or *grande*	*grandi*
Santa	*Sant'* or *Santa*	*Sante*

The indefinite article *un* (a, an) changes to *uno* when followed by s+cons., *z*, *ps* and *gn*, in the masculine. In the feminine, *una* may change to *un'* when followed by a vowel. A similar pattern is also followed by the adjective *buono* (good) in the singular:

Masculine singular	Masc. sing. before s+cons., z, ps and gn	Feminine singular	Fem. sing. followed by vowel
un (a, an)	*uno*	*una*	*un'* or *una*
buon (good)	*buono*	*buona*	*buon'* or *buona*

ADJECTIVES

Except for those mentioned above, adjectives usually follow nouns and agree with them. They may precede them, if more emphasis is required or for other stylistic reasons.

Adjectives generally fall into two categories:

(a) adjectives ending in *-o* (masc. sing.), *-a* (fem. sing.), *-i* (masc. pl.) and *-e* (fem. pl.);
(b) adjectives ending in *-e* (sing.) and *-i* (plural), e.g.

nuovo, nuova, nuovi, nuove (new)
vècchio, vècchia, vecchi, vècchie (old)
famoso, famosa, famosi, famose (famous)
brutto, brutta, brutti, brutte (ugly, nasty)
caro, cara, cari, care (dear; expensive)
interessante, interessanti (interesting)
notèvole, notèvoli (remarkable)

forte, forti (strong; heavy)
pesante, pesanti (heavy)

Demonstrative and indefinitive adjectives, such as *questo* (this), *quello* (that), *codesto* (that, near you), *molto* (much), *parècchio* (several), *vari, vàrie* (various), *qualùnque, qualsìasi* (any, whatever), *qualche* (some), *poco, poca* (little), *pochi, poche* (few, a few), *tanto, tanta* (so much), *tanti, tante* (so many), *troppo, troppa* (too much), *troppi, troppe* (too many), *certo, certa, certi, certe*, (certain), *alcuno, alcuna* (no), *alcuni, alcune* (some), always precede the nouns they qualify, e.g.

Certi vecchi e buoni amici generosi (Certain old, good and generous friends)
Parècchie persone interessanti (Several interesting people)

PRESENT TENSE OF ÈSSERE (TO BE) AND AVERE (TO HAVE)

(Io) sono (I am)	*(Io) ho* (I have)
(Tu) sei or *(Lei) è* (you are)	*(Tu) hai* or *(Lei) ha* (you have)
(Egli, lui, lei, esso, essa) è (he, she, it is)	*(Egli, lui, lei, esso, essa) ha* (he, she, it has)
(Noi) siamo (we are)	*(Noi) abbiamo* (we have)
(Voi) siete or *(Loro) sono* (you are)	*(Voi) avete* or *(Loro) hanno* (you have)
(Loro, essi, esse) sono (they are)	*(Loro, essi, esse) hanno* (they have)

The *tu* and *voi* forms are used when addressing children, relatives and friends, in the singular and in the plural respectively. Otherwise, the more formal, *Lei* (sing.) and *Loro* (pl.) forms must be used. The *Loro* form in the plural, however, tends to be regarded as a bit too formal and to be confined to official situations and to waiters and shop-assistants attending customers. An extremely formal alternative of *Lei* is *Ella*, which is normally reserved for bureaucratic usage, e.g.

È Lei il Signor Conti? (Are you Mr Conti?)
Sono Loro, signorine? (Is it you, young ladies?)

Tu sei la sorellina di Marisa (You are Marisa's little sister)

Lui (he) is more colloquial than *egli*, and so is *loro* with regard to *essi* and *esse* (they). *Egli, lui, lei* and *loro* refer only to people.

The subject personal pronouns have been put between brackets to show that they are often omitted in Italian, unless they are required for emphasis, contrast or because they stand in isolation, e.g.

Chi è? Sono io (Who is it? It is me)
Il dottore è lei non lui (The doctor is she, not he)
Sei Carla? (Are you Carla?)
Sei tu, Carla (Is it you, Carla?)
Chi ha la màcchina? Io (Who has got a car? I have)

Finally, it may be interesting to know that the curious use of *Lei, Ella* and *Loro* when addressing people formally can be traced back to the medieval custom of addressing feudal lords and princes as *Vostra Signoria* or *la Signoria Vostra* (Your Lordship), plural *le Signorie Vostre*, followed by the third persons of verbs. This is still the way of addressing persons in bureaucratic documents in Italy today. The use was reinforced in past centuries by Spanish influence. Ordinary people, however, especially when illiterate, may continue calling each other *voi* throughout Italy, as they find the use of *Lei* and *Loro* almost as difficult as students of Italian often do. During the Fascist period, the use of *voi* was made compulsory, but it was discarded after the war, as an authoritarian imposition.

The verb *avere* is also used to replace 'to be' in such phrases as: *avere fame* (to be hungry), *avere sete* (to be thirsty), *avere sonno* (to be sleepy), *avere vergogna* (to be ashamed), *avere paura* (to be afraid) and *avere fretta* (to be in a hurry).

Ciò, questo, quello

Ciò and *questo* are used to mean 'it, this, this fact, this thing', e.g. *Ciò è insopportàbile* (This is unbearable).

Quello, quella, quelli, quelle are used to mean 'the one, the ones', e.g. *Vorrei quella* (I'd like that one).

Exercise 1

Turn the following sentences into the plural:

(a) *C'è un tàvolo lìbero?*
(b) *Questo formàggio è buono ma troppo caro.*
(c) *È un po' ubriaco.*
(d) *Ho vino bianco casalingo.*
(e) *Ecco lo zio.*

Exercise 2

Combine the articles and prepositions between brackets as appropriate:

(a) *C'è minestrone (in il) menù?*
(b) *Avete ravioli (a la) panna?*
(c) *Il conto (di il) ristorante è alto.*
(d) *Quali sono i piatti (di la) casa?*
(e) *Cameriere, frutta (su il) tàvolo.*

Exercise 3

Place the correct form of the adjective between brackets:

(a) *È un (santo) uomo,*
(b) *È una (grande) bella donna.*
(c) *(Santo) Antònio.*
(d) *Il gatto è un (buono) e (bello) animale.*
(e) *Un (bello) arrosto di vitello e un (buono) vino bianco dolce.*

Exercise 4

Turn the following familiar or informal sentences into formal ones:

(a) *Hai fretta?*
(b) *Sei ubriaca.*
(c) *Quanti siete?*
(d) *Voi siete psicanalisti?*
(e) *Come stai, ragazzo?*

LESSON 3

◼ PRESENTAZIONI

Ciao, Fabbri, come va?

Beh, così così. E tu?
Si tira avanti. Non c'è male.
Conosci John Carpenter?
John, scusa, questo è il mio collega Giòrgio Fabbri. È bancàrio come me.

Piacere.
Molto lieto.
E Lei, Signor Carpenter, che cosa fa?
Fàccio il professore di stòria in un istituto superiore inglese, ma qui fàccio lo studente di italiano ora.
Ah, capisco, allora Lei è pròprio inglese.
Ma, veramente sono scozzese.
Però vivo in Inghilterra, vicino a Londra, da anni.

Ah, sì? Come parla bene l'italiano!
Gràzie del complimento, ma fàccio molta fatica.

Possiamo darci del tu, no?

INTRODUCTIONS

Hello, Fabbri, how are things?
Well, so so, and you?
One carries on. Not bad.
Do you know John Carpenter? John, excuse me, this is my colleague Giorgio Fabbri. He's a bank clerk like me.

Pleased to meet you.
Very glad to meet you.
What do you do, Mr Carpenter?
I'm a history lecturer in an English institute of higher education, but I'm an Italian student here now.
Oh, I understand (I see), you're really English, then.
In point of fact I'm Scottish, but I have been living in England, near London, for years.

Oh, really? You speak Italian very well!
Thank you for the compliment but it is very hard for me.
We can call each other *tu*, can't we?

Ma certo. È più sĕmplice   Sure we can, it's simpler for
per me.   me.

PRESENT TENSE INDICATIVE

Italian verbs are used in a number of tenses and persons. Considering the Italian infinitives ending in *-re* as corresponding to the English infinitives, i.e. 'to + verb', then Italian verbs are divided into three different conjugations, according to the vowels *a*, *e* and *i* preceding the ending *-re*. These characteristic vowels are kept, or vary or disappear in a consistent way throughout the tenses and forms of the verbs. So, for example, *parlare* (to speak) belongs to the first conjugation, because its characteristic vowel is *a*; *vĕndere* (to sell) to the second, as the characteristic vowel is *e*; *dormire* (to sleep) to the third, as the characteristic vowel is *i*. The present tense indicative of these verbs will be as follows:

(Io) parlo (I speak)	*vendo* (I sell)	*dormo* (I sleep)
(Tu) parli or *(Lei) parla* (you speak)	*vendi* or *vende* (you sell)	*dormi* or *dorme* (you sleep)
(Egli, lui, lei, esso, essa) parla (he, she, it speaks)	*vende* (he, she, it sells)	*dorme* (he, she, it sleeps)
(Noi) parliamo (we speak)	*vendiamo* (we sell)	*dormiamo* (we sleep)
(Voi) parlate or *(Loro) părlano* (you speak)	*vendete* or *vĕndono* (you sell)	*dormite* or *dŏrmono* (you sleep)
(Loro, essi, esse) părlano (They speak)	*vĕndono* (they sell)	*dŏrmono* (they sleep)

Notice that the stress falls on the root vowel in the third person plural.

The verbs belonging to the *i* or third conjugation are not many in number. The main ones are: *cucire* (to sew), *divertire* (to amuse), *fuggire* (to flee), *consentire* (to agree), *conseguire* (to achieve), *partire* (to leave), *seguire* (to follow), *sentire* (to hear; to feel), *servire* (to serve), *vestire* (to dress), *svestire* (to undress), *sfuggire* (to escape), *rifuggire* (to skirt), *proseguire* (to continue), *scucire* (to unpick).

The present tense of the indicative is used:

(a) in general statements;
(b) to describe events taking place now;
(c) to give immediacy to past events;
(d) to indicate future events;
(e) instead of the English perfect, when the duration or the beginning of the event is mentioned; this is a very remarkable difference between English and Italian and one that should not be overlooked.

For example:

(a) *Dormite troppo* (You sleep too much)
(b) *Dov'è? Dorme* (Where is he? He's sleeping)
(c) *Garibaldi parte con mille uŏmini e conquista il Regno delle Due Sicĭlie* (Garibaldi leaves with one thousand men and conquers the Kingdom of the Two Sicilies)
(d) *Domani vendo la mắcchina* (Tomorrow I shall sell my car)
(e) *Vive a Firenze da anni* (She has been living in Florence for years)
(f) *Aspettiamo da mezzogiorno* (We have been waiting since noon)

Notice the use of *da* in Italian, instead of the English 'for' or 'since'.

There is an alternative way of saying this kind of sentence, by starting the sentence with a form of the verb *ĕssere* (to be) followed by the time and *che* (that) and the main verb, e.g.

Sono molti anni che vive a Londra (He has been living in London for many years)
È da mezzogiorno che aspettiamo (We have been waiting since noon)
È dal 1970 che non torno in Italia (I have not gone back to Italy since 1970)
Sono settimane che non guardo la televisione (It is weeks since I last watched television)

NUMBERS FROM 1 TO 12

Cardinal numbers (*numeri cardinali*) are invariable, while ordinal numbers (*numeri ordinali*) are adjectives agreeing with the noun they refer to:

■ Cardinal numbers

		Ordinal numbers	
1, *uno*	(one)	1°, *primo, prima, primi, prime*	(first)
2, *due*	(two)	2°, *secondo*	(second)
3, *tre*	(three)	3°, *terzo*	(third)
4, *quattro*	(four)	4°, *quarto*	(fourth)
5, *cinque*	(five)	5°, *quinto*	(fifth)
6, *sei*	(six)	6°, *sesto*	(sixth)
7, *sette*	(seven)	7°, *settimo*	(seventh)
8, *otto*	(eight)	8°, *ottavo*	(eighth)
9, *nove*	(nine)	9°, *nono*	(ninth)
10, *dieci*	(ten)	10°, *decimo*	(tenth)
11, *undici*	(eleven)	11°, *undicesimo*	(eleventh)
12, *dodici*	(twelve)	12°, *dodicesimo*	(twelfth)

THE DAYS OF THE WEEK

■ *I giorni della settimana sono sette* (The days of the week are seven):

lunedì (Monday), *martedì* (Tuesday), *mercoledì* (Wednesday), *giovedì* (Thursday), *venerdì* (Friday), *sabato* (Saturday), *domènica* (Sunday).

I giorni della settimana si scrivono con la lettera minuscola (The days of the week are written with a small letter)

They can be preceded by an article:

Il lunedì è il primo giorno della settimana, la domènica l'ultimo (Monday is the first day of the week, Sunday the last)

The article *il, la* or the preposition *di* precede them if the meaning is 'every':

Il sabato andiamo a fare la spesa (On Saturdays we go to do our shopping)
Di domènica i negozi sono chiusi (Shops are closed on Sundays)

Un, *una* precede them when the reference is to 'one': *Un giovedì vengo a trovarti* (I'm going to see you one Thursday)

Per or *entro* precede them to mean 'by' or 'within': *Lo prepariamo entro venerdì* (We shall prepare it by Friday)

Otherwise no preposition precedes them: *Vacci martedì* (Go there on Tuesday)

MONTHS

■ *I mesi dell'anno sono dòdici* (The months of the year are twelve):

gennàio (January), *febbràio* (February), *marzo* (March), *aprile* (April), *màggio* (May), *giugno* (June), *lùglio* (July), *agosto* (August), *settembre* (September), *ottobre* (October), *novembre* (November), *dicembre* (December).

They are written with small letters, like the days.

Di or *in* translate 'in':

Di sòlito andiamo in vacanza in agosto (We usually go on holiday in August)

Per or *entro* translate 'by' or 'within': *Entro giugno deve essere finito* (It must be over by June)

SEASONS

■ *Le stagioni dell'anno sono quattro* (The seasons of the year are four):

primavera (spring)
estate (summer)
autunno (autumn)
inverno (winter)

Un mese ha un po' più di quattro settimane (A month has a little more than four weeks)
Agli ùltimi del mese (In the last days of the month)
Ai primi di gennàio (Early in January)

Di or *in* translate 'in'; *per* or *entro* 'by' or within':

Natale viene d'inverno, Pasqua di primavera (Christmas comes in winter, Easter in spring)

Notice the adjectives: *primaverile* (of spring), *estivo* (of summer), *autunnale* (of autumn), *invernale* (of winter):

Oggi è una giornata primaverile (Today is a spring-like day)
C'è una svendita di abiti estivi (There is a sale of summer clothing)

ADVERBS

Adverbs of manner usually end in *-mente*, just as in English they end in -ly. They are formed from adjectives, after changing the final vowel *-o* to *-a* or dropping the final vowel *-e* if preceded by *l* or *r*, e.g.

freddamente (coldly, coolly), from *freddo* (cold)
caldamente (warmly), from *caldo* (warm)
cortesemente (courteously), from *cortese* (courteous)
gentilmente (kindly), from *gentile* (kind)

Some adverbs have distinct forms, e.g.

male (badly; unwell)	*molto* (much, very much, a lot)
malamente (badly; awkwardly)	*poco* (little, a little)
bene (well, good)	*abbastanza* (enough)
piuttosto (rather)	*troppo* (too much)

Some adjectives can be used as adverbs, e.g.

veloce or *forte* (quickly, speedily, fast)	*vicino* (nearby)
forte (loud)	*lontano* (far away)
	distante (far off)

All these adverbs are normally placed after verbs or at the end of the sentence.

Adverbs of time and frequency also have distinct forms, e.g.

oggi (today) *domani* (tomorrow) *ieri* (yesterday)
posdomani or *dopodomani* (the day after tomorrow)
l'altro ieri or *ieri l'altro* (the day before yesterday)

una volta (once) *ogni tanto* (every now and then)
ora or *adesso* (now), *poi* or *dopo* or *più tardi* (then, later)
stasera or *questa sera* (tonight) *pròprio* or *pròprio ora* (just)
immediatamente or *sùbito* (immediately, at once)
stamattina or *questa mattina* (this morning)
improvvisamente (suddenly) *sempre* (always)
tutto d'un tratto or *tutto ad un tratto* (all of a sudden)
di mattina (in the morning) *di sera* (in the evening)
di notte (at night, by night) *nel pomeriggio* (in the afternoon)
tutto il giorno (all day long) *tutti i giorni* (every day)
a quest'ora or *ormai* (by now)
in tempo or *puntualmente* (in time, punctually)
in ritardo or *tardi* (late)
domènica scorsa or *la scorsa domènica* (last Sunday)
domènica pròssima or *la pròssima domènica* (next Sunday)
nel gennàio scorso or *lo scorso gennàio* (last January)
la pròssima primavera or *la primavera pròssima* (next spring)
spesso (often) *mai* (never, ever)
talvolta or *qualche volta* or *alle volte* (at times, sometimes)
ancora (still, yet, some more) *tuttora* (so far)
generalmente (generally) *di sòlito* or *solitamente* (usually)
normalmente (normally, as a rule)

These adverbs are preferably placed after a verb or at the end of the sentence, but they can be found at the beginning of the sentence too. The adverbs *sempre* (always), *mai* (never, ever), *già* (already), *spesso* (often), *ancora* (still, yet), and *più* (no longer, no more) follow auxiliaries in compound tenses, e.g.

Ho già mangiato (I have already eaten)
Dormi sempre (You always sleep)
Ho ancora soldi (I have some more money)
Di sòlito sono puntuale, ma oggi sono in ritardo (I am usually punctual, but today I am late)
Guardo spesso la televisione (I often watch television)

UNSTRESSED OBJECT PRONOUNS

When not preceded by prepositions, personal, reflexive and reciprocal pronouns, as well as the two place pronouns *ci* and *vi* both meaning 'here' or 'there', are placed before verbs. But they are placed after infinitives, gerunds, past participles in isolation, imperatives and *ecco* (here is, there is, here are, there are) forming one word with them. This is the full list:

mi (me; to me; myself; to myself)
ti or *Le* (you; to you; yourself; to yourself)
lo (him, it)
la (her, it)
gli (to him, to it)
le (to her, to it)
si (himself, herself, itself; to himself, to herself, to itself; themselves; to themselves; each other; to each other)
ci (us; to us; ourselves; to ourselves; each other; to each other; here; there)
vi (you; to you; yourselves; to yourselves; each other; to each other; here; there)
ne (some; about it, about him, about her, about them)

Loro (them; to them) always follows verbs.

Ti presento il mio amico (I'd like to introduce my friend to you)
Le passo il Signor Conti (I'll put Mr Conti through to you)
Si àmano molto (They love each other very much)
Viene a trovarci or *Ci viene a trovare* (He comes to see us)
Perchè non vi decidete (Why don't you make up your mind?)
Ne parla sempre (She always speaks about it (or them))
Èccomi (Here I am)
Ne vorrei altri due (I'd like two more)

The pronouns mentioned above can be found in pairs, in which case the first pronoun is an indirect object while the second is the direct object. Besides, the pronouns *mi, ti, si, ci* and *vi* change to *me, te, se, ce* and *ve* before *lo, la, li, le* and *ne*. *Gli* and *le* change to *glie*, which combines with *lo, la, li, le* and *ne*. All these pronouns are combined together and with the verbs, when they follow:

me lo (him to me)
me la (her to me)
me li (them to me)
me le (them to me)
me ne (some to me; to me about it or them)
mi ci (to me here or there; myself here or there)

te lo or *Glielo* (him to you)
te la or *Gliela* (her to you)
te li or *Glieli* (them to you)
te le or *Gliele* (them to you)
te ne or *Gliene* (some to you; to you about it or them)
ti ci or *Le ci* (to you there or here; yourself here or there)

glielo (him to him)
gliela (her to her, him to her; her to him)
glieli (them to him; them to her)
gliele (them to him; them to her)
gliene (some to him or her; to him or her about it or them)
gli ci (to him here or there)
le ci (to her here or there)

se lo (him to himself; him to herself; him to themselves)
se la (her to himself; her to herself; her to themselves)
se li (them to himself; them to herself; them to themselves)
se le (them to himself; them to herself; them to themselves)
se ne (some to himself; some to herself; some to themselves; people about it; people about them)
ci si (himself here or there; herself here or there; people to us)

ce lo (him to us)
ce la (her to us)
ce li (them to us)
ce le (them to us)
ce ne (some to us; to us about it or them)

ve lo (him to you)
ve la (her to you)
ve li (them to you)
ve le (them to you)
ve ne (some to you; to you about it or them)
vi ci (you here or there)

Il cameriere ve lo porta (The waiter will bring it to you)
Me li mandi? (Will you send them to me?)
Signore, Gliene porto una bottiglia (Sir, I'll bring a bottle of it to you)

Che ve ne sembra? (What do you think about them?)
Gliene parlo io (I'll speak to her about it)
Le caramelle se le prèndono i bambini (The children will take the toffees for themselves)
È un bel cappotto. Vorrei provàrmelo (It is a fine overcoat. I'd like to try it on myself)
Se volete andare in campagna, vi ci porto io (If you want to go into the country, I'll drive you there)
Non vende la màcchina. Se la tiene (He won't sell his car. He'll keep it for himself)

Pronoun ci with èssere and avere

A particular use of the pronoun *ci* (here, there) is found with verbs *èssere* (to be) and *avere* (to have); *c'è* (there is), *ci sono* (there are), e.g.

C'è qualcuno alla porta (There is someone at the door)
Oggi ci sono spaghetti (There is spaghetti today)
C'è Màrio? (Is Mario there?) *No, non c'è* (No, he isn't there)

With the verb *avere*, the forms are colloquial alternatives to the plain verb meaning 'to have something' or 'to be the matter, to be wrong', e.g.

Che ci hai nella borsa? (What have you got in the bag?)
Che ci avete oggi? (What's the matter with you today? or What have you got today?)
Ci ho la màcchina nuova (I've got a new car)

Exercise 1

Rewrite the dialogue at the beginning of the lesson as a passage.

Exercise 2

Insert the adverb between brackets in the appropriate place:

(a) *Lei è scozzese.*   *(pròprio)*
(b) *Puoi darmi del tu.*   *(ormài)*
(c) *Parliamo in italiano.*   *(spesso)*

(d) *Conosciamo John.* *(bene)*
(e) *Parlano di Lei.* *(sempre)*

Exercise 3

Fill the gaps with the appropriate preposition or article, if required:

(a) *Il settimo giorno della settimana è . . . domenica.*
(b) *Di solito faccio giardinaggio* (gardening) *. . . domenica.*
(c) *. . . primavera la temperatura è mite.*
(d) *Partiamo . . . giugno.*
(e) *Andateci . . . giovedì mattina.*

Exercise 4

Replace the direct and/or indirect object(s) with pronoun(s):

(a) *Viviamo in Inghilterra.*
(b) *Hanno due appartamenti.*
(c) *Trova una casa al professore.*
(d) *Diciamo questo al portiere.*
(e) *Hanno finestre a ghigliottina* (sash windows).

Exercise 5

In the following sentences you find a pronoun and a noun. Replace the latter with a second pronoun:

(a) *Che ti sembra della mia casa?*
(b) *Ti riscaldo la manina.*
(c) *Mi dici la verità?*
(d) *Si parla molto di voi.*
(e) *Le passo il sale.*

Exercise 6

Answer the following questions with a full sentence:

(a) *Da quanto tempo non andate più in Italia?*
(b) *Da quando non avete più rivisto Roma?*

(c) *Da quanto è ammalata?*
(d) *Per quanto tempo restate in Itàlia?*
(e) *Da quanto tempo è che fai il professore?*

Exercise 7

Turn the following sentences into equivalent ones starting with *è* or *sono*, as required:

(a) *Àbito a Firenze da anni ormai.*
(b) *C'è terrorismo da molto tempo.*
(c) *Studiamo a Perùgia da giovedì scorso.*
(d) *L'ascensore non funziona da una settimana.*
(e) *Sono in vacanza da lùglio.*

LESSON 4

■ IN PIZZERIA

*Può darsi che la pizzeria sia aperta stasera. Andiamo?
Per me va bene. E tu, Giovanni?
Io prendo solo un toast, però. Non ho molta fame.*

Buona sera, signori. Va bene questo tàvolo qui? C'è pizza alla napoletana, margherita, ai funghi, quattro stagioni e capricciosa. Volete che vi porti il menù?

Dùnque, due pizze quattro stagioni e un toast. Da bere, tre birre grandi alla spina.

AT THE PIZZERIA

The pizzeria may be open tonight. Shall we go?
It's all right with me. How about you, John?
I'll have only a toasted sandwich. I'm not very hungry.

Good evening, ladies and gentlemen. Is this table here all right? There is pizza Neapolitan-style, margherita, mushroom, four seasons and capricciosa. Would you like me to bring you the menu?
Well, two pizzas four-seasons and a toasted sandwich. For drink, three large draught beers.

Restaurants are usually more elaborate and expensive than *tratto-rie, pizzerie, rosticcerie* (specializing in fried fish) and *tàvole calde* (usually self-service).

Other eating places are *gelaterie* (ice-cream parlours) and *past-iccerie* (confectioners'). *Gelati* (ice-cream) can be *di panna* or *di panna montata* (whipped cream), *alla cioccolata* (chocolate), *alla crema* (cream), *alla vaniglia* (vanilla), *al pistàcchio* (pistachio), *alla nocciola* (hazelnut), *alla màndorla* (almond). Pastries include *torte* (cakes) and *paste* (fancy cakes).

Restaurant menus are divided into such sections as: *antipasti* (hors d'oeuvres); *primi* (first courses) including *minestre* (soups), *pasta, riso* (rice), *gnocchi* (potato noodles), etc.; *secondi* (second courses) including *carne* (meat), *pesce* (fish) and *contorni* (side-dishes, i.e. vegetables); *dolci* (desserts); *bevande* (drinks).

PRESENT SUBJUNCTIVE

Instead of the indicative, at times it is either necessary or stylisti-cally more acceptable to use the subjunctive. The forms of the present subjunctive do not vary remarkably from those of the present indicative:

First conjugation
(Io) parli (I speak)
(Tu) or *(Lei) parli* (you speak)
(Egli, lui, lei, esso, essa) parli (he, she, it speaks)
(Voi) parliate or
(Loro) pàrlino (you speak)
(Loro, essi, esse)
pàrlino (they speak)

Second conjugation
venda (sell)
venda (you sell)
venda (he, she, it sells)
vendiamo (we sell)
vendiate or *vèndano* (you sell)
vèndano (they sell)

Third conjugation
dorma (I sleep)
dorma (you sleep)
dorma (he, she, it sleeps)
dormiamo (we sleep)
dormiate or *dòrmano* (you sleep)
dòrmano (they sleep)

As can be noticed, the first three forms are all the same. Therefore, it may be necessary to use the subject personal pronouns for clarity.

The subjunctive is used instead of the indicative in a number of cases, either depending on certain expressions or after verbs or phrases indicating possibility, doubt, uncertainty, wish, regret, fear, hope, dissatisfaction and other states of mind. At times its use is mainly a question of elegant style. Here are a number of cases when the subjective is either necessary or preferable:

(1) After *può darsi, può anche darsi, potrebbe darsi, potrebbe anche darsi* (it may be, it might be):

Può darsi che lei sia stanca (She may be tired)

(2) After *sperare* (to hope), *dubitare* (to doubt), *sospettare* (to suspect), *chièdersi* or *domandarsi* or *meravigliarsi* (to wonder), *nella speranza che* (in the hope that), *nel dùbbio che* (doubting that), as an alternative to the future:

Speriamo che non piova (Let's hope it won't rain)
Mi domando perchè sia così (I wonder why he is like that)

(3) After *volere* (to want), *desiderare* (to wish), *preferire* (to prefer), *piacere* (to like), *dispiacere* (to be sorry), *non vedere l'ora* (to look forward to), *aspettarsi* (to expect), *augurare* or *augurarsi* or *esprimere l'augùrio* (to express a wish):

Marisa si aspetta che le parli (Marisa expects me to talk to her)
Non vediamo l'ora che lui parta (We look forward to his leaving)
Vi auguriamo che siate felici (We wish you to be happy)

(4) After *parere* or *sembrare* (to seem), *avere l'idea* (to have an idea), *venire in mente* (to occur):

Pare che non sia affatto vero (It appears that it is not at all true)

Mi sembra che suoni il telefono (It seems to me that the telephone is ringing)

(5) After *accadere* or *succedere* or *capitare* (to happen), *èssere possìbile* (to be possible, likely), *èssere impossìbile* (to be impossible, unlikely), *èssere probàbile* (to be probable), *èssere improbàbile* (to be improbable), *èssere insòlito* (to be unusual), *èssere naturale* (to be natural), *èssere giusto* (to be right), *èssere ingiusto* (to be unfair), *èssere fàcile* (to be easy), *èssere diffìcile* (to be difficult), *èssere bene* (to be a good thing), *èssere male* (to be a bad thing), *èssere òvvio* (to be obvious), *èssere una bella cosa* (to be good):

Accade che non dorma per tutta la notte (As it happens I do not sleep all night)
È bene che vi rendiate conto di ciò (It is a good thing that you realize that)

(6) After *bisogna* or *occorre* (it is necessary), *conviene* (it is convenient), *importa* (it matters), *basta* (it is sufficient), *è sufficiente* (it is sufficient), *è essenziale* (it is essential), *è importante* (it is important), *è necessàrio* (it is necessary), *è vantaggioso* (it is advantageous), *è indispensàbile* (it is indispensable), *tanto vale* (I might as well), *è mèglio* (it is better), *è una buona idea* (it is a good idea), *corre voce* (there is a rumour), *c'è bisogno* (there is a need):

Bisogna che stìano zitti (They must be quiet)
Tanto vale che io parta (I might as well leave)
Basta che compili il mòdulo (You need only fill in the form)
Corre voce che si spòsino (There is a rumour that they will get married)

(7) After *è ora* or *è tempo* (it is high time):

È tempo che lavoriate (It is high time you should work)
È ora che andiate (it is time you went)

(8) After *lasciare* or *permèttere* (to let, allow), *supporre* (to suppose), *ammèttere* (to admit), *concèdere* (to grant), *impedire* (to prevent), *proibire* (to forbid), *ordinare* or *comandare* (to order), *pregare* or *supplicare* or *implorare* (to beg, to pray), *insìstere* (to

insist), *prèmere* (to urge; to matter), *illùdersi* (to delude oneself), *immaginare* (to imagine), *rischiare* or *còrrere il rìschio* (to risk), *manca poco* (hardly to avoid), *badare* or *stare attento* or *fare attenzione* (to be careful, to pay attention), *cercare* (to try), *richièdere* (to request):

Lasciate che i pìccoli vengano a me (Let the children come to me)
Bada che non sia troppo caldo (Be careful that it is not too hot)
Manca poco che (non) cada (I've hardly avoided falling down)

The subjunctive is also used after the following expressions:

(1) *Che* (that), at the beginning of a question, to signify doubt (though the future tense indicative can be used instead), e.g.

Che sia nel bagno? (Could he be in the bathroom?)
Che piova? (Will it rain?)

(2) *Che* or *che non* or *di quanto* or *di quanto non* (than) in a comparison (though the indicative is possible), e.g.

È più divertente di quanto non crediate (It's more amusing than you think)

(3) *Che* (who, which, what, that), *dove* (where), *di dove* (from where), *in cui* (in which), *da cui* (from which), *per cui* (for which, for whom), *a cui* (to which, to whom), when necessity is implied, e.g.

Qualcuno che decida (Someone who should decide)

(4) *Benchè*, *sebbene*, *quantùnque*, *per quanto* (although), *qualùnque*, *qualsìasi* (any, whatever, whichever), *qualsìasi cosa*, *qualùnque cosa* (whatever), *comùnque* (however), *ovùnque*, *dovùnque* (wherever), e.g.

Benchè sia vècchio ha molta energia (Although he is old, he is very energetic)

(5) *Sia che . . . o che, sia che . . . sia che* (whether . . . or), e.g.

Torni a casa stanco o costi molto, a teatro ci vado sempre (Whether I come back home tired or it costs a lot, I always go to the theatre)

(6) *Purchè, sempre che, a condizione che, a patto che* (provided

that, as long as, on condition that), *qualora, in caso, nel caso che* (in case), *a meno che* or *a meno che non* (unless), *senza che* or *senza che non* (without), e.g.

Ti porto al ristorante, sempre che tu ne àbbia vòglia (I shall take you to the restaurant, as long as you want to)

(7) *Affinchè, perchè, che, allo scopo che* (so that), *in modo che, in maniera che, sì che* (in such a manner as), *a tal punto che* (to such an extent that), e.g.

Gli do mille lire che si prenda qualcosa da mangiare (I'll give him a thousand lire, that he may get himself some food)

(8) *Che* or *per quanto* (as far as), e.g.

Che io ricordi, non ci àbita nessuno qui (As far as I can remember, nobody lives here)

(9) *Se* (whether, if), *perchè, la ragione per cui* (why, the reason why), *come* (how), *quando* (when), *dove* (where), *chi* (who), *quanto* (how much), *che cosa, che, cosa* (what), in the indirect speech, implying doubt or uncertainty, e.g.

Mi domando che diàvolo àbbia (I wonder what the hell is the matter with him)

(10) *Come se* or *come* (as if), *quasi che* (as if, as though), e.g.

Mi guarda come se vòglia dirmi qualcosa (He looks at me as if he wanted to say something to me). The imperfect subjunctive is more commonly used.

(11) *Il solo, l'ùnico* (the only), *il primo* (the first), *l'ùltimo* (the last, the latest), *il migliore* (the better, the best), *il peggiore* (the worse, the worst) and other comparatives, e.g.

È la persona più fidata che conosca (He is the most reliable person that I know)

(12) *Prima che* (before), *finchè, finchè non, fino a che, fino a quando, fino al momento che* (until, till), *finchè, fintanto che* (as long as), *dopo che* (after), *una volta che* (once), *quand'anche* (even when), when the idea of possibility needs to be stressed or for

stylistic reasons. But *prima che* usually requires the subjunctive, e.g.

Prima che il gallo canti (Before the cock crows)

(13) *Che* (that) and the imperative, in the first persons singular and plural, in the third persons singular and plural, and in the formal ways of addressing. *Che* is often omitted. *Pure* is sometimes added to an imperative expressing invitation, e.g.

Tenga le mani a posto (Keep your hands off me)
Che non ti metta le mani addosso (Don't let him put his hands on you)
Che mi telefonino pure a casa (Let them ring me up at home)

NEGATIVES

To make a sentence negative, *non* (not) has to precede the verb:

Non capisco (I do not understand)

A second or even a third negative may be found in the same sentence. The following are the main negatives:

niente or *nulla* (nothing)
nessuno, nessuna (nobody, none; no, followed by a countable noun)
ne . . . nessuno, nessuna (none)
nè . . . nè (neither . . . nor)
che (only, nothing, no one but)
più (no more, no longer)
affatto or *per nulla* or *niente affatto* or *punto* (at all, in the least)
niente followed by a noun (no)
mica (at all) very colloquial
alcuno, alcun, alcuna (no, followed by a countable noun)
neanche or *nemmeno* (not even)
neanche per sogno or *manco per niente* or *manco per il cavolo* – this is considered rather vulgar – (not in the least):
Non abbiamo niente da dire (We have nothing to say)
Non ho mica fretta (I am not at all in a hurry)
Non ne ho·più voglia (I don't want any more of it)
Non c'è alcun bisogno di noi (There's no need for us)
Non pensate mai al futuro (You never think of the future)

Non desìdero che te (I don't want anyone but you)
Non le telèfono nemmeno per sogno (I don't even dream of phoning her)

After *finchè* (until), *di quanto* or *di quello che* or *che* (than), *non* may be added for stylistic reasons, without making the sentence negative:

Anna è migliore di quello che non pensiate (Anna is better than you think)
Non mi sento tranquillo finchè non torna (I won't feel relaxed until she comes back)

Non is always omitted whenever another negative precedes the verb for special emphasis, e.g.

Nessuno ha il diritto di giudicare (Nobody has the right to judge)
Mica sono fesso (I'm not a fool)

Exercise 1

Transform the following pairs of sentences using the subjunctive:

(a) *Mi piace andare al ristorante se la cucina è casalinga.*
(b) *Forse non hanno più pesce.*
(c) *State zitti. È necessàrio.*
(d) *È una casa vècchia, ma è còmoda.*
(e) *Non rispòndere al telèfono, anche se succede qualsìasi cosa.*

Exercise 2

Change the verbs between brackets into the correct subjunctive forms:

(a) *Prima che (fare) qualcosa, pensaci.*
(b) *Può anche darsi che (avere) fretta.*
(c) *Speriamo che non si (spaventare).*
(d) *Avete paura che vi (rapinare)?*
(e) *Non sappiamo se (finire) oggi o domani.*

Exercise 3

Change the verbs between brackets into the appropriate imperative formal forms:

(a) *Mi (dare) un caffè espresso, per favore.*
(b) *Si (accomodare) pure a questo tàvolo, signori.*
(c) *(Prèndere) la specialità della casa, signora.*
(d) *Mi (fare) un favore, cameriere.*
(e) *(Stare) pure seduti, prego.*

Exercise 4

Write a short dialogue between two people who are going to order something to eat at a restaurant, using at least five subjunctive forms.

Exercise 5

Turn the following short passage to negative:

Oggi dobbiamo fare un mùcchio di cose, perchè il tempo è bello. Abbiamo denaro e possiamo permètterci di comperare tutto quello che vogliamo. Possiamo andare nei migliori negozi, che oggi sono aperti.

LESSON 5

■ ALLA STAZIONE FERROVIÀRIA

AT THE RAILWAY STATION

(In strada)
Scusi, dov'è la stazione ferroviària?
In fondo alla via, giri a sinistra e poi prenda la seconda a destra.

(In the street)
Excuse me, where is the railway station?
At the end of the street turn left, then take the second street on the right.

Ho capito. Gràzie mille.	I've got it. Many thanks.
Buon giorno.	Good-bye.
Buon giorno	Good-bye.

(Alla biglietteria)   **(At the booking office)**

Sì, mi dica.

Yes? What can I do for you?
(Yes, tell me)

Firenze, andata e ritorno.
seconda classe, prego.
Cinquemiladuecento lire.

A return ticket to Florence,
second class, please.
Five thousand two hundred
lire.

Ecco il resto.
A che binàrio è?

Here is your change.
What platform does it leave
from?

Binàrio quattro.
C'è un ràpido ora, mi pare,
no?
No, signore, il ràpido è in
partenza, non fa più in
tempo. Comùnque bisogna
che prenoti e fàccia il
supplemento ràpido. Quello
delle otto e cinquanta è
espresso. È in ritardo. Fa
ancora in tempo a prènderlo,
purchè corra.

Platform 4.
There is a 'very fast' train,
now, I think, isn't there?
No sir, the *rapido* train is
leaving right now, you
haven't time to get it. In any
case you need to book and
pay the supplementary charge
for the *rapido*. The 8.50 is an
'express' train. It is late. You
are still in time to catch it,
provided you run.

(Sul treno)   **(On the train)**

Ah, ecco finalmente uno
scompartimento di seconda.
Scùsino, è lìbero quel posto
vicino al finestrino?
Credo di sì.

Oh, here's a second class
compartment at last. Excuse
me, is that seat near the
window free?
I think so.

Scusi (excuse), *mi scusi* (excuse me), *ci scusi* (excuse us), or, when
talking to relatives, friends and children, *scusa, scùsami, scùsaci,*
are used in addressing one person only. When more than one
person are addressed, *scùsino, mi scùsino, ci scùsino*, or, familiarly,

scusate, scusàtemi, scusàteci, are used. They can be replaced by *mi dispiace* (I am sorry), *ci dispiace* (we are sorry), e.g.

■ *Mi scusi, è occupato questo posto?* (Excuse me, is this seat taken?)
Scusi se la disturbo (Sorry for bothering you)
Scusate il disturbo (Sorry for the bother)
Mi dispiace disturbarLa (I am sorry to bother you)
Scusa il ritardo (Sorry for the delay)
Scusa, che cosa hai detto? (I beg your pardon, what did you say?)
Scusi, non capisco (I am sorry, I don't understand)
Ci dispiace dell'accaduto (We are sorry for what happened)
Mi dispiace, ma non sono italiano (I am sorry, I am afraid I am not Italian)
La prego di accettare le mie scuse (Please accept my apologies)
Con le nostre scuse (With our apologies)

Therefore, *scusi* and the other forms are used: (a) to call the attention of people, (b) to apologize for something, (c) to ask somebody to repeat what has just been said.

Dov'è is short for *dove è* (where is).

La ferrovia (railway); *le Ferrovie dello Stato (FS)* (Italian State Railways); *il ferroviere* (railwayman); *il bigliettàrio* (booking clerk; conductor); *il conduttore* (conductor); *il macchinista* (train engine driver); *il treno* (train); *il capostazione* (station-master); *la polizia ferroviària* (railway police).

There are four kinds of trains in Italy. *Il ràpido (Rap.)*, the fastest, stops at main cities only and requires a supplementary charge (*il supplemento ràpido*) and sometimes also compulsory booking (*la prenotazione obbligatòria*) and/or a first class ticket. A special type of *ràpido* is the TEE (Trans Europe Express). *L'espresso (Expr.)* is a fast train stopping at about the same main towns as the *ràpido*, though it is usually not so comfortable and fast; it may require second class passengers to travel a minimum distance, usually either a hundred and fifty or two hundred kilometres. *Il diretto (Dir.)* stops at fairly large or important towns. *Il locale (Loc.)* stops at all or almost all stops, including very small towns, and is the slowest and often consists of carriages similar to those of a city underground train or suburban train. The traveller should check carefully with the timetable for the features of trains. Once you have bought your ticket, you can board your train and leave your station of destination without your ticket being checked, except on board by the conductor. Tickets may be bought on board a train, but a surcharge is made. Conductors should preferably be informed that you are boarding a train without a ticket, in order to avoid possible charges of fraud.

Fare in tempo or *èssere in tempo* (to be in time); *c'è tempo* (there is still time); *fare tardi* or *èssere in ritardo* (to be late).

IMPERATIVE

The imperative forms of verbs are used when commands are given, or polite requests are made, or something is wished to happen:

First conjugation
parla or *parli* (speak!)
parli or *che parli* (let him, her, speak)
parliamo (let's speak)
parlate or *pàrlino* (speak!)
pàrlino or *che pàrlino* (let them speak)

Second conjugation
vendi or *venda* (sell!)
venda or *che venda* (let him, her sell)
vendiamo (let's sell)
vendete or *vèndano* (sell!)
vèndano or *che vèndano* (let them sell)

Third conjugation
dormi or *dorma* (sleep!)
dorma or *che dorma* (let him, her sleep)
dormiamo (let us sleep)
dormite or *dòrmano* (sleep!)
dòrmano or *che dòrmano* (let them sleep)

The student will have noticed that the formal forms of the imperative, i.e. *parli, pàrlino* (speak!), *venda, vèndano* (sell!) and *dorma, dòrmano* (sleep!), as well as *parli, pàrlino* (let him, her, them speak), *venda, vèndano* (let him, her, them sell) and *dorma, dòrmano* (let him, her, them sleep), are taken from the subjunctive. The other forms are the same as in the indicative, except for *parla* (speak!) which is *parli* (you speak, you are speaking) in the indicative.

Imperatives may be intensified by adding *pure* (do), or *suvvia, avanti, dai* (come on), or *prego* (please):

Vendete tutto! (Sell everything!)
Non tocchi niente! (Don't touch anything!)
Dormi pure (Do sleep!)
Avanti, parlate! (Come on, speak up!)
Dai, muòviti (Come on, hurry up)
Prego, si accòmodi (Sit down, please)

Polite alternatives to the imperative forms are sentences starting with *vuoi?, vuole?, volete? vògliono?*, or *vòglia, vogliate, vògliano*, all meaning 'will you please, would you please', or *vorresti?, vorrebbe?, vorreste?, vorrèbbero?* (would you please), or *ti dispiacerebbe, vi dispiacerebbe, Le dispiacerebbe* (would you mind), or *ti dispiace, vi dispiace, Le dispiace* (do you mind), or *vuoi èssere così gentile da, vuole èssere così gentile da*, etc.:

Vòglia accomodarsi, prego (Will you come in, please?)
Vorrebbe èssere così gentile da passarmi il sale?
(Would you be so kind as to pass me the salt?)
Le dispiacerebbe dirmi il suo nome? (Would you mind telling me your name?)

The second person familiar of the imperative, like *parla, vendi* and *dormi*, is replaced by the infinitive when the sentence is negative:

Non parlargli (Don't talk to him)
Non dormire (Don't sleep)
Non chiùdere la porta (Don't shut the door)
Non aprire la finestra (Don't open the window)

As previously mentioned, the unstressed pronouns are placed after imperatives, except for the formal forms. They combine with the verb to form one word:

Àmami (Love me)
Domàndaglielo (Ask him or her, that)

Vendeteceli (Sell them to us)
But *Me la venda, per favore* (Sell it to me, please)
Ce lo mostrino (Show it to us)

When imperatives combine with pronouns, doubling of the consonant occurs in the following forms:

Fa (do, make) followed by *mi, ti, lo, la, li, le* and *ci*:
Fammi vedere (Let me see)
Facci strada (Lead us)
Facceli conoscere (Introduce us to them)
Fammici pensare (Let me think it over)

Da (give) followed by *mi, ti, lo, la, li, le* and *ci*:

Dacci oggi il nostro pane (Give us today our bread)
Dammelo quando vuoi (Give it to me when you like)
Dallo a me (Give it to me)

VERBS WITH DIFFERENT FORMS OF PRESENT TENSE

A number of Italian verbs form their present tenses of the indicative, subjunctive and imperative with different variations in their roots or endings. These have been grouped and the group numbers have been kept throughout the book for the convenience of the student:

Group 1: verb *avere* (to have)

Indicative	Subjunctive	Imperative
ho	abbia	
hai	abbia	abbi
ha	abbia	abbia
abbiamo	abbiamo	abbiamo
avete	abbiate	abbiate
hanno	abbiano	abbiano

Group 2: verb *essere* (to be)

sono	sia	
sei	sia	sii
è	sia	si
siamo	siamo	siamo

siete	siate	siate
sono	sĩano	sĩno

Group 3: the majority of verbs in *-ire* add *-isc-* before some endings, e.g. *finire* (to finish)

finisco	finisca	
finisci	finisca	finisci
finisce	finisca	finisca
finiamo	finiamo	finiamo
finite	finiate	finite
finĩscono	finĩscano	finĩscano

More verbs:

abolire (to abolish)
agire (to act)
ammonire (to warn)
appassire (to wither)
applaudire (to applaud)
arrossire (to blush)
arrostire (to roast)
assalire (to assail)
attribuire (to attribute)
capire (to understand)
chiarire (to clarify)
colpire (to hit)
concepire (to conceive)
condire (to season)
contribuire (to contribute)
costituire (to constitute)
costruire (to construct)
custodire (to look after)
definire (to define)
demolire (to demolish)
digerire (to digest)
diminuire (to diminish)
distribuire (to distribute)
esaurire (to exhaust)
favorire (to favour)
ferire (to wound)

fiorire (to flourish, blossom)
fornire (to supply)
garantire (to guarantee)
gestire (to administer)
guarire (to recover)
impaurire (to scare)
impedire (to prevent)
indebolire (to weaken)
infastidire (to annoy)
ingrandire (to enlarge)
inserire (to insert)
istruire (to instruct)
marcire (to rot)
nutrire (to nourish)
obbedire (to obey)
preferire (to prefer)
progredire (to make progress)
proibire (to forbid)
pulire (to clean)
punire (to punish)
rapire (to abduct, kidnap)
restituire (to give back)
riferire (to report)
riunire (to reunite)
seppellire (to bury)
sostituire (to substitute)

sparire (to disappear)	*suggerire* (to suggest)	
spedire (to send off)	*tossire* (to cough)	
stabilire (to establish)	*tradire* (to betray)	
starnutire (to sneeze)	*unire* (to unite)	
stordire (to stun, daze)		

Group 4: verbs doubling *c* in some forms, e.g. *tacere* (to keep silent)

tàccio	*tàccia*	
taci	*tàccia*	*taci*
tace	*tàccia*	*tàccia*
tacciamo	*tacciamo*	*tacciamo*
tacete	*tacciate*	*tacete*
tàcciono	*tàcciano*	*tàcciano*

More verbs:

piacere (to like)
dispiacere (to be sorry; to displease)
giacere (to lie down)
nuòcere (to harm)

Group 5: verbs inserting double *cc* in certain forms, e.g.

fare (to do, to make)

fàccio	*fàccia*	
fai	*fàccia*	*fa* or *fai*
fa	*fàccia*	*fàccia*
facciamo	*facciamo*	*facciamo*
fate	*facciate*	*fate*
fanno	*fàcciano*	*fàcciano*

More verbs:

disfare (to undo)
soddisfare (to satisfy)

Group 6: verbs changing -*n*- into -*ng*- in certain forms, e.g. *venire* (to come)

vengo	*venga*	
vieni	*venga*	*vieni*
viene	*venga*	*venga*

veniamo	*veniamo*	*veniamo*
venite	*veniate*	*venite*
v̶ę̈ngono	*v̶ę̈ngano*	*v̶ę̈ngano*

More verbs:

contenere (to contain)
convenire (to suit; to agree)
mantenere (to maintain, keep)
ritenere (to think; to retain)
svenire (to faint)

Group 7: verbs changing -*l*- into -*lg*- and -*gli*- in certain forms, e.g. *valere* (to be worth)

valgo	*valga*	
vali	*valga*	*vali*
vale	*valga*	*valga*
vagliamo	*vagliamo*	*vagliamo*
valete	*vagliate*	*valete*
v̶ălgono	*v̶ălgano*	*v̶ălgano*

Also:

prevalere (to prevail)

Group 8: verbs changing -*gli*- into -*lg*- in certain forms, e.g. *c̶ǫ̈gliere* (to pick)

colgo	*colga*	
cogli	*colga*	*cogli*
coglie	*colga*	*colga*
cogliamo	*cogliamo*	*cogliamo*
cogliete	*cogliate*	*cogliete*
c̶ǫ̈lgono	*c̶ǫ̈lgano*	*c̶ǫ̈lgano*

More verbs:

acc̶ǫ̈gliere (to welcome)
racc̶ǫ̈gliere (to collect)
t̶ǫ̈gliere (to remove)

Group 9: verbs changing *-l-* into *-lg-* in certain forms, e.g. *salire* (to go up)

salgo	*salga*	
sali	*salga*	*sali*
sale	*salga*	*salga*
saliamo	*saliamo*	*saliamo*
salite	*saliate*	*salite*
sàlgono	*sàlgano*	*sàlgano*

More verbs:

assalire (to assail, to assault)
risalire (to date back; to go up again)

Group 10: verbs alternating the hard and the soft sounds of *-g-*, e.g. *dipìngere* (to paint)

dipingo	*dipinga*	
dipingi	*dipinga*	*dipingi*
dipinge	*dipinga*	*dipinga*
dipingiamo	*dipingiamo*	*dipingiamo*
dipingete	*dipingiate*	*dipingete*
dipìngono	*dipìngano*	*dipìngano*

More verbs:

aggiùngere (to add)
avvòlgere (to wrap up; to wind)
coinvòlgere (to involve)
costrìngere (to force)
fìngere (to pretend, feign)
mùngere (to milk)
piàngere (to weep, cry)
rivòlgersi (to apply to)
sconvòlgere (to upset, unsettle)
strìngere (to grasp, clench, hug, grip, hold tightly)
ùngere (to grease, oil)

Group 11: verbs changing -rr- into -n- and -ng-, e.g. *supporre* (to suppose)

suppongo	*supponga*	
supponi	*supponga*	*supponi*
suppone	*supponga*	*supponga*
supponiamo	*supponiamo*	*supponiamo*
supponete	*supponiate*	*supponete*
suppòngono	*suppòngano*	*suppòngano*

More verbs:

comporre (to compose)
deporre (to depose; to lay down)
disporre (to arrange)
esporre (to expose; to expound)
porre (to set)
proporre (to propose)
scomporre (to break up)
sovrapporre (to superimpose)

Group 12: verbs changing -rr into -gg in certain forms, e.g. *trarre* (to draw)

traggo	*tragga*	
trai	*tragga*	*trai*
trae	*tragga*	*tragga*
traiamo	*traiamo*	*traiamo*
traete	*traiate*	*traete*
tràggono	*tràggano*	*tràggano*

More verbs:

attrarre (to attract)   *estrarre* (to extract)
detrarre (to deduce)   *sottrarre* (to subtract; to purloin)

Group 13: verbs alternating the hard and the soft sounds of -gg-, e.g. *distrùggere* (to destroy)

distruggo	*distrugga*	
distruggi	*distrugga*	*distruggi*
distrugge	*distrugga*	*distrugga*

distruggiamo	*distruggiamo*	*distruggiamo*
distruggete	*distruggiate*	*distruggete*
distrŭggono	*distrŭggano*	*distrŭggano*

More verbs:

frĭggere (to fry)
inflĭggere (to inflict)
lĕggere (to read)
protĕggere (to protect)
redĭgere (to draw up)
rĕggere (to hold upright)
sconfĭggere (to defeat)

Group 14: verbs alternating the hard and the soft sounds of -sc-, e.g. *conoscere* (to know, to be acquainted with)

conosco	*conosca*	
conosci	*conosca*	*conosci*
conosce	*conosca*	*conosca*
conosciamo	*conosciamo*	*conosciamo*
conoscete	*conosciate*	*conoscete*
conŏscono	*conŏscano*	*conŏscano*

More verbs:

crĕscere (to grow, to grow up)   *născere* (to be born)

Group 15: verbs inserting either hard or soft -c- in most forms, e.g. *dire* (to say, to tell)

dico	*dica*	
dici	*dica*	*di'* or *dici*
dice	*dica*	*dica*
diciamo	*diciamo*	*diciamo*
dite	*diciate*	*dite*
dĭcono	*dĭcano*	*dĭcano*

More verbs:

benedire (to bless)
contraddire (to contradict)
disdire (to cancel)

maledire (to curse)
predire (to anticipate, forecast)

Group 16: verbs changing *-rr-* into either hard or soft *-c-* in all forms, e.g. *tradurre* (to translate)

traduco	traduca	
traduci	traduca	traduci
traduce	traduca	traduca
traduciamo	traduciamo	traduciamo
traducete	traduciate	traducete
tradŭcono	tradŭcano	tradŭcano

More verbs:

condurre (to lead) *ridurre* (to reduce)
dedurre (to deduce, infer) *sedurre* (to seduce)
produrre (to produce)

Group 17: verbs alternating the hard and soft sounds of *-c-*, e.g. *vĭncere* (to win)

vinco	vinca	
vinci	vinca	vinci
vince	vinca	vinca
vinciamo	vinciamo	vinciamo
vincete	vinciate	vincete
vĭncono	vĭncano	vĭncano

More verbs:

avvĭncere (to thrill) *distŏrcere* (to distort)
convĭncere (to convince)

Group 18: verbs keeping the hard sound of *-c* and *-g-* throughout, with the insertion of *-h-* if required, e.g. *giocare* (to play)

gioco	giochi	
giochi	giochi	gioca
gioca	giochi	giochi
giochiamo	giochiamo	giochiamo
giocate	giochiate	giocate
giŏcano	giŏchino	giŏchino

More verbs:

caricare (to load)
cercare (to try; to look for)
fregare (to rub, scrub; to swindle, cheat, dupe, take in)
imbiancare (to whiten)
legare (to bind, to tie)
mancare (to lack; to miss)
negare (to deny)
pregare (to pray, to beg)
soffocare (to suffocate, suppress)
toccare (to touch)

Group 19: verbs keeping the soft sound of *-c-* throughout, with the insertion of *-i-* when required, e.g. *cuŏcere* (to cook)

cuŏcio	*cuŏcia*	
cuoci	*cuŏcia*	*cuoci*
cuoce	*cuŏcia*	*cuŏcia*
cuociamo	*cuociamo*	*cuociamo*
cuocete	*cuociate*	*cuocete*
cuŏciono	*cuŏciano*	*cuŏciano*

Group 20: verbs changing *-r-* to *-i-* in certain forms, e.g. *morire* (to die), which also changes *-o-* to *-uo-* when stressed.

muŏio	*muŏia*	
muori	*muŏia*	*muori*
muore	*muŏia*	*muŏia*
moriamo	*moriamo*	*moriamo*
morite	*moriate*	*morite*
muŏiono	*muŏiano*	*muŏiano*

More verbs:

apparire (to appear, turn up)   *parere* (to seem)
comparire (to turn up)   *scomparire* (to disappear)

Group 21: verbs distinguished by double *-n-* in the third person plural of the indicative and by final *-a-* in the three singular forms of the subjunctive and the third person of the imperative, e.g. *dare* (to give)

do	dia	
dai	dia	dà or dai
dà	dia	dia
diamo	diamo	diamo
date	diate	date
danno	dïano	dïano

stare (to stay; to stand)

This verb has no accent on the third person singular or in the imperative.

Group 22: the verb *bere* (to drink) inserts -*v*- throughout:

bevo	beva	
bevi	beva	bevi
beve	beva	beva
beviamo	beviamo	beviamo
bevete	beviate	bevete
bĕvono	bĕvano	bĕvano

Group 23: the verb *andare* (to go) has forms deriving from the ancient verb *vădere*:

vado	vada	
vai	vada	va or vai
va	vada	vada
andiamo	andiamo	andiamo
andate	andiate	andate
vanno	vădano	vădano

Group 24: the verb *uscire* (to go out) changes -*u*- into -*e*- when this vowel is stressed, and the soft sound of -*sc* into the hard one:

esco	esca	
esci	esca	esci
esce	esca	esca
usciamo	usciamo	usciamo
uscite	usciate	uscite
ĕscano	ĕscano	ĕscano

The verb *riuscire* (to succeed) follows the same pattern.

Group 25: the verb *udire* (to hear) changes the vowel *-u-* into *-o-* when this vowel is stressed:

odo	oda	
odi	oda	odi
ode	oda	oda
udiamo	udiamo	udiamo
udite	udiate	udite
ŏdono	ŏdano	ŏdano

Group 26: the verb *sapere* (to know, to know how) shows various irregularities, including the disappearance or the doubling of *-p-*:

so	sặppia	
sai	sặppia	sappi
sa	sặppia	sặppia
sappiamo	sappiamo	sappiamo
sapete	sappiate	sappiate
sanno	sặppiano	sặppiano

Group 27: the verb *sedere* (to sit) changes the vowel *-e-* into *-ie-* when this is stressed:

siedo or seggo	sieda or segga	
siedi	sieda or segga	siedi
siede	sieda or segga	sieda or segga
sediamo	sediamo	sediamo
sedete	sediate	sedete
sièdono or sèggono	sièdano or sèggano	sièdano or sèggano

Group 28: the verb *dovere* (to have to, must, should, ought to) changes *-o-* into *-e-* when this vowel is stressed and *-v-* into *-bb-* in certain unstressed forms:

devo or debbo	deva or debba	no imperative
devi	deva or debba	
deve	deva or debba	
dobbiamo	dobbiamo	
dovete	dobbiate	
dèvono or dèbbono	dèvano or dèbbano	

Group 29: the verb *potere* (to be able, to be possible, to be likely, can, may) is characterized by the change of *-t-* to *-ss-* or by its

disappearance in certain forms and by the change of -o- into -uo- when this is stressed:

posso	possa	no imperative
puoi	possa	
può	possa	
possiamo	possiamo	
potete	possiate	
pòssono	pòssano	

Group 30: the verb *volere* (to want) is characterized by either the disappearance of -*l*- or its change into -*gli*- and by the change of -*o*- into -*uo*- when stressed:

vòglio	vòglia	no imperative
vuoi	vòglia	
vuole	vòglia	
vogliamo	vogliamo	
volete	vogliate	
vògliono	vògliano	

■ PRESENTAZIONI: read and translate

Ti presento la Signorina Làura Negri.
Piacere di conoscèrLa, Signorina. Molto lieta.
Mi chiamo Giorgio Conti, e Lei?
Io sono Giovanni Ferrari. Ma diàmoci del tu. Chiàmami pure Gianni.
Sì, è mèglio. Sei italiano anche tu, vero?
No, sono svìzzero, ticinese.
Davvero?

Exercise 1

Give instructions to someone who wants to take a train and go somewhere.

Exercise 2

Turn the following sentences into imperative:

(a) *Me lo vendi?*
(b) *Glielo dite voi?*
(c) *Glieli chiediamo sùbito.*
(d) *Perchè non ce ne dai un po'?*
(e) *Mi ci fate sedere su questa poltrona?*

Exercise 3

Answer the following questions with prohibitions:

(a) *Apriamo le finestre?*
(b) *Mamma, prendo un po' di dolce?*
(c) *Si può fumare qui?*
(d) *Rimango ancora un po'?*
(e) *Dico tutto?*

Exercise 4

Turn the following informal imperatives into formal ones:

(a) *Dimmi che cosa vuoi.*
(b) *Traduci questo, per favore.*
(c) *Non morire!*
(d) *Non andàrtene!*
(e) *Esci da qui immediatamente.*

Exercise 5

Write a dialogue between two people who are going to go somewhere by train and express their fears, hopes, doubts and similar psychological states (implying the use of the imperative and the subjunctive).

LESSON 6

■ ALL' ALBERGO

Il signore desìdera?
Ha una càmera dòppia, con bagno o dòccia?

Le dispiace darmi un documento, per cortesia? Il passaporto. . . .
Basta la patente?

Sì, certo.
Èccola.
Per quanto la vuole?

Mi fermo tre notti.
Prende la colazione domattina?
Vorrei fare mezza pensione: colazione e pranzo.
Bene, signore. La colazione si serve tra le sette e mezza e le nove, il pranzo tra mezzogiorno e le due. Vuole la svèglia alla mattina?
Sì, alle sette e un quarto, per cortesia.
Pietro, prendi le valìgie e accompagna il signore alla stanza ventidue.

AT THE HOTEL

What can I do for you, sir?
Have you got a double bedroom, with a bath or shower?

Do you mind giving me a document, please? Your passport. . . .
Is my driving-licence sufficient?
Yes, certainly.
Here you are.
How long do you want it for, sir?

I'll stay three nights.
Will you have breakfast tomorrow morning?
I'd like to have half board: breakfast and lunch.
Good, sir. Breakfast is served between half past seven and nine, lunch between noon and two. Do you wish to be woken up in the morning?
Yes, at quarter past seven, please.
Peter, take the suitcases and see the gentleman to room no. 22.

There are *càmere sìngole* (single rooms), *dòppie* (double), *a due letti* (two beds), etc.

A document of identity (*documento di identità*) is requested when booking into a hotel or guest-house.

Basta, plural *bástano*, are forms of the verb *bastare* (to be enough, sufficient). *Basta!* (That's enough; enough of it! Stop it!). *Bástano pochi soldi* (A little money is enough).

Si serve (is served): *si* (one, people) is often used to make a sentence passive.

ORDER OF WORDS

The subject of a sentence may be either at the beginning or at the end of a sentence, as the verb form usually makes the meaning unambiguous, e.g.

La gente ci conosce e ci tratta bene (People know us and treat us well), or
Ci conosce e ci tratta bene la gente (People know us and treat us well)

The subject may be at the beginning, at the end or after the verb when it is a question, e.g.

Il cameriere parla l'inglese? or
Parla il cameriere l'inglese? or
Parla l'inglese il cameriere? (Does the waiter speak English?)

The intonation of questions is rising. But it is falling, if the question starts with an interrogative word or expression such as: *chi?* (who), *quale*, plural *quali?* (which, what), *che*, or *che cosa*, or *cosa?* (what), *di chi?* (whose), *dove?* (where), *come?* (how), *quando?* (when), *da quando?* (since when), *da quanto tempo?* or *da quanto?* (how long), *perchè?* (why), *come mai?* (how come), *fino a quando?* (until when), *fino a che punto?* (to what extent), *per quanto?* or *per quanto tempo?* (how long), *per quale ragione?* or *per quale motivo?* (for what reason), *quanto, quanta*, plural *quanti, quante?* (how much, how many).

Notice such question-tags as *vero?* or *è vero?* or *non è vero?* or *no?* or *eh?* (this is very colloquial), all of which mean 'is it? isn't it?, does he?, doesn't she?' and similar short questions used to ask for confirmation, and *davvero?* or *veramente?* (really?, is that so?). All of these have a rising intonation, e.g.

Capite l'italiano, vero? (You understand Italian, don't you?)
Davvero non capisci l'italiano? (Is it really true that you don't understand Italian?)

PARTITIVES

In order to indicate an unspecified or limited quantity, such as 'some', 'a few', or 'a little', Italian nouns are used without articles, or they may be preceded by *del, dello, dell', della* (some, a little), *dei, degli, delle* (some, a few), or *alcuni, alcune* (some, a few), or *qualche* (a few) followed by a singular noun, e.g.

Vorrei àcqua minerale or *vorrei dell'àcqua minerale* (I would like some mineral water)
Cerco testi di chìmica or *Cerco dei testi di chìmica* or *Cerco qualche testo di chìmica* or *Cerco alcuni testi di chìmica* (I am looking for some chemistry textbooks)

If the sentence is negative the noun is either without any article or preceded by *alcun, alcuno, alcuna* or *nessun, nessuno, nessuna,* if the noun is countable, e.g.

Non ho àcqua minerale (I have not got any mineral water)
Non abbiamo testi di chìmica or *Non abbiamo alcun testo di chìmica* or *Non abbiamo nessun testo di chìmica* (We have not got any chemistry textbooks)

When the noun is omitted, the pronoun *ne* (some of) is used, followed or not by *qualcuno, qualcuna,* or a number or another pronoun, if the indefinite noun is countable, or by *alcuno, alcuna* or *nessuno, nessuna,* if the sentence is negative and the noun is countable, e.g.

Ha testi di chìmica? (Have you got any chemistry textbooks?)
Sì, ne abbiamo or *Sì, ne abbiamo qualcuno* (Yes, we have got some) or *Sì, ne abbiamo due* (Yes, we have got two) or *Sì, ne abbiamo molti* (Yes, we have got many)
Mi dà dell'àcqua minerale? (Could I have some mineral water?)
Mi dispiace, non ne abbiamo (I am sorry, we have not got any)
Ha testi di chìmica? (Have you got any chemistry textbooks?)
Mi dispiace, ma non ne abbiamo or *non ne abbiamo alcuno* (I am sorry, we have not got any)

STRESSED PRONOUNS

The following pronouns are used instead of the unstressed ones listed in Lesson 5 when they are preceded by a preposition, or are set in contrast with another pronoun or noun, or are emphatic, or are in isolation, or are the second part of a comparison:

me (me)	*se* (oneself, oneselves)
te or *Lei* (you)	*noi* (us)
lui (him)	*voi* or *Loro* (you)
lei (her)	*loro* (them)

For example:

Vengo con te, se vuoi (I'm coming with you, if you like)
Ama te, non me (She loves you, not me)
Siete voi i colpèvoli (It is you who are guilty)
Sai chi vogliono premiare? Te (Do you know who they want to give a prize to? You)
Sono più alto di te e di tutti voi (I'm taller than you and all of you)

For special emphasis, the adjective *stesso, stessa,* plural *stessi, stesse,* which corresponds to pronoun forms ending in self, may follow the pronouns, or the adverb *pròprio* (just, exactly) may precede them, e.g.

Conosci te stesso (Know yourself)
Pènsano solo a se stessi (They only think of themselves)
Cerco pròprio voi (I'm looking for *you*)

Both stressed and unstressed pronouns can be reinforced by *l'un l'altro, l'una l'altra,* plural *gli uni gli altri, le une le altre,* or by the adverb *reciprocamente* (mutually), if they mean 'each other, one another', e.g.

Amàtevi gli uni gli altri (Love one another)

PRONOMINAL VERBS

These consist of verb and one or two unstressed pronouns, the first of which may be a reflexive *si* or the place pronoun *ci* (there), while the second is either the feminine pronoun *la,* possibly standing for *cosa* (thing), or the pronoun *ne* (from there, or of it):

Avèrcela con (to have it in for)
Avèrsene a male (to take it amiss)
Andàrsene (to go off)
Aspettàrsela (to expect it)
Dàrsela a gambe (to take to one's heels)
Fàrcela (to make it, to scrape through)
Cavàrsela (to scrape through)
Fàrselo dire (to be told repeatedly)
Fàrsene di (to do with)
Farla finita, or *smètterla* or *piantarla* or *finirla* (to stop it)
Farla a, or *farla in barba a* (to get the better of)
Farsi vedere (to be seen; to show up)
Godèrsela (to have fun)
Mèttercela, or *mèttercela tutta* (to do the utmost)
Fregàrsene, or, less vulgar, *infischiàrsene* or *non importàrsene* (not to care a damn)
Filàrsela, or *svignàrsela*, or *bàttersela* (to take French leave)
Immaginàrsela, or *figuràrsela*, or *immaginarsi*, or *figurarsi* (to picture to oneself)
Prèndersela, or *prèndersela a male* (to take umbrage, offence)
Prèndersela (to be worried, concerned)
Prèndersela còmoda (to take it easy; to take one's time)
Prèndersela a cuore, or *prèndersi a cuore* (to take things to heart)
Spassàrsela (to have a good time)
Vedèrsela da sè (to see to it, about it)
Darsi da fare (to bestir oneself, bustle about, be active)
Farsi in quattro (to go out of one's way)
Farci caso (to take notice)

For example:

Con chi ce l'hai? (Who do you have it in for?)
Non avèrtene a male (Don't take it amiss)
Ce ne andiamo, siamo stufi (We'll go off, we're fed up)
Vàttene (Go away)
Ce la fai? (Can you manage?)
Non ce la faccio più (I cannot go on any more)
È ora di finirla (It's high time all this came to an end)
Non vi fate mai vedere (You never drop in)
Non me l'aspettavo da te (I wouldn't have expected this from you)

Me ne frego (I don't give a damn)

Non te ne importa pròprio niente? (Don't you care at all?)

Te l'immàgini Carlo ballare? (Just think of Charles dancing)

Se la prende troppo, gli viene l'esaurimento nervoso (He gets too worried, he'll get nervous exhaustion)

Non ci fare caso se non saluta (Don't take any notice if he doesn't say hello)

Ce la godiamo pròprio qui; ce la spassiamo tutto il santo giorno (We have lots of fun here; we have a marvellous time all day long)

Exercise 1

Turn the following sentences into negative ones:

(a) *Vòglio un po' d'àcqua minerale.*
(b) *Abbiamo anche testi di chìmica.*
(c) *Sì, ne abbiamo molti.*
(d) *Cerchiamo qualche persona che vòglia collaborare.*
(e) *Ci sono dei cioccolatini e delle caramelle.*

Exercise 2

Insert a pronoun or an adjective or an adverb, to make the sentence more emphatic:

(a) *Penso a tutto.*
(b) *Non sono i colpèvoli.*
(c) *Aiutàtevi.*
(d) *Telèfonami, quando arrivi.*
(e) *Lo amo molto.*

Exercise 3

Ask a person you have met what he does by profession and what he is doing here, where he is staying, how he travels around, when he plans to go back home, how long he has been staying in Florence, why he likes to stay in Italy.

Exercise 4

Translate:

(a) You are joking, aren't you?
(b) Am I?
(c) I think you are.
(d) You don't think so, do you?
(e) She isn't too tired, is she?

Exercise 5

Turn the following sentences into imperatives:

(a) *Ve lo fate sempre dire due volte.*
(b) *Te ne vai?*
(c) *Devi aspettàrtela da uno come lui.*
(d) *Te ne freghi di tutto.*
(e) *Noi ce la svigniamo sùbito.*

LESSON 7

■ COME HA PASSATO IL TEMPO?

HOW DID YOU SPEND YOUR TIME?

Ha passato bene il week-end, Signor Fabbri?
Non ho fatto niente di speciale. Sabato sono stato tutta la mattina a far còmpere, al supermercato, con mia mòglie e mia fìglia.
Poi sono passato dal fotògrafo a ritirare le fotografie della gita che abbiamo fatto in montagna.

Did you have a nice weekend, Mr Fabbri?
I did nothing special. On Saturday I went shopping all morning, to the supermarket, with my wife and daughter.

Then I called at the photographer's to collect the pictures of the trip we took to the mountains.

Cos'altro ho fatto? Nel pomeriggio ho aiutato mia moglie nelle pulizie, ho riparato il campanello d'ingresso e infine ho guardato i cartoni animati alla televisione con mia figlia. Alla sera sono rimasto a casa a vedere un film alla televisione. Domenica mattina sono andato a messa e a giocare al tennis, e, nel pomeriggio, vista la giornata magnifica, abbiamo fatto un giro in macchina in campagna.

What else did I do? In the afternoon I helped my wife with the housework, repaired the doorbell and eventually I watched the cartoons on television with my daughter. In the evening I stayed at home to watch a film on television.
On Sunday morning I went to Mass and to play tennis and, in the afternoon, when we saw what a splendid day it was, we went for a drive in the country.

E Lei, che cosa ha fatto di bello?
Sono andato in macchina in montagna.

What about you? What did you do?
I drove to the mountains.

Niente di speciale (nothing special): *di* is to be added after *niente*, *nulla* (nothing), *qualcosa* (something), *qualunque cosa* (anything, whatever) followed by an adjective.

Passare means 'to pass; to spend (time); to call at'. *Essere* may mean 'to go' when used in the past. Both verbs, as well as other verbs of motion, are followed by *da* and person, or by *in* or *a* and a place. *A* is not usually accompanied by an article, e.g.

Passo da te domani (I'll drop in at your house tomorrow)
Sono stato a casa sua ieri (I was at his house yesterday)
È andato in città (He went to town)
Resta all'ospedale (He is staying in hospital), or *in ospedale*

In macchina or *con la macchina* or *in auto* or *con l'auto* (by car, in a car). *In treno* or *col treno* (by train). *In motocicletta* or *in moto* or *con la motocicletta* or *con la moto* (by motorcycle). *In bicicletta* or *con la bicicletta* (by bicycle). *In aereo* or *con l'aereo* (by plane). *In autobus* or *con l'autobus* (by bus). *In nave* or *con la nave* (by ship). *A piedi* (on foot, walking).

PERFECT TENSE

The perfect is one of the most frequent ways of referring to past events, in particular when speaking or writing informally. It is used to denote something which was completed in the recent past and can also be used to denote something which happened a long time ago, but with which the speaker is still psychologically involved. It is more widely used by northern Italians than central or southern Italians.

It is often dependent on such phrases as *ieri* (yesterday), *poco fa* (a little while ago), *pròprio ora* or *pròprio adesso* (just now), *un giorno* (one day), *la settimana scorsa* (last week) and other expressions with the adjective *scorso, passato* (last), *dieci anni fa* (ten years ago) and other expressions with *fa* (ago), specific times of the day, or such adverbs of time and frequency as *mai* (never), *sempre* (always), *già* (already), *ancora* (still, yet), *più* (no longer), which are all placed between the auxiliary and the main verb, and *finora* (so far), *tante volte* (so many times), *in quel momento, allora* (at that time, then).

The implied idea is also that the event described by the verb was brief, almost instantaneous, or is anyway thought of as a single occurrence, rather than a prolonged or continuous or constantly repeated action or state of mind.

This tense, called in Italian *passato pròssimo*, is a compound tense, consisting of the present tense of *avere* (to have) followed by the past participle of the main verb. *Èssere* (to be) is used, instead of *avere*, if the verb is reflexive, or passive, or impersonal, or with a few intransitive verbs, i.e. verbs which cannot be followed by a direct object, such as *andare* (to go), *venire* (to come), *entrare* (to go in), *uscire* (to go out), *salire* (to go up), *scèndere* (to go down), *restare* or *stare* or *rimanere* (to stay, remain), *partire* (to depart, leave), *arrivare* (to arrive), *cadere* (to fall), *èssere* (to be), *nàscere* (to be born), *morire* (to die), *accòrrere* (to rush), *ritornare* or *tornare* or *tornare indietro* (to return, come back), *scappare* or *fuggire* (to flee, escape), *sparire* (to disappear), *svanire* (to vanish), *scomparire* (to disappear), *sembrare* or *parere* or *apparire* (to seem, appear), *comparire* or *apparire* (to turn up, appear), *diventare* or *divenire* (to become), *piacere* (to please, like), *riuscire* (to succeed, to manage), *succèdere* (to happen; to succeed), *emèrgere* (to emerge), *evàdere* (to evade), *àrdere* or *bruciare* (to burn).

The past participle (*particìpio passato*) has the form of an adjective ending in *-to* in the masculine singular, e.g. *parlato* (spoken), *venduto* (sold), *dormito* (slept). The student will have noticed that verbs ending in *-ere*, like *vèndere* (to sell), change the *-e-* into *-u-* before the ending *-to*.

Past participles vary in gender and number if the auxiliary verb is *èssere,* e.g.

La posta non è ancora arrivata oggi (The mail has not yet arrived today)
Gli òspiti sono tutti partiti (The guests have all left)

Past participles do not vary in gender and number with the auxiliary verb *avere*, unless this is preceded by the direct object pronouns *la* (her), *li* (them, m.), *le* (them, f.), or, optionally, *mi* (me), *ti* (you), *ci* (us), *vi* (you) and *che* (whom, which), e.g.

Li avete già conosciuti? (Have you met them before?)
L'ho vista una volta (I saw her once)
I bambini hanno mangiato (The children have had their meal)
Non ci hanno riconosciuto or *riconosciuti* (They did not recognize us)

PERFECT TENSE OF REFLEXIVE, RECIPROCAL AND IMPERSONAL VERBS

Reflexive and reciprocal verbs (see Lesson 3), impersonal verbs and phrases, as well as sentences starting with the impersonal *si* (see Lesson 10), all form their perfect tense with the auxiliary *essere* (to be):

Ci siamo già conosciuti (We have already met)
Vi siete lavati bene? (Have you washed yourselves well?)
Non è mai successo prima (It has never happened before)
Si sono dette molte cose sul suo conto (They have told a lot of stories about him)

PERFECT SUBJUNCTIVE

This tense is formed with *àbbia, àbbia, àbbia, abbiamo, abbiate, àbbiano* or *sia, sia, sia, siamo, siate, stano*, as required, followed by the past participle. It replaces the perfect indicative in the cases detailed in Lesson 4:

Spero che àbbia capito e si comporti bene (I hope he has understood and will behave well)
Che se ne sia dimenticata? (Could she have forgotten about it?)

■ **L'ITÀLIA. ORDINAMENTO AMMINISTRATIVO: read and translate**

L'Itàlia è una repùbblica. Il Presidente della Repùbblica è eletto dal Parlamento e dai rappresentanti delle regioni ogni sette anni. I suoi poteri sono molto limitati.

Il Governo, formato dal Presidente del Consiglio dei Ministri e dai Ministri e Sottosegretari, è nominato dal Presidente della Repùbblica, ma deve ottenere la fidùcia del Parlamento, cioè della Camera dei Deputati e del Senato. Questi sono eletti a suffràgio diretto universale in elezioni polìtiche, almeno ogni cinque anni. Ci sono 630 deputati e circa 315 senatori.

Almeno ogni cìnque anni si dèvono anche tenere le elezioni amministrative, cioè quelle per elèggere i consigli comunali, provinciali e regionali. Ci sono venti regioni in Itàlia, di cui cìnque a statuto speciale e quìndici a statuto ordinàrio. Le prime sono: la Valle d'Aosta, bilìngue italiana-francese, il Trentino-Alto Adige, bilìngue tedesco-italiano con una minoranza ladina, il Friuli-Venèzia Giùlia, con una minoranza slovena, la Sicìlia e la Sardegna. Le seconde sono: il Piemonte, la Ligùria, la Lombardia, l'Emìlia-Romagna, il Vèneto, la Toscana, le Marche, l'Ùmbria, il Làzio, l'Abruzzo, il Molise, la Pùglia, la Basilicata, la Campània e la Calàbria.

Exercise 1

Turn the following sentences into ones with the perfect tense:

(a) *Oggi non fàccio niente di speciale.*
(b) *Tra poco vendo la casa.*

(c) *Ora mángia.*
(d) *Quest'inverno scio molto.*
(e) *Che cosa accade?*

Exercise 2

Replace the present subjunctive with the perfect subjunctive in the following sentences:

(a) *Speriamo che non se ne diméntichi.*
(b) *Credi che parta?*
(c) *Non lo so se ci vóglia andare.*
(d) *È importante che veniate anche voi.*
(e) *È una città pericolosa, nonostante ti possa sembrare tranquilla.*

Exercise 3

Write the past participles between brackets in the appropriate form, i.e. masculine or feminine, singular or plural:

(a) *Maria, ti sei (lavato) le mani bene?*
(b) *Sì, mamma, me le sono (lavato) bene.*
(c) *Non c'è nessuno; chissà se sono tutti (morto).*
(d) *Improvvisamente la luce è (scomparso).*
(e) *Li ho (aiutato) io a salire.*
(f) *L'abbiamo (venduto), perchè abbiamo bisogno di una casa più grande.*
(g) *Vi ho (visto) entrare.*
(h) *La ragazza è (fuggito) di casa.*

Exercise 4

Tell what you did last weekend.

Exercise 5

Tell what you are going to do next weekend, using the present tense as a way to tell future events.

LESSON 8

■ DAL PARRUCCHIERE

Buon giorno, signora. Prego?

Vorrei tagliarmi i capelli e farmi la permanente, o almeno la messa in piega. Ha tempo ora?
No, signora, mi dispiace. Oggi non è possibile. Posso prenotarLa per dopodomani mattina alle dieci, se vuole.

Dopodomani? Dunque, vedo nel mio diàrio. Va bene, d'accordo.
ArrivederLa a dopodomani, allora, signora, e gràzie.

■ DAL BARBIERE

Si accòmodi, signore. Come li vuole?
Me li accorci dietro e attorno alle orècchie, ma non troppo.
Vuole lo shàmpoo o una lozione?
Niente, gràzie.

AT THE HAIRDRESSER'S

Good morning, madam. What can I do for you?
I'd like to have my hair cut and to have a perm, or at least have it set. Can you do it now?
No, madam, I'm sorry. I can't do it today. I can book you for the day after tomorrow, in the morning, at ten, if you like.
The day after tomorrow?
Well, I'll have to look in my diary. All right, fine.
Good-bye until the day after tomorrow, then, madam, and thank you.

AT THE BARBER'S

Please sit down, sir. How would you like it cut?
Short at the back and sides, but not too short, please.
Would you like a shampoo or a lotion on it?
No, thank you.

POSSESSIVES

These are usually preceded by an article and are generally placed before nouns:

il mio	la mia	i miei	le mie (my, mine)
il tuo	la tua	i tuoi	le tue (your, yours)
il Suo	la Sua	i Suoi	le Sue (your, yours)
il suo	la sua	i suoi	le sue (his, her, hers, its)
il nostro	la nostra	i nostri	le nostre (our, ours)
il vostro	la vostra	i vostri	le vostre (your, yours)
il Loro	la Loro	i Loro	le Loro (your, yours)
il loro	la loro	i loro	le loro (their, theirs)
di chi?			(whose?)
il cui	la cui	i cui	le cui (whose)

Loro never changes.

The singular definite articles (*il, lo, l', la*) are usually omitted when possessives precede nouns referring to relatives, unless *loro* occurs or unless accompanied by other adjectives or by other modifiers, such as diminutives.

For example:

mia madre (my mother), *tuo padre* (your father), *nostra sorella* (our sister), *vostro fratello* (your brother), *suo zio* (his or her uncle), *mia zia* (my aunt), *nostro cognato* (our brother-in-law), *vostra cognata* (your sister-in-law), *tuo gènero* (your son-in-law), *nostra nonna* (our grandmother), *vostro nonno* (your grandfather), *mio cugino* (my cousin), *tua cugina* (your cousin), *vostro nipote* (your nephew, or grandson), *sua nipote* (his or her granddaughter, *tua nuora* (your daughter-in-law).

But:

i miei genitori (my parents), *i tuoi cugini* (your cousins), *i suoi zii* (his or her uncles, or uncle and aunt), *i nostri generi* (our father- and mother-in-law), *i miei nonni* (my grandfather and grandmother), *i tuoi fratelli* (your brothers, or brothers and sisters); *la loro zia* (their aunt); *la tua cuginetta* (your young cousin); *la nostra cara nonnina* (our dear old grandmother).

The definite articles are also usually omitted whenever the possessives precede or follow nouns in exclamations:

amore mio! (my love!), *mamma mia!* (my mother!, or good heavens!), *padre mio!* (my father!), *papa* or *babbo mio!* (my daddy!), *mammina mia!* (my dear mummy!), *figlio mio!* (my child!), *bambina mia!* (my child! or my baby!), *tesoro* or *tesoruccio mio!* (honey! sweetheart!), *Londra mia!* (my London!), *Italia nostra!* (our Italy!), *Signor nostro!* (our Lord!), *ragazze mie!* (my girls!), *belli miei!* (my dear ones!), *belle mie!* (my fair ones!), *caro mio!* (my dear fellow!), *vita mia!* (my life!)

The definite articles are also often omitted in titles and lists.

Possessive nouns, as are found in English when 's is added, do not exist in Italian. So, they must be translated by *di* followed by the noun; or by *quello, quella, quelli, quelle di* (that, those, the one, the ones of):

La villa dei Rossi è stupenda (The Rossis' villa is fantastic)
'La pastorale' di Beethoven mi piace moltissimo (Beethoven's 'Pastoral' symphony pleases me very much)
Questa non è la vostra stanza, è quella degli altri ospiti (This is not your room, it belongs to the other guests)
Di chi è questa macchina? Credo che sia (quella) di Ferrari (Whose car is this? I believe it is Mr Ferrari's)
Il clima di Londra non è male (London's climate is not bad)

Actual possession can also be expressed by using the phrase *appartenere a qualcuno* (to belong to somebody):

Questa casa appartiene ai miei genitori, ma l'auto appartiene a me (This house belongs to my parents, but the car belongs to me)
Non mi appartiene niente, non ho niente di mio (Nothing belongs to me, nothing is mine)

IRREGULAR PAST PARTICIPLES

The following groups of verbs have special forms of past participles: (The group numbers refer to Lesson 5.)

(2) *Èssere* (to be), past participle *stato* (been, aux. *èssere*)

(5) Past participle ending in *-tto*:
fare (to do, to make), p.p. *fatto*
disfare (to undo; to melt away), p.p. *disfatto*
soddisfare (to satisfy), p.p. *soddisfatto*

(6) *Venire* (to come), p.p. *venuto* (aux. *èssere*)

(7) Past participle ending in *-lso*:
valere (to be worth), p.p. *valso* (aux. *èssere*)
prevalere (to prevail), p.p. *prevalso* (aux. *èssere*)

(8) Past participle ending in *-lto*:
cògliere (to pick up), p.p. *colto*
accògliere (to welcome), p.p. *accolto*
raccògliere (to collect), p.p. *raccolto*
tògliere (to remove), p.p. *tolto*

(10) Past participle ending in *-nto* or *-lto*:
dipìngere (to paint), p.p. *dipinto*
aggiùngere (to add), p.p. *aggiunto*
avvòlgere (to wrap up; to wind), p.p. *avvolto*
coinvòlgere (to involve), p.p. *coinvolto*
fìngere (to pretend, to feign), p.p. *finto*
piàngere (to weep, to cry), p.p. *pianto*
mùngere (to milk), p.p. *munto*
rivòlgersi (to apply to), p.p. *rivolto*
sconvòlgere (to upset), p.p. *sconvolto*
strìngere (to grasp, clench, hug, grip, hold tightly), p.p. *stretto*
ùngere (to grease, to oil), p.p. *unto*

(11) Past participle ending in *-sto*:
supporre (to suppose), p.p. *supposto*
deporre (to depose; to lay down), p.p. *deposto*
comporre (to compose), p.p. *composto*
disporre (to arrange), p.p. *disposto*
esporre (to expose; to expound), p.p. *esposto*

porre (to set), p.p. *posto*
proporre (to propose), p.p. *proposto*
scomporre (to break up), p.p. *scomposto*
sovrapporre (to superimpose), p.p. *sovrapposto*
rimanere (to remain), p.p. *rimasto*

(12), (13), (15), (16), (19), (21) Past participle ending in *-tto*:
trarre (to draw), p.p. *tratto*
attrarre (to attract), p.p. *attratto*
detrarre (to deduce), p.p. *detratto*
estrarre (to extract, to pull out), p.p. *estratto*
sottrarre (to subtract; to purloin), p.p. *sottratto*
distrüggere (to destroy), p.p. *distrutto*
friggere (to fry), p.p. *fritto*
lĕggere (to read), p.p. *letto*
protĕggere (to protect), p.p. *protetto*
costringere (to compel), p.p. *costretto*
sconfiggere (to defeat), p.p. *sconfitto*
dire (to say, to tell), p.p. *detto*
benedire (to bless), p.p. *benedetto*
contraddire (to contradict), p.p. *contraddetto*
disdire (to cancel), p.p. *disdetto*
indire (to announce, to summon), p.p. *indetto*
maledire (to curse), p.p. *maledetto*
predire (to anticipate, to forecast), p.p. *predetto*
tradurre (to translate), p.p. *tradotto*
condurre (to lead), p.p. *condotto*
dedurre (to deduce, to infer), p.p. *dedotto*
indurre (to induce, to lead), p.p. *indotto*
produrre (to produce), p.p. *prodotto*
ridurre (to reduce), p.p. *ridotto*
sedurre (to seduce), p.p. *sedotto*
cuŏcere (to cook), p.p. *cotto*
rŏmpere (to break), p.p. *rotto*
corrŏmpere (to corrupt), p.p. *corrotto*

(17) Past participle ending in *-nto* or *-rto*:
vincere (to win), p.p. *vinto*
avvincere (to thrill), p.p. *avvinto*
distŏrcere (to distort), p.p. *distorto*

(20) *Morire* (to die), p.p. *morto*
   but:
   aprire (to open), p.p. *aperto* (aux. *avere*)
   apparire (to appear), p.p. *apparso* (aux. *èssere*)
   comparire (to turn up, to show up), p.p. *comparso* (aux. *èssere*)
   parere (to seem), p.p. *parso* (aux. *èssere*)
   scomparire (to disappear), p.p. *scomparso* (aux. *èssere*)

(22) *Bere* (to drink), p.p. *bevuto*

(34) *redìgere* (to draw up, edit), p.p. *redatto*

(35, 40) Past participle ending in -*sso*:
   mèttere (to put), p.p. *messo*
   ammèttere (to admit), p.p. *ammesso*
   compromèttere (to compromise), p.p. *compromesso*
   dimèttersi (to resign), p.p. *dimesso*
   permèttere (to permit), p.p. *permesso*
   promèttere (to promise), p.p. *promesso*
   sottomèttere (to submit), p.p. *sottomesso*
   concèdere (to grant), p.p. *concesso*
   muòvere (to move), p.p. *mosso*

(36) Past participle ending in -*uso*:
   fòndere (to smelt, to fuse), p.p. *fuso*
   confòndere (to confuse), p.p. *confuso*
   diffòndere (to spread, to diffuse), p.p. *diffuso*

(37) *Espèllere* (to expel, to evict), p.p. *espulso*

(38) *Vìvere* (to live), p.p. *vissuto*
   convìvere (to live together), p.p. *convissuto*

(39) *Attèndere* (to wait), p.p. *atteso*

(41) *Esìstere* (to exist), p.p. *esistito*

Past participles can be used in Italian instead of a full sentence, e.g.

Vista la situazione, ho pensato di andàrmene (After seeing what the situation was like, I thought of leaving)

Arrivato a casa, sono andato sùbito a letto (No sooner was I back home than I went to bed)
I libri spedìtimi non sono ancora arrivati (The books that were sent to me have not yet arrived)
Avuta l'informazione, sono contento (Having got the information, I am happy)

LESSON 9

■ **ALL'ÒPERA**

AT THE OPERA

Mi piacerebbe andare a teatro sàbato sera a vedere la 'Tosca'. È un sacco di tempo che non la vedo. Vieni anche tu? Andiamo sùbito al botteghino a prèndere i biglietti?

I'd like to go to the theatre to see *Tosca* on Saturday evening. I haven't seen it for ages. Are you coming along? Shall we go right away to the box office and get the tickets?

Mah, se vuoi, andiamo pure. (Più tardi)

Well, if you like, let's go then. (Later)

Ah, bene, abbiamo dei buoni posti di platea. Mi diverto pròprio. Che te ne pare del tenore? A me sembra una cannonata. Anche la soprano non è mica male. A me piàcciono tutti e due.

Oh, good, we have good stalls seats. I am really enjoying it. What do you think of the tenor? To me he seems smashing. The soprano is not bad, either. I do like both of them.

A me piace di più un bel concerto. Delle òpere lìriche mi piàcciono soprattutto le romanze, sai, quelle famose.

As for me, I like a good concert better. I like the arias of operas particularly, you know, the famous ones.

L'òpera is short for *l'òpera lìrica* (opera). *La lìrica* can mean 'opera' in general, or a lyric poem. *L'òpera*, short for *il teatro d'òpera* or *il teatro dell'òpera*, means 'opera theatre', e.g. *Andiamo all'òpera* (Let's go to the opera, to the opera theatre, or to see an opera). Literally, *òpera* refers to any work of art or craft, such as *un'òpera d'arte* (a work of art), *un'òpera letterària* (a literary work), *un'òpera di ingegneria* (an engineering work), e.g.

Di chi è òpera questo? È òpera dei ladri (Who was this done by? It was done by the thieves)
Gli operai sono all'òpera (The workers are working)

È un sacco di tempo che non vedo la 'Tosca' (I haven't seen *Tosca* for a long time). As the student noticed in Lesson 3, the present tense is used to describe an action which began in the past and is continuing in the present. An alternative way of expressing the sentence above would be the following:

Non vedo la 'Tosca' da un sacco di tempo (I haven't seen *Tosca* for ages). Further examples:
Sono due anni che la conosco, or *La conosco da due anni* (I have known her for two years)
È dal millenovecento ottanta che non vado al mare, or *Non vado al mare dal millenovecento ottanta* (I have not gone to the seaside since 1980).

Mi piacerebbe (It would please me, I'd like) is a conditional, like *vorrei* (I'd like).

USE OF THE VERB PIACERE

This verb, meaning 'to like, to please, to be pleasing to, to be likeable to' may be confusing to the student of Italian, as it follows the pattern of the English verb 'to please', rather than 'to like', so that the direct object of 'like' becomes the subject of *piacere*. Thus, instead of saying 'I like you', the student must say 'you are pleasing to me'. This verb is mainly used in the third persons singular and plural.

Present indicative and subjunctive

Mi piace or *A me piace* (*piàccia*)	+ singular noun, or	(I like)
Ti piace or *a te piace* (*piàccia*)	infinitive,	(You like)
Gli piace or *a lui piace* (*piàccia*)	or *che* (that)	(He likes)

Le piace or *a lei piace (piàccia)*	(She likes; you like)
Ci piace or *a noi piace (piàccia)*	(We like)
Vi piace or *a voi piace (piàccia)*	(You like)
Piace loro or *a loro piace (piàccia)*	(They, you like)

Mi piàcciono or *A me piàcciano (piàcciano)* + plural noun (I like).

A Giovanni piace il gelato (John likes ice-cream)
Alla gente piace divertirsi (People like to have fun)
Agli italiani piàcciono le àuto veloci (Italians like fast cars)
Agli inglesi piàcciono i giardini e i fiori (The English like gardens and flowers)
Non piace a nessuno èssere preso in giro (Nobody likes to be made fun of)
Ci piace che stiate con noi (We like you to stay with us)

Here is the full present tense of the verb *piacere*, indicative and subjunctive:

(Io) piàccio (piàccia) alla gente (People like me)
(tu) piaci (piàccia) a tutti (Everybody likes you)
(Lei) piace (piàccia) agli inglesi (The English like you)
(lui) piace (piàccia) agli italiani (The Italians like him)
(noi) piacciamo (piacciamo) a voi (You like us)
(voi) piacete (piacciate) molto (You are liked very much)
(Loro) piàcciono (piàcciano) al direttore (The manager likes you)
(loro) piàcciono (piàcciano) al capoufficio (The head of the office likes them)

More examples:

(Tu) mi piaci poco (I don't like you much)
Come vi piace (As you like it)
Ad alcuni piace caldo (Some like it hot)
Vi piàccia o no (Whether you like it or not)
È una ragazza che piace (She is a girl one likes)
Ti piàccio con questo cappello? No, non mi piaci pròprio per niente (How do you like me in this hat? I don't like you at all like that)
Io mi piàccio come sono. Non mi importa anche se non piàccio a te. (I like myself as I am. I am not bothered if you don't like me, or if I don't please you)

Non credo che al bambino piàcciano questi giocàttoli (I don't think the child likes these toys)

Il piacere, pl. *i piaceri* means 'pleasure', but *fare un piacere* or *un favore* or *una cortesia* means 'to do a favour', e.g.

Prima il dovere e poi il piacere (First duty and then pleasure)
Fammi un piacere (Do me a favour), but *Ma fammi un piacere!* (If you don't mind!)
Se Le fa piacere (If you like), or *se ha piacere* (If it doesn't bother you)
Piacere (di conòscerLa) or *Piacere di fare la Sua conoscenza*, or *Molto piacere* (Pleased to meet you; how do you do?)
Piacere mio (It's my pleasure; how do you do?)
Con piacere (With pleasure!)
Per piacere = per favore = per cortesia (please!, if you please)
Apprendo con piacere (I am pleased to learn)

But: 'Do as you like' would be translated into *Fa come ti pare,* or *Fa come vuoi* (Do as you like), and 'If you like' *Se ti pare* or *Se vuoi*.

The opposite of *piacere* is usually *non piacere* (not to like, to dislike), e.g.

Non mi piàcciono queste sinfonie (I do not like these symphonies)
Se non ti piace, vàttene (If you do not like it, go away)

The verb *dispiacere* means 'to be displeasing, unpleasant', 'to object to', 'to mind', 'to be sorry', or, rarely, 'not to like', e.g.

Non mi dispiace la nuova scuola (I do not dislike the new school)
Mi dispiace disturbarLa (I am sorry to trouble you; I do not like to bother you)
Se non vi dispiace, me ne vado (If you do not mind, I shall leave)
Il tuo comportamento ci dispiace molto (Your behaviour displeases us very much)
Le dispiace chiùdere la porta? (Do you mind closing the door?)
Le dispiace se apro la finestra? (Do you mind if I open the window?)

In the sense of 'to be sorry', an alternative verb to *dispiacere* is *essere spiacente*, which is more elegant in style, e.g.

Ci dispiace davvero (or *pròprio*) *che non veniate* (We are really sorry that you will not come)

Siamo davvero (or *pròprio*) *spiacenti che non possiamo accontentarLa* (We are really sorry that we cannot satisfy you)

Sono spiacente di dover informarLa che la visita è annullata (I am sorry to have to inform you that the visit is cancelled)

Non si può entrare? (Can't I go in?) *No, spiacente* (No, sorry).

Il dispiacere means 'affliction, sadness, sorrow, grief'.

Le esprimiamo il nostro dispiacere per la pèrdita della nonna (We express to you our grief for the passing away of your grandmother)

Mia figlia mi dà tanti dispiaceri (My daughter is a great worry to me)

Con nostro gran dispiacere, abbiamo appreso la notìzia
(Much to our regret, we have learnt the news)

■ CORRISPONDENZA FAMILIARE: LÈTTERA AI GENITORI: read and translate

Londra, 12/7/1982

Carìssimi papa e mamma,

èccomi arrivato in questa grande e magnìfica città. Il viàggio è andato abbastanza bene, anche se ci sono stati dei forti ritardi e qualche altro inconveniente. Ora allòggio in una pensione vicina al centro con Gianni e Giòrgio e non paghiamo molto, per èssere a Londra.

Ci piàcciono molto le abbondanti colazioni all'inglese, a base di fiocchi d'avena, uova à la coq, all'òcchio di bue, strapazzate o in camìcia, pancetta, fette di pane tostato e imburrato con marmellate d'arància e varie, tutte buonissime, e naturalmente tè in abbondanza, tazze su tazze.

Sto imparando ad orientarmi. Vado molto in metropolitana e con gli àutobus a due piani, che mi piàcciono tanto. Gli inglesi sono piuttosto riservati, ma quando si mèttono a raccontàrtela non li ferma più nessuno.

Ora devo uscire. Abbiamo un sacco di cose da fare e da vedere.

Spero che stiate bene e che non vi preoccupiate per me. Non ho bisogno di niente ed anche con i soldi me la cavo. Per ora mi diverto molto.

Vi abbràccio e vi bacio con tanto affetto.

Màrio

Exercise 1

Answer the following questions, saying that the person mentioned does not like what is asked:

(a) *A Sua mòglie piace l'òpera lìrica?*
(b) *Nemmeno a Lei piace?*
(c) *E ai Suoi figli piace?*
(d) *E a me crede che piàccia?*
(e) *I concerti vi piàcciono, invece?*

Exercise 2

Rewrite the following passage, replacing the verbs *amare* (to love) and *preferire* (to prefer) with *piacere*:

Gli stranieri di sòlito àmano molto la Toscana. Àmano il Chianti, le dolci colline e le stòriche città. Forse la preferìscono alle altre regioni italiane perchè àmano l'arte e il Rinascimento.
Naturalmente àmano anche molto Venèzia, Roma e le altre città e regioni stòriche d'Itàlia. Il mio amico preferisce la Sicìlia, per la sua mistura di greco, romano, àrabo, normanno e spagnolo, oltre che per le sue bellezze naturali. Io amo anche l'Ùmbria, il Vèneto e tanti altri posti. E tu quali regioni o città preferisci? Non è sempre fàcile dire quale si ama di più perchè veramente la scelta è troppo grande.

Exercise 3

Write a dialogue in which two or more people express their likes and dislikes in Italy.

Exercise 4

Replace the verbs and phrases used in the following sentences with *dispiacere*, either as a verb or as a noun:

(a) *Vuole riempire questi mòduli?*
(b) *La prego di uscire.*
(c) *Siamo spiacenti di comunicarLe che la sua domanda non è accettata.*
(d) *È con vivo rincrescimento che ho appreso la notizia.*
(e) *Scusate se vi disturbo.*
(f) *Per favore, vorrei una birra.*
(g) *Mi passa il pepe, per cortesia?*

LESSON 10

■ UNA TELEFONATA

Come si fa a telefonare da una cabina pùblica?
Si dèvono avere dei gettoni telefònici. Si prèndono alla SIP, dal tabaccàio o mettendo delle monete da cento lire nella appòsita macchinetta da gettoni.
Ho capito. Allora, prima gettoni e poi si fa il nùmero: sessantasette, quarantuno, ventidue, sei. (6741226)
Pronto, chi parla?
Sei tu Mario? Ah, scusi, signora. Sono John. Si ricorda? L'amico inglese di Suo marito. Come sta? C'è Suo marito?

A TELEPHONE CALL

How can I phone from a telephone booth?
You must have some tokens. You get them from SIP, or from a tobacconist, or by inserting one-hundred lire coins into the appropriate token slot machine.
I've got it. So, first the tokens and then I dial the number: six, seven, four, one, double two, six.
Hello, who's speaking?
Is it you, Mario? Oh, I'm sorry, madam. This is John speaking. Do you remember? Your husband's English friend. How are you? Is your husband in?

Bene, gràzie, e Lei? Sì, mio marito è in casa. Vuole che Glielo passi? Attenda un àttimo che Glielo chiamo. ArrivederLa a presto. Màrio, c'è il Signor Carpenter al telèfono per te!

Well, thank you, and how are you? Yes, my husband's in. Shall I get him? Hold on a second, please, I'll see where he is. See you soon. Mario, Mr Carpenter is on the telephone!

SIP is the acronym for the Italian telephone corporation. It is pronounced as a word, i.e./seep/.

IMPERSONAL EXPRESSIONS

The pronoun *si*

The student has already encountered *si* as a reflexive pronoun, but it is also an indefinite one. It may also replace passive sentences, as they are often felt to be cumbersome and a bit awkward in Italian:

Si parla inglese qui (English is spoken here)
Per Castel Sant'Angelo si gira a destra, poi si va diritto e si attraversa il ponte (To get to Castel Sant'Angelo you turn right, go straight on and then cross the bridge)
Mi si dice che non vuoi più studiare (I am told that you do not want to study any more)
Che si fa stasera? (What shall we do tonight?)
Si va al cìnema o al bar? (Shall we go to the cinema or to the cafe?)

The verb agrees in number with the noun which follows:

Si vede una casa da qui (You can see a house from here)
Si vèdono anche àlberi (You can see trees too)

Other ways to express a general statement, i.e. one that is not definite about who is involved in the action, are by starting the sentence with:

la gente (people), which is singular in Italian,
qualcuno (somebody),
alcuni (some people),

certi or *certuni* (some, or certain people),
altri (others),

or simply by using the plural form of the verb:

La gente dice che non sta bene (People say she is not well)
Qualcuno dice che non sta bene (Somebody says that she is not well)
Dicono che non sta (or *stia*) *bene* (She is said not to be well)
Mi dicono che non sta bene (I am told she is not well)
Si dice che non sta bene (They say she is not well)
Questo libro si vende bene (This book sells well)
Si lèggono volentieri giornali come questo (You enjoy reading newspapers like this)
Si sta bene qui, seduti al tavolino a bere il caffè e a guardare le ragazze che pàssano (It is nice here, sitting at a café table sipping coffee and watching girls strolling)
Si vende (For sale)
Si affitta (To let)
Si sta costruendo una nuova scuola (A new school is being built)
Si stanno facendo grandi progetti (Great plans are being made)

The unstressed object pronouns precede *si*, except for *loro*, e.g.

Mi si dice (I am told)

but:

Se ne parla (People talk about it)

IMPERSONAL VERBS

These usually refer to weather condition:

piove (it rains)
piove a dirotto or *dilùvia* (it pours)
nèvica (it snows)
spiove (it stops raining)
gela (it freezes)
gràndina (it hails)
albèggia (it dawns)
pioviggina (it drizzles)
ghiàccia (it ices)
viene a piòvere (it is going to rain)

c'è (la) nèbbia or *è nebbioso* (it is foggy)
c'è foschia or *c'è nebbiolina* (it is misty)

c'è la neve (there is snow, it is snowing)
c'è nevìschio or *viene giù nevìschio* (it sleets)
ci sono le stelle (it is a starry night)
c'è il sole or *è soleggiato* (it is sunny)
c'è la luna (it is a moonlit night)
c'è vento or *è ventoso* or *tira vento* (it is windy)
ci sono le nùvole or *è nuvoloso* (it is cloudy)
c'è caldo or *fa caldo* or *è caldo* (it is warm, hot)
c'è fresco or *fa fresco* or *è fresco* (it is cool)
c'è freddo or *fa freddo* or *è freddo* (it is cold)
c'è chiaro or *fa chiaro* or *è chiaro* (it is daylight)
c'è bùio or *fa bùio* or *è bùio* (it is dark)
c'è scuro or *fa scuro* or *è scuro* (it is dark)
è piovoso (it is rainy)
è bello or *fa bello* or *fa bel tempo* (it is good weather)
è brutto or *fa brutto* or *fa brutto tempo* (it is bad weather)
è ùmido (it is damp, wet)
è caldo ùmido (it is humid)
è bagnato (it is wet)
è sereno or *fa sereno* (it is clear)
è tiepido or *fa tiepido* (it is mild, slightly warm)
è mite (it is mild)
si rannùvola (it becomes cloudy)
si rasserena (it clears up)
si rischiara or *si schiarisce* (it opens up)
si oscura or *si rabbùia* (it gets dark)
sembra che vòglia piovere (it looks like rain)
sembra che vòglia nevicare (it looks like snow)

Other impersonal verbs and phrases refer to what is suitable, convenient, necessary, sufficient, apparent, etc. These expressions are followed by a noun, or by an infinitive, or by *che* and subjunctive, or, less often, by *che* and indicative:

a chi tocca? tocca a (whose turn is it? it is the turn of)
spetta a or *tocca a* (it is the duty of, it is up to)
bisogna or *occorre* or *è necessàrio* or *si deve* (it is necessary)
importa or *ha importanza* (it matters)
basta or *è sufficiente* (it suffices)
interessa or *è interessante* (it is of interest)

non occorre (one need not)
sembra or *pare* (it seems)
accade or *avviene* or *succede* (it happens)
mi viene in mente (it comes to mind, it occurs to me)
ci vuole or *occorre* or *è necessàrio* (it is required)
è bene or *è una buona cosa* or *è una bella cosa* (it is all right)
va bene (it is all right)
va da sè (it goes without saying)
è inutile dire (it is useless to say)
sta male (it is not fitting), *sta bene* (it is proper)
è chiaro or *è evidente* (it is clear, evident)
è opportuno or *è conveniente* or *conviene* (it is convenient)
è necessàrio or *è essenziale* or *è indispensàbile* (it is essential)
è urgente or *urge* (it is urgent)
è bello (it is good), *è brutto* (it is wrong)
è un fatto or *sta di fatto* (as a matter of fact)
è vero (it is true) *è falso* (it is false)
è la prima volta (it is the first time)
è inutile or *è vano* (it is useless), *è utile* (it is useful)
è incredìbile (it is unbelievable)
è vietato or *è proibito* or *non si può* or *non si deve* or *non
è permesso* (it is not allowed)
è mèglio (it is better), *è pèggio* (it is worse)

The compound tenses of impersonal verbs and phrases are formed
with *èssere*, except for those expressions containing the verbs *tirare*
and *fare*, e.g.

Mi viene in mente che ho un appuntamento (It occurs to me that I
have an appointment)
Mi va bene domènica (Sunday is all right with me)
È piovuto tutto il giorno (It has been raining all day)
Mi è sembrato che faccia sul serio (It seemed to me that he is
serious)
Non occorre forse che Le spieghi tutto quello che è successo (I need
not explain to you perhaps all that happened)
È bello sciare (It is nice to ski)
Basta così per oggi! (That's enough for today!)
Ci vuole coràggio (We need to be daring)

Non me ne importa niente (It does not matter to me at all)
Mi sembra che sia ora (It seems to me that it is time)
Ci sembra ammalato (He looks ill)
A chi tocca lavare i piatti? A me no (Whose turn is it to wash the dishes? Not mine)
Mi tocca sempre lavare i piatti (It is always up to me to wash the dishes)
Non mi tocca (It does not affect me)
Spetta a loro organizzare tutto? (Is it their duty to plan everything?)
A chi spetta? (Whose duty is it?)
Che t'importa? Fregatene (Why should you care? Don't bother!)
A me importa molto, invece (I, on the other hand, do care a lot)

INDEFINITES

ogni (every, each), only singular
un altro, un'altra, altri, altre (another, others)
certo, certa, certi, certe (certain)
certuni, certune or *taluni, talune* (certain people)
un tale, una tale, dei tali, delle tali (a certain, some people)
qualsiasi (any, whatever)
qualunque (any, whatever)
chiunque (whoever, anyone, anybody)
ognuno, ognuna (everyone, everybody, each one)
alcuno, alcuna (no one, none), singular
alcuni, alcune (some, a few), plural
ciascuno, ciascuna (each one)
qualcuno, qualcuna (someone, somebody)
tutto, tutta, tutti, tutte (all, the whole, every)
tutto, or *ogni cosa* (everything)
qualunque cosa or *qualsiasi cosa* (anything, whatever)
niente (nothing)
qualcosa (something)
dovunque or *ovunque* or *dappertutto* or *da ogni parte* (everywhere, anywhere)

For example:

Ad alcuni piace caldo (Some like it hot)

Sono tutti impazziti (Everybody's gone crazy)
Dappertutto, in tutto il mondo c'è gente come me e te (Everywhere, all over the world there are people like you and me)

PASSIVE VERBS

Verbs that can be followed by a direct object can be used in the passive, i.e. the direct object becomes the new subject of the verb. In this case the various tenses will be formed with the auxiliary verb *essere* followed by the past participle. The English 'by' is translated by *da*, e.g.

I cinema sono molto frequentati da tutti in Italia (Cinemas are much attended by everybody in Italy)
I biglietti sono stati acquistati (The tickets have been bought)
Siamo stati fermati dalla polizia stradale (We have been stopped by the highway police)
Quel film è stato girato in questi posti (That film has been shot in these places)

Alternative auxiliaries of passive sentences are *venire*, except for the perfect and pluperfect passive tenses, and *andare*, which also implies obligation to do something, unless in the perfect and pluperfect tenses, e.g.

I soldi della tredicesima vengono spesi in un baleno (The Christmas bonus money is spent in a jiffy)
Il denaro va speso bene (Money should be spent wisely)
Le donne vanno trattate con riguardo (Women are to be treated with consideration)

The pronoun *si*, as has been seen previously (see Lesson 10), may often replace passive sentences, as these are often felt too cumbersome by Italian speakers), e.g.

Si riparano scarpe (Shoes are mended here)
Si sono fatti grandi progressi (Great progress has been made)

■ ANDARE IN AUTOMOBILE: read and translate

Ricordi di controllare che tutto sia a posto quando va in Italia:

assicurazione, motore, ŏlio, pneumătici, tergicristalli, impianto elĕttrico.

Ho fatto la carta verde e ho portato la măcchina dal meccànico. È ancora in officina. Vado a riprĕnderla stasera.

Stia attento al cŏdice stradale. Ci sono almeno tre polizie in Itălia: i carabinieri, la polizia stradale e i vĭgili urbani che le pŏssono fare la multa.

Notes

Vĭgili urbani (the urban police) is a municipal body which is empowered with the enforcement of the highway code and other local regulations and by-laws.

The *carabinieri* are a police body which is under the supervision of the Ministry of Defence. Therefore they can be employed as a regular army corps, also during wartime.

The *pŭbblica sicurezza* (public security) is a police body, usually called simply *polizia* (police) which is under the control of the Home Ministry, through local *questura* (police headquarters). It includes *polizia stradale* (highway police), *polizia ferroviăria* (railway police) and *cĕlere* (flying squad).

Vĭgili urbani, carabinieri and *polizia* can all give fines (*la multa* or *la contravvenzione*) and intervene in case of car crashes. *Carabinieri* and *polizia* have also similar duties in all other emergencies. Call 113 on the telephone for special emergencies or prompt police intervention.

Other polices in Italy consist of *guărdia di finanza* (finance police), including *polizia di frontiera*, and *guărdia forestale* (forest police).

Exercise 1

Turn the verbs in the following passage into sentences introduced by *si*:

In Itălia telĕfonano dalle cabine pŭbbliche, dai telĕfoni pŭbblici nei bar e ristoranti e dagli uffici della SIP. Negli apparecchi a gettoni, questi vengono inseriti nelle apposite feritŏie. I gettoni sono venduti dagli uffici della SIP e da certi bar e tabaccherie o vĕngono distribuiti da macchinette. Per fare telefonate interurbane dovete prima fare il prefisso di teleselezione. L'elenco dei prefissi lo trovate all'inizio dell'elenco telefonico. Nel caso di telefonate internazionali, o fate il prefisso oppure, se non riuscite ad avere il collegamento, chiedete la linea al centralino.

Exercise 2

Translate:

This morning, when I got up, it was quite foggy. But, then, if it is foggy in the early morning, it usually clears up later in the day. In fact it became sunny, as the fog disappeared. It has been a very quiet day; there has been no wind at all, nor has it been cloudy. It has also been mild. It has got dark very late and we have enjoyed the day very much.

Exercise 3

Rewrite the following sentences, preceding them with *è evidente,* or *spetta a me, è ora, tocca a me, va bene, va da sè:*

(a) *Non stai bene.*
(b) *Andiamo a teatro.*
(c) *Non si ricorda più di me.*
(d) *Devo comperarle un regalo.*
(e) *Vado in ufficio sàbato.*
(f) *Prende la tua màcchina.*
(g) *Paga tu.*
(h) *Finalmente mi hanno riparato l'àuto.*

Exercise 4

Rewrite the following sentences, replacing the plural (or singular) indefinite pronouns or adjectives with singular (or plural) ones of the same meaning:

(a) *Ad alcuni piace caldo.*
(b) *Lassù qualcuno mi ama.*
(c) *Ognuno ha il suo posto.*

(d) *Ogni settimana ho ricevuto inviti.*
(e) *Un altro ha fatto come me.*

Exercise 5

Turn the following sentences to passive ones:

(a) *In Italia vendono il sale nelle tabaccherie.*
(b) *Hanno fatto molti progressi, ma non ancora abbastanza.*
(c) *Hanno migliorato il traffico in centro.*
(d) *Abbiamo dipinto le pareti di rosa.*
(e) *Gli studenti hanno prodotto delle cose stupende.*

Exercise 6

Describe what you can buy at the post office or at the tobacconist's in Italy.

LESSON 11

■ **DESCRIZIONE DI GENTE**

Mario Fabbri ha trent'anni e lavora come tecnico nelle Ferrovie dello Stato. È sposato da quattro anni con una ragazza della sua stessa età, Giovanna Carli, che lavora come segretària-dattilògrafa alla Pirelli, dove lavorava anche Mario quando è arrivato a Milano sei anni fa.

DESCRIPTION OF PEOPLE

Mario Fabbri is thirty and works as a technician with the State Railways. He has been married four years to a girl the same age as he is, Giovanna Carli, who works as a secretary-typist with Pirelli, where Mario used to work too, when he arrived in Milan six years ago.

Mário non è alto, è di média statura ed ha capelli e occhi castani. Giovanna è di statura normale ed ha capelli e occhi scuri. Àbitano a Milano con il loro figlioletto, un bambino di pochi mesi che si chiama Luca. Sono molto contenti di Luca. Giovanna naturalmente è in aspettattiva per maternità.

Mario is not tall, he is of average height and has brown hair and eyes. Giovanna is of normal height and has dark hair and eyes. They live in Milan with their little son, a baby a few months old who is called Luca. They are very pleased with Luca. Of course Giovanna is on maternity leave of absence.

Vìvono in un appartamento in affitto di due stanze, cucina e servizi e pàgano molto di affitto. Vògliono comperarsi un appartamento con i loro risparmi e magari con un mùtuo, che però non è fàcile da ottenere. Le banche fanno pagare alti interessi indicizzati.

They live in a rented flat of two rooms, kitchen and bathroom, and pay a high rent. They wish to buy a flat with their savings and perhaps with a loan, which, however, is not easy to obtain. Banks charge high, index-linked interest.

RELATIVE PRONOUNS

There are two sets of relative pronouns and adjectives. Those in the list on the left-hand side below are used more frequently and are also more colloquial. Those in the list on the right-hand side are more formal and are mainly used in writing, but also in speaking, for clarity or for emphasis. The latter are also preceded by a comma and a definite article, and agree in gender and number, like other adjectives:

chi	*colui il quale*	(he, she, they,
colui che, colei che	*colei la quale*	the one, the
coloro che	*coloro i quali*	ones, those who)
quello che, quella che	*quello il quale*	
quelli che, quelle che	*quella la quale*	
	quelli i quali	

che	*il quale, la quale,*	(who, which,
il cui, la cui, i cui, le	*i quali, le quali*	that)
cui, di cui'	*del quale, della*	(whose, of which,
	quale, dei quali,	of whom)
	delle quali	

(Similarly, other prepositions may precede *cui*)

il che, la qual cosa (which)
ciò che or *quello che* (what)
tutto ciò che or *tutto quello che* (all that)

For example:

La città che mi piace di più è senz'altro Venèzia (The city I like best is, without any doubt, Venice)
Mi piace la gente che non fa tante stòrie (I like people who are not fussy)
La ditta con cui ho lavorato tanti anni è fallita (The company I worked with for so many years went bankrupt)
È bello conoscere gente di cui si conosce la lingua (It is nice to meet people whose language we know)
I Ferrari, la cui casa è accanto alla nostra, fanno troppo rumore (The Ferraris, whose house is next to ours, are too noisy)

EXCLAMATIVES

Che is also exclamative, e.g.

Che uomo fortunato! (What a lucky man!)
Che bello! (How nice!)
Che tardi che è! (How late it is!)

Instead of *che*, *come* (how) and *quanto* (how much) may be used:

Com'è fortunato quell'uomo! or
Quant'è fortunato quell'uomo! (How lucky that man is!)
Quant'è bello! (How nice it is!)
Com'è tardi! (How late it is!)

GERUND

The gerund corresponds roughly to the English '-ing' form of the verb. It has the endings:

-*ando*, for the verbs with the characteristic vowel -*a*, such as *parlare* (to speak), *parlando*; *odiare* (to hate) *odiando*; *amare* (love), *amando*; *continuare* (to continue), *continuando*; *fermarsi* (to stop), *fermàndosi*; *lavarsi* (to wash oneself), *lavàndosi*; *guidare* (to guide, to drive), *guidando*;

-*endo*, for all other verbs, such as *temere* (to fear), *temendo*; *vèndere* (to sell), *vendendo; finire* (to end), *finendo*; *dormire* (to sleep), *dormendo*; *capire* (to understand), *capendo*.

The past gerund is formed with *avendo* or *essendo* followed by the past participle.

The gerund is used in the following cases:

(a) After *stare* (to stay, stand), particularly in its present and imperfect tenses; to indicate a continuous or progressive action; as alternative forms for the simple present and the imperfect indicative and subjunctive;

Sta arrivando qualcuno (Somebody is arriving)
Sta suonando il campanello (The bell is ringing)
Stavo dicendo che così non mi va (I was saying that this does not suit me)

(b) After *andare* (to go) or *venire* (to come), to emphasize a constantly repeated or gradually increasing action:

Ma che vai dicendo? (What on earth are you saying?)
Il sole va tramontando (The sun is gradually setting)

(c) To replace a sentence expressing the time when something happened, or the means through which something can be achieved, or the cause for some occurrence.

Scendendo le scale, sono scivolato (While coming down the stairs, I slipped)
Studiando s'impara (You learn if you study, *or* by studying)
Andando al lavoro, mi còmperi il giornale? (On your way to work, will you buy me a newspaper, please?)

*Avendo esaminato la situazione attentamente, non mi resta che
concludere che non c'è niente da fare* (As I have examined the
situation carefully, the conclusion to be drawn is that nothing
can be done about it)
*Essendo ammalato il pianista, il concerto ha dovuto essere an-
nullato* (As the pianist was ill, the concert had to be cancelled)
Ti comprometti facendo ciò (By doing so, you will compromise
yourself)

The object personal pronouns follow gerunds and are written as
one word with them, but may precede the auxiliary verb:

Lavàndovi bene i denti, prevenite la càrie (If you brush your teeth
well, you prevent tooth decay)
Stai lavàndoti i denti? or *Ti stai lavando i denti?* (Are you brushing
your teeth?)

The subject of a gerund must be the same as that of the main
clause.

USE OF INFINITIVES AS NOUNS

Infinitives, with or without article, are used to replace English
'-ing' forms functioning as subject or object of a sentence. The past
infinitive is formed with *avere* or *èssere* followed by the past participle, e.g.

Camminare, or *Il camminare fa bene alla salute* (Walking is good
for your health)
Amo molto ascoltare buona mùsica (I very much like listening to
good music)
Smettètela di chiacchierare (Stop talking)
Mi piace lèggere or *Il lèggere mi piace* (I enjoy reading)
Il mio passatempo preferito è coltivare fiori (My favourite hobby
is growing flowers)
Vietato fumare (No smoking)
Vietato andare in bicicletta (No cycling)

At times, it is possible for verbs to be replaced by equivalent nouns:

Il fumo fa male (Smoking is bad for one's health)

Lo sci è un gran bello sport (Skiing is a fabulous sport) means the same as *Sciare*, or *Lo sciare è un gran bello sport*
Le passeggiate fanno bene (Walks are good for one's health)
Uno dei miei passatempi preferiti è la lettura (One of my favourite hobbies is reading)
Vietato il parchèggio (No parking)

After a preposition you can only have an infinitive, or an equivalent noun:

Prima di partire telèfonagli (Before leaving, phone him)
Nello scèndere le scale è scivolata e si è rotta una gamba (While coming down the stairs, she slipped and broke a leg)
Sono riuscito a convìncerlo (I succeeded in convincing him)
Sono stanca di alzarmi così presto al mattino (I am tired of getting up so early in the morning)

Gerunds often replace '-ing' verbs, particularly when preceded by 'in, while, on, by':

Sbagliando s'impara (You learn by making errors)
Camminando ho avuto un'idea (While walking I had an idea)
Vedendo ciò, mi sono detto che era tutto sbagliato (On seeing that, I said to myself that it was all wrong)

Another way of translating '-ing' forms is by full sentences:

Mentre attraversa la strada, viene investita da un'àuto in corsa (While crossing the street, she is run over by a fast moving car)
Ci ho pensato dopo che sei uscito (I thought of it after your leaving)

Exercise 1

Join the following pairs of sentences with relatives:

(a) *L'Itàlia è ricca di tesori d'arte. Quest'arte è stata creata nel corso di molti sècoli.*
(b) *Una conseguenza di ciò è che è stata spesso invasa. Mi dispiace di questa conseguenza.*
(c) *Mi ricordo i nomi di alcune importanti città. Queste città sono Firenze, Venèzia, Roma, Torino, Milano, Nàpoli e Palermo.*
(d) *È una bellìssima ragazza. Ti ho visto uscire con lei.*
(e) *Quel tipo è mio amico. Ti piace la sua màcchina.*

Exercise 2

Use the relative *cui*, with or without preposition, in the following sentences to replace other relatives:

(a) *Sai, il signore al quale ho fatto lezione di italiano è andato in Itàlia.*

(b) *Il mio fidanzato, del quale non so più niente da mesi, si è trovato qualcun'altra.*

(c) *La Signora Tedeschi, della eleganza della quale non fate altro che parlare, è una miliardària.*

(d) *Alcuni, fra i quali tuo cugino, sono stati arrestati dopo la dimostrazione.*

(e) *La galleria del Monte Bianco, attraverso la quale si arriva in Itàlia dalla Frància, è la più lunga galleria autostradale del mondo.*

Exercise 3

Replace the simple present tense in the following sentences with the progressive present with *stare* followed by gerund:

(a) *Arriva qualcuno.*

(b) *Pranzi?*

(c) *Che cosa fai?*

(d) *Silènzio! Dorme.*

(e) *Aspettate un po', ci prepariamo.*

Exercise 4

Replace the gerunds in the following sentences with a full sentence or phrase:

(a) *Cadendo, mi sono rotto un bràccio.*

(b) *Comperàndoti la casa, risolvi i tuoi problemi.*

(c) *Conoscèndolo, mi piace di più.*

(d) *Stai attento attraversando la strada.*

(e) *Abitando a Firenze si è quasi al centro d'Itàlia.*

Exercise 5

Translate:

(a) I am tired of waiting.
(b) We look forward to getting to the seaside.
(c) After leaving I did not do anything.
(d) She enjoys walking and window-shopping.
(e) Parking is not easy in this town.

LESSON 12

■ UN LITIGIO

Buon compleanno, Daniela.
Perchè non mi hai telefonato
che non potevi fare in tempo?
Su, rispondi.
Scusami, cara; non me ne ero
dimenticato. Solamente che
dovevo andare in questura per
il rinnovo del permesso di
soggiorno e poi c'era un
traffico indescrivibile. Un
caos. Si andava a passo
d'uomo.
Tutte storie. Sono tutte scuse.
Sapevi che oggi compivo gli
anni e che a casa ti
aspettavano tutti a pranzo.

Su, avanti, Daniela, non fare
così. Andiamo a festeggiare.

A QUARREL

Happy birthday, Daniela.
Why didn't you ring me to
say you couldn't be here on
time? Come on, answer.
Excuse me, darling. I had not
forgotten about it. The fact is
that I had to go to the police
station for the renewal of my
residence permit and then the
traffic was unbelievable.
Chaos. I drove at a snail's
pace.
This is all nonsense. They are
all excuses. You knew that
today was my birthday and
everyone was waiting for you
for lunch at home.
Come on, Daniela, don't be
like that. Let's go and
celebrate.

THE IMPERFECT TENSE

This tense indicates events in the course of their taking place in the past, but without a definite reference to their conclusion. So it may refer to:

(a) events which did or did not occur habitually or repeatedly in the course of time:

Anche Mário lavorava alla Pirelli (Mario used to be employed by Pirelli, too)
Come si comportava? Taceva sempre, non diceva mai una parola (How did he behave? He was always silent, he never said a word)
Dovevi pensarci prima (You should have thought of it before)

(b) events which, though initiated in the past, are continued in the present, or in polite requests or newspaper accounts:

Volevo un gelato (I'd like to have an ice-cream)
Che cosa volevate dire con ciò? (What did you mean by that?)

(c) states of mind, health, physical and mental condition:

Aveva ancora la febbre, quando è partita (She still had a temperature when she left)
Come eravamo? Stavamo bene, eravamo contenti anche se avevamo poco (How were we? We were all right, we were happy even though we didn't have much)
Volevamo prèndere i biglietti, ma non abbiamo potuto perchè era tutto esaurito (We wanted to buy tickets, but we couldn't, as it was all sold out)

(d) events which were or were not taking place when something else began to happen:

Guardavamo sempre la televisione mentre cenavamo (We always watched television while we were having our supper)
Quando mi hai chiamato al telèfono, facevo la dòccia (When you rang me up, I was having a shower)

Notice that this particular use of the imperfect can be replaced by the imperfect of the verb *stare* followed by the gerund of the verb:

Stavate mangiando? (Were you having your meal?)
Che cosa stavo dicendo? (What was I saying?)

Another alternative way is using the imperfect of *stare* followed by *a* and the infinitive of the verb:

Stavo a bàttere a macchina tutto il giorno senza sosta (I kept typing all day without interruption)
Che cosa stavi a fare quando ti ho chiamato al telèfono? (What were you doing when I rang you up?)

For special emphasis, the imperfect of *andare* or *venire* followed by the gerund of the verb could be used, too:

L'anno scolàstico andava finendo (The school year was coming to an end)
Le giornate venìvano allungàndosi (The days were becoming longer)

(e) expressions such as *mancava poco, per poco (non), quasi quasi, a momenti (non)* (almost), *tanto valeva* (I might as well), *valeva la pena* (it was worth while):

Mancava poco che ci investiva (He almost ran us over)
Per poco non ci ammazzava (He might have killed us)
Quasi quasi piangeva (He almost burst into tears)

(f) situations where the past conditional would normally be used, with the verbs *dovere* (to have to), *potere* (to be possible, to be in a position to), *volere* (to want):

Dovevo capirlo prima (I should have understood it before)
Come potevi rispòndere sùbito? (How would it have been possible for you to answer straight away?)
Non volevamo disturbarLa (We wouldn't have liked to bother you)

(g) verbs and phrases meaning 'to be necessary, suitable, easy, sufficient, high time, better, worse', when used impersonally:

Occorrèvano tempo e denaro (Time and money were needed)
Era ora di muòversi (It was high time to get moving)
Era pèggio del previsto (It was worse than anticipated)

(h) opinions or beliefs:

Non me l'aspettavo da te (I didn't expect that from you)
Lo supponevo; lo sospettavo da tempo (I supposed so; I'd been suspecting it for some time)

(i) requests and polite offers:

Cercavo pròprio Lei (I was just looking for you)
Voleva qualcosa, signore? (Would you like something, sir?)

(j) action that had started in the earlier past and was still going on at the time implied by the main clause:

La conoscevo da quando siamo andati al mare (I had known her ever since we went to the seaside)
Era dal 1980 che non andavo in Itàlia (I hadn't gone to Italy since 1980)

The endings of the imperfect are the following:

-vo, -vi, -va, -vamo, -vate, -vano.

First conjugation	Second conjugation	Third conjugation
parlavo (I used to speak)	*vendevo* (I used to sell)	*dormivo* (I used to sleep)
parlavi	*vendevi*	*dormivi*
parlava	*vendeva*	*dormiva*
parlavamo	*vendevamo*	*dormivamo*
parlavate	*vendevate*	*dormivate*
parlàvano	*vendèvano*	*dormìvano*

PLUPERFECT INDICATIVE TENSE

This tense consists of the imperfect of *avere* or *essere* followed by the past participle, e.g.

Era tardi e l'àutobus era già passato (It was late and the bus had already gone)
Quando siamo arrivati, avèvano già finito tutto (When we arrived, they had already finished everything)

Some verbs have different forms of the imperfect tense:

G2 Verb *èssere* (to be)
ero (I was; I used to be)
eri
era
eravamo
eravate
èrano

G5 Verbs *fare* (to do, to make), *disfare* (to undo), *soddisfare* (to satisfy), e.g.

facevo (I was doing; I used to do)
facevi
etc.

G11 Verbs *supporre* (to suppose), *porre* (to put), *comporre* (to compose), *deporre* (to depose), *disporre* (to arrange), *esporre* (to expose; to expound), *proporre* (to propose), *scomporre* (to break up), *sovrapporre* (to superimpose), e.g.

supponevo (I was supposing; I used to suppose)
supponevi
etc.

G12 Verbs *trarre* (to draw), *attrarre* (to attract), *detrarre* (to deduce), *distrarre* (to distract), *sottrarre* (to subtract; to purloin), e.g.

traevo (I was drawing, I used to draw)
traevi
etc.

G15 Verbs *dire* (to say, to tell), *benedire* (to bless), *contraddire* (to contradict), *disdire* (to cancel), *maledire* (to curse), *predire* (to anticipate, to forecast), e.g.

dicevo (I was saying, I used to say)
dicevi
etc.

G16 Verbs *tradurre* (to translate), *condurre* (to lead), *dedurre* (to deduct; to infer), *indurre* (to induce, to lead), *produrre* (to produce), *ridurre* (to reduce), *sedurre* (to seduce), e.g.

traducevo (I was translating, I used to translate) etc.

G22   Verb *bere*

bevevo (I was drinking, I used to drink) etc.

■ **CRÒNACA CITTADINA: read and translate**

È partito sotto il sole il week-end della neve. Sciatori, però, delusi: gli impianti di molte stazioni invernali non sono ancora aperti. Visibilità buona su tutte le autostrade.
(Dal quotidiano 'Il Corriere della Sera' di Milano)

Una splendida giornata, l'assenza della nèbbia, la temperatura gradèvole (13° di màssima) hanno favorito la prima parte dell'èsodo per il 'ponte' di Sant'Ambrogio. Una 'fuga' dalla città ordinata, ma non massìccia. Molti milanesi pàrtono oggi. È cominciata ufficial-mente la stagione dello sci, anche se in alcune stazioni invernali gli impianti di risalita non sono ancora in funzione.

Su tutte le strade e le autostrade lombarde ieri il traffico è stato scorrèvole. I caselli d'ingresso nelle principali autostrade non sono stati presi d'assalto. Non si è registrato il tradizionale effetto-imbuto. A Melegnano si sono formate code di una certa consistenza soltanto nel pomerìggio. Visibilità buona ovùnque. La nèbbia si è addensata però sull'autostrada Milano–Venèzia nei dintorni di Verona, dove ci sono stati incidenti di una certa gravità.

Folla, ma non a livelli eccezionali, alla Stazione Centrale: i re-sponsàbili del Compartimento hanno rinforzato soprattutto i treni per il Sud. Il Roma (TEE) delle ore 16.50 si è rivelato insufficiente per ospitare tutti i passeggeri in partenza. In pochi minuti è stato allestito un convoglio straordinàrio. Spintoni e ricerca disperata del posto anche sui treni per Venèzia, in partenza alle ore 16.55 e 18.30 e per la Sicìlia delle 17.15. Molte le richieste per Parigi e aggiunta di carrozze letto sull''internazionale' delle 22. Sui treni diretti a Lecce (20.30 e 21.02) sòlita ressa e occupazione di tutti gli spazi disponìbili.

In funzione regolarmente Linate e Malpensa. Ritardi e cancella-zioni sono stati causati dalle condizioni del tempo sfavorèvoli su altri scali (come Roma e Pisa). I passeggeri per Gènova con il volo delle 18.40 sono partiti in treno: l'equipàggio aveva terminato l'arco di lavoro giornaliero.

Le previsioni del tempo per oggi: cielo sereno o poco nuvoloso, possibile formazione di banchi di nèbbia in Lombardia nelle prime ore del mattino.

Exercise 1

Replace the verbs between brackets with either the imperfect or the perfect, as appropriate:

Màrio, che (vivere) a Milano da vari anni, si (trasferire) nella sua città. Sua mòglie (essere) contenta del trasferimento. A Milano (pagare) molto di affitto, ma (risparmiare) abbastanza perchè (lavorare) tutti e due. Così (potere) comperarsi un appartamento nella nuova città. A Màrio non (piacere) Milano, non gli (piacere) mai. Ma Milano (essere) più interessante, anche se (essere) più rumorosa e meno tranquilla. Quando (essere) a Milano, Màrio (venire) spesso a trovare i suoi genitori. Di sòlito (viaggiare) in treno, di cui (avere) l'abbonamento mensile.

Exercise 2

Rewrite the following passage in the past; taking care to use the pluperfect, the imperfect or the perfect, as appropriate:

La luna illùmina tutto a giorno. I due uòmini màngiano seduti l'uno di fronte all'altro e, dopo, Guglielmo offre una sigaretta all'altro. Ma questi preferisce accèndere la pipa. Fino a questo momento hanno scambiato solo poche parole. Ma ora Guglielmo gli chiede quanti anni sono che fa quel mestiere. 'Quaranta', risponde l'uomo. 'Ho cominciato ad andare con mio padre quando avevo quìndici anni.'
Quel mestiere se lo trasmèttono di padre in fìglio.

Exercise 3

Turn the following imperfect verb forms into imperfect forms of *stare*, *andare* or *venire* plus gerund, as seems most fitting:

(a) *L'estate finiva lentamente.*
(b) *La sigaretta si spegneva.*

(c) *Il tràffico diventava sempre più forte.*

(d) *Col passare delle ore del giorno, il caldo aumentava in modo insopportàbile.*

(e) *Dopo quella dura giornata, sentivo la stanchezza cadermi addosso.*

LESSON 13

■ **AL CONCERTO**

AT THE CONCERT

Vorrei andare ad un concerto, e tu no?

I'd like to go to a concert, wouldn't you?

Anche a me piacerebbe.

So would I. Let's see what is on. Here we are, look:

Vediamo cosa c'è. Ecco, guarda: Beethoven, Mozart e Boccherini. Bello, no?

Beethoven, Mozart and Boccherini. Good, isn't it?

Certo! Mi piace di più la mùsica sinfònica settecentesca ed ottocentesca.

It certainly is. I like symphonic music of the eighteenth and nineteenth centuries best.

Sono rimasti solo posti di platea da sedicimila lire.

Only stalls seats at sixteen thousand lire are left.

Sono carìssimi, ma prendiàmoli lo stesso.

They are extremely expensive, but let's buy them all the same.

Ti piace di più la mùsica leggera o quella clàssica?

Do you like pop music better than classical music?

Tutta la mùsica mi piace, ma mi piàcciono di più le sinfonie. Più di tutto mi piace Beethoven. La mùsica da camera mi piace meno di tutto.

I like all music, but I like symphonic music best. I like Beethoven best of all. I like chamber music least of all.

Che ti è sembrato dell'orchestra?

How did the orchestra sound to you?

*Mi è parsa buona. Mi è
piaciuto soprattutto il
direttore. Formidàbile!
È stata una bella serata.
Valeva la pena spèndere
tanto.*

It seemed good to me. I liked
the conductor in particular.
Terrific!
It has been a good evening.
It was worth spending so
much.

COMPARISONS AND SUPERLATIVES

Comparisons are expressed with *più* (more) or *meno* (less) in the
first part and *di* followed by a noun, or *che* followed by an infinitive,
or *di quello che (non)*, *di quanto che (non)*, *di quanto (non)* before
a verb in the subjunctive or in the indicative, e.g.

È più basso e magro di me (He is shorter and thinner than me)
Màngia (di) più di tutti noi (He eats more than all of us)
È più interessante restare a vedere la mostra che andare a casa (It
is more interesting to stay and see the exhibition than to go home)
Penso che stano meno ricchi di quello che (non) si creda
(I think they are less rich than people believe)

Comparisons are also expressed with *così* or *tanto* (as, so), in the
first part, and *come* or *quanto* (as), in the second part. *Così* and
tanto in the first part can be omitted, e.g.

Sono (tanto) alto quanto te (I am as tall as you)
Fa caldo come l'anno scorso (It is as hot as last year)

A few adjectives and adverbs have special comparative and super-
lative forms:

buono (good)	*migliore* (better)	*il migliore* (best)
bene (good, well)	*mèglio* (better)	*il mèglio* (the best)
cattivo (bad)	*peggiore* (worse)	*il peggiore* (the worst)
male (badly, unwell)	*pèggio* (worse)	*il pèggio* (the worst)
poco (little)	*meno* (less)	*il meno* (the least)
grande (great, big)	*maggiore* or *più grande* (greater, bigger)	*il più grande* or *il maggiore* or *il màssimo* (greatest, biggest)

Colloquial Italian is also available in the form of a course pack (ISBN 0-415-03892-8), containing this book and an accompanying audio cassette. The pronunciation guide, readings, conversations and idiomatic phrases contained in the book have been recorded by native speakers of Italian, making the cassette an invaluable aid to speaking and comprehension.

If you have been unable to obtain the course pack the cassette can be ordered separately through your bookseller or, in case of difficulty, cash with order from Routledge Ltd, ITPS, Cheriton House, North Way, Andover, Hants SP10 5BE, price £7.99 including VAT, or from Routledge Inc., 29 West 35th Street, New York, NY 10001, USA, price $14.95.

For your convenience an order form is attached.

CASSETTE ORDER

Please supply one/two/ . . . . cassette(s) of

Andreis, *Colloquial Italian*
ISBN 0-415-03891-X
Price £7.99 inc. VAT or US $14.95

☐ I enclose payment with order.

☐ Please debit my Access/Mastercharge/Visa/American Express account number

☐☐☐☐☐☐☐☐☐☐☐☐☐☐☐☐☐☐☐☐   Expiry date ....

Name ....

Address ....

....

Order to your bookseller or to . . .

ROUTLEDGE
ITPS
North Way
Andover, Hants.
SP10 5BE
ENGLAND

ROUTLEDGE INC.
29 West 35th Street
New York
NY 10001
USA

| pìccolo (small, little) | minore or più pìccolo (smaller; minor) | il mìnimo or il minore or il più pìccolo (the smallest) |
| grandemente (greatly) | maggiormente or di più (more) | massimamente (most) |

For example:

È nelle peggiori condizioni possìbili (It is in the worst possible condition)
Facciamo il màssimo possìbile (We do our utmost)
Tanto pèggio tanto mèglio (The worse, the better)
Non tòllera il mìnimo rumore (He can't stand the slightest noise)
Carla è la maggiore della famìglia (Carla is the eldest of her family)
È il meno che mi possa aspettare (It is the least I can expect)

When the meaning of an adjective or adverb is intensified in the extreme, this is expressed either by the endings *-ìssimo, -ìssima, -ìssimi, -ìssime*, or by such adverbs as *molto, assai* (very), *piuttosto* (rather), *estremamente* (extremely), *straordinariamente* (extraordinarily), e.g.

Bravìssimo! (Very good, excellent, very clever)
Fa caldìssimo (It is extremely hot)
Siamo molto contenti di voi (We are very satisfied with you)

CARDINAL AND ORDINAL NUMBERS

Nùmeri cardinali   *Nùmeri ordinali*

trèdici	13	tredicèsimo	13th
quattòrdici	14	quattordicèsimo	14th
quìndici	15	quindicèsimo	15th
sèdici	16	sedicèsimo	16th
diciassette	17	diciassettèsimo	17th
diciotto	18	diciottèsimo	18th
diciannove	19	diciannovèsimo	19th
venti	20	ventèsimo	20th
ventuno	21	ventunèsimo	21st

ventidue	22	ventiduèsimo	22nd
trenta	30	trentèsimo	30th
quaranta	40	quarantèsimo	40th
cinquanta	50	cinquantèsimo	50th
sessanta	60	sessantèsimo	60th
settanta	70	settantèsimo	70th
ottanta	80	ottantèsimo	80th
novanta	90	novantèsimo	90th
cento	100	centèsimo	100th
centouno	101	centunèsimo	101st
duecento	200	duecentèsimo	200th
novecentonovantanove	999	novecentonovantavèsimo	999th
mille	1,000	millèsimo	1,000th
milleuno	1,001	milleunèsimo	1,001st
duemila	2,000	duemillèsimo	2,000th
un milione	1,000,000	milionèsimo	1,000,000th
dieci milioni		dieci milionèsimo	10,000,000th
trecentomila	10,300,000	miliardèsimo	1,000,000,000th
un miliardo	1,000,000,000		
cento miliardi e due			
milioni	100,002,000,000		

For example:

Il déficit della bilancia commerciale ha raggiunto i diecimila miliardi di lire (The deficit of the trade balance has reached ten thousand billion lire)

Il metro è la quarantamilionèsima parte del meridiano terrestre (The metre is the forty millionth part of the earth's meridian)

Un miglio ha milleseicentonove metri (A mile consists of one thousand six hundred and nine metres)

Un milionàrio in dòllari o in sterline è un miliardàrio in lire (A millionaire in dollars or pounds is a billionaire in lire)

Negli anni bisestili febbràio ha ventinove giorni (February has twenty-nine days in leap years)

Il venticinquèsimo anniversàrio delle nozze viene chiamato 'nozze d'argento', il cinquantèsimo 'nozze d'oro', il sessantèsimo 'nozze di diamante' (The twenty-fifth wedding anniversary is called a silver wedding, the fiftieth a golden wedding and the sixtieth a diamond wedding)

Ogni dieci giorni (every ten days)
Siamo in tanti, siamo in dòdici, compreso il cane (There are so many of us, there are twelve of us, including the dog)

COLLECTIVE NUMBERS

These indicate approximation to a certain number. They can also be used in the plural and are feminine:

decina (about ten)	*cinquantina* (about fifty)
dozzina (about twelve)	*sessantina* (about sixty)
quindicina (about fifteen)	*settantina* (about seventy)
ventina (about twenty)	*ottantina* (about eighty)
trentina (about thirty)	*novantina* (about ninety)
quarantina (about forty)	

The following are masculine in the singular and feminine, ending in *-a*, in the plural:

centinàio (about a hundred), pl. *centinàia*
migliàio (about a thousand), pl. *migliàia*

The meaning of 'about, approximately' is otherwise conveyed by the use of the article *un*, or by *circa, all'incirca, approssimativamente, suppergiù* (about, approximately), e.g.

Ci dèvono èssere un quìndici persone (There must be about fifteen people)
Roma ha circa tre milioni di abitanti (Rome has about three million people)

FRACTIONS (FRAZIONI)

These consist of a cardinal followed by an ordinal number. The latter can become plural, e.g.

¼ *un quarto*
¹/₃ *un terzo*
½ *una metà*, or *un mezzo*, or *metà*, or *mezzo*
²/₃ *due terzi*
¾ *tre quarti*

For example:

Ho mangiato metà mela (I've eaten half of an apple)
È una bottiglia da tre quarti (It is a three-quarter litre bottle)
Si è messo a piòvere a un quarto dalla fine dello spettàcolo (It started raining three-quarters of the way through the performance)

ARITHMETIC

Addition (addizione)

Due e due fanno quattro (Two and two are four)
Tre più quattro fa sette (Three and four are seven)
Cinque più due è uguale sette (Five plus two equals seven)

Subtraction (sottrazione)

Due meno uno fa uno (One from two is one)

Multiplication (moltiplicazione)

Sei per quattro fa ventiquattro (Six times four is twenty-four)
Due moltiplicato per tre fa sei (Two multiplied by three is six)
Quattro volte quattro è uguale a sèdici (Four times four equals sixteen)

Division (divisione)

Nove diviso tre fa tre (Nine divided by three is three)
Il tre nel nove ci sta tre volte (Three goes into nine three times)

Square and cube roots

La radice quadrata di trentasei è sei (The square root of thirty-six is six)
La radice cùbica di sessantaquattro è quattro (The cube root of sixty-four is four)

ORDINAL NUMBERS IN TITLES

No article precedes ordinal numbers in titles, unlike in English, e.g.

Elisabetta II, read *Elisabetta Seconda* (Elizabeth II)
Napoleone I, read *Napoleone Primo* (Napoleon I)
Giovanni XXIII, read *Giovanni Ventitreèsimo* (John XXIII)
la Regina Elisabetta I (Queen Elizabeth I)
(il) Re Giòrgio VI (King George VI)
(il) Papa Giovanni Paolo II (Pope John Paul II)
l'Imperatore Napoleone III (the Emperor Napoleon III)
Such titles as *Regina* (Queen), *Imperatore* (Emperor), *Duca* (Duke), *Prìncipe* (Prince), *Principessa* (Princess) must be preceded by the article, while *Re* (King) and *Papa* (Pope) may or may not.

HEIGHT OF PERSONS

This is given in metres and centimetres, the average range for men being roughly between 1 metre 60 centimetres and 1 metre 90 centimetres. For women, the range may be between 1 metre 50 centimetres and 1 metre 80 centimetres, e.g.

Quanto sei alto? Uno e settantacìnque (How tall are you? 1 metre 75 centimetres)

AGE

Instead of saying 'to be so many years old', the Italians use the expression 'to have so many years', e.g.

Quanti anni hai? Ho vent'anni (How old are you? I'm 20)
Avrà settant'anni (She may be 70)

When an approximate age is meant, the collective numbers may be used preceded by the expression *'èssere sulla'*, e.g.

È sulla sessantina (He is in his sixties)

SIZES OF CLOTHING AND FOOTWEAR

Men's shoes range from 40 to 44, women's from 36 to 39, e.g.

Vorrei un paio di scarpe marrone, misura quarantadue (I'd like a pair of brown shoes, size 42)
Che misura porta? (What's your size?)

Men's clothes range from about 40 to about 54, women's from about 40 to about 48. In some instances, sizes range from one to six, e.g.

Che numero porta, signora? Porto il quarantaquattro (What's your size, madam? I wear size 44)
In Inghilterra porto il dodici. A che numero corrisponde qui?
(I wear size 12 in England. What size does that correspond to here?)
Che taglia ha? Il quarantasei (What's your size? 46)
Che misura porta? Porto la quarta misura (What's your size? I wear size four)

BIRTH

Nascere (to be born) is seldom used in the present. It is normally used in the perfect, i.e. *sono nato* (I was born), or, more formally, in the past definite, i.e. *nacqui* (I was born), or in the pluperfect, i.e. *ero nato* (I had been born), or in the gerund, i.e. *nascendo* (being born), *essendo nato* (having been born), or in the infinitive, i.e. *nascere* (to be born), *essere nato* (to have been born). The imperfect, i.e. *nascevo*, is sometimes used instead of the past definite in literary or historical texts, e.g.

Dove e quando siete nate, ragazze? (Where and when were you born, girls?)
Io sono nata a Siena il 12 ottobre 1968 e lei a Torino il 30 settembre 1970 (I was born in Siena on 12 October 1968 and she in Turin on 30 September 1970)
Data e luogo di nascita, prego! (Your date and place of birth, please)
Napoleone nacque ad Ajaccio (Napoleon was born in Ajaccio)
Era nato prima della guerra (He had been born before the war)
Essendo nato a Venezia, amo il mare (Having been born in Venice, I love the sea)
Leopardi nasceva a Recanati nel 1798 (Leopardi was born in Recanati in 1798)

DATES

Except for *il primo* (the 1st) of each month, cardinal numbers are used in Italian in the dates. No article is mentioned in heading dates. The simple article is used, instead, to replace the English 'on':

Oggi è il ventidue ottobre 1981 (Today is 22 October 1981)
Domani è il 23 novembre 1980 (Tomorrow is 23 November 1980)
La nave parte il 16 giugno e deve arrivare il 2 luglio (The ship is leaving on 16 June and is due to arrive on 2 July)

In letters and other headings, dates are written as follows, usually on the right-hand side:

Milano, 4/6/1982
(Milan, 4 June 1982)
Firenze, 4 giugno 1982
(Florence, 4 June 1982)

No article or preposition is used when the day of the week is also mentioned in a date:

Venerdì 12 luglio veniamo a trovarvi (We shall come and see you on Friday, 12 July)

but:

Veniamo a trovarvi il venerdì or *di venerdì* (We shall come and see you on a Friday, on Fridays)
Il venerdì va bene per venire a trovarci (Fridays are all right to come and see us)
Andiamo a fargli visita il martedì che avete libero (We are going to visit him on your Tuesday off)
Ho libero il lunedì della settimana prossima
(Monday of next week is free for me)

In or *di* (in) is used with reference to months and seasons, *tra* or *fra* (between or within) is used when a period of time is expressed, *per* (for) to indicate the duration, *da* (from or since) to indicate the starting time, and *a* (to) to indicate the time of end:

Il dottore è assente dal primo luglio al trentuno compresi. Si prega di rivolgersi al suo sostituto, Dott. Giorgio Giacometti (The doctor will be away from 1 to 31 July inclusive. You are kindly requested to apply to his substitute, Dr G. Giacometti)

A partire da (as from) is used if the moment when an event started is to be stressed. *Per* or *entro* (by) indicates a specific time within which something is bound to happen, e.g.

A partire dalla mezzanotte di sàbato 23, a càusa dell'ora legale, gli orari dei treni càmbiano (As from midnight, Saturday 23, because of the introduction of summer time, the times of trains are going to change)
Entro venerdì dobbiamo consegnare la denùncia dei rèdditi (By Friday we must fill in the tax return form)
Ti assicuro che la preparo per domani (I can assure you that I shall get it ready by tomorrow)

DISTANCES

They are measured in kilometres (*chilòmetri*) and metres *(metri)*, e.g.

È lontana la stazione? È a circa mezzo chilòmetro (Is the station far away? It's about half a kilometre away)
Quanto dista Milano? Cento chilòmetri (How far is Milan? 100 kilometres)
A che distanza è Firenze? È a pochi chilòmetri (How far is Florence? It is a few kilometres away)
Vado a cento chilòmetri all'ora (I'm driving at 100 km. an hour)

Il mìglio (mile) has the feminine plural *le mìglia*, e.g.

Londra dista tre mìglia (London is three miles away)
Venticìnque mìglia all'ora (25 miles an hour)

TEMPERATURES

These are measured in degrees centigrade (*gradi centìgradi*), zero (*zero*) being freezing point. Body temperatures may be between 35 and over 40 degrees, 37 being the normal temperature, e.g.

Ho la febbre. Ho trentotto e due lìnee (I have a fever. My temperature is 38.2)

Che freddo, dev'èssere sotto zero! (How cold, it must be below zero!)

L'estate scorsa ha fatto un caldo insopportàbile. C'èrano anche quaranta gradi all'ombra (Last summer it was unbearably hot. It was up to 40 in the shade).

WEIGHTS AND CAPACITY

Weights are expressed in kilos (*chili* or *chilogrammi*), grammes (*grammi*), hundreds of grammes (*etti*), hundreds of kilos (*quintali*), thousands of kilos or metric tons (*tonnellate*). Liquids are measured in litres (*litri*) and hundreds of litres (*ettòlitri*). Pounds (*libbre*) are rarely used, e.g.

Quanto pesi? Peso quasi ottanta chili. Che grasso!
(How much do you weigh? I weigh almost 80 kilos. How fat!)
Quanto costa la benzina al litro? (How much is petrol per litre?)

■ HOURS AND TIMES

Che ore sono? or *Che ora è?* (What time is it?)
È l'una (It's one o'clock)
È l'una esatta or *in punto* or *precisa* or *spaccata* (It's one sharp)
Sono le due (It's two)
Sono le tre e venticìnque (minuti) (It's three twenty-five)
Sono le quattro e mezza or *le quattro e trenta* (It's half past four)
Sono le cìnque meno venti or *Màncano venti minuti alle cìnque* (It's twenty to five)
Sono le sei e quarantacìnque or *Sono le sette meno un quarto* or *Manca un quarto alle sette* (It's a quarter to seven)
Sono le otto e un quarto or *Sono le otto e quìndici* (It's a quarter past eight)
Un quarto d'ora (A quarter of an hour)
Tre quarti d'ora (Three-quarters of an hour)
Un secondo (A second)
Un minuto (A minute)
Un orològio (A clock; a watch), *una svèglia* (an alarm-clock)
Il pèndolo fa le nove precise (It is nine o'clock sharp at the pendulum)

Il mio orolõgio resta indietro di tre minuti al giorno
(My watch is three minutes slow every day)
Il tuo orologio non va bene, è avanti di dieci minuti
(Your watch is not right, it is ten minutes fast)
La svèglia non funziona, va avanti (The alarm-clock does not work
properly, it is fast)
Da quanto aspetti? Da ore (How long have you been waiting?
For hours)
Aspetto dalle tre (I've been waiting since three)
Èrano sècoli che non ti vedevo (I had not seen you for centuries!)

■ **FILASTROCCA: read and translate**

Trenta giorni ha novembre,
con aprile, giugno e settembre;
ventotto ne ha uno,
tutti gli altri ne hanno trentuno.

■ **ACQUISTI: read and translate**

(Nel negõzio di calzature)

Buon giorno, signorina, mi dica!
Volevo vedere le scarpe in vetrina, quelle marroni.
Quelle con la fìbbia o con i lacci?
Con la fìbbia.
Che misura porta?
Il trentasette.
Ecco, le provi. Le vanno bene?

(Nel negõzio di abbigliamento)

Prego, signorina? Desìdera?
Mi fa vedere una camicetta di seta sul rosa?
Ecco, questi sono gli ùltimi modelli.
Posso provare questa? È la terza misura, vero?
Prego, si accòmodi.

Mi va bene, la prendo.
Bene, gràzie e arrivederLa.

(In farmacia)

Desìdera?
Mi dà un tubetto di aspirine e dei cerotti, per favore?
Ecco, paghi alla cassa, prego.

Exercise 1

Join the following pairs of sentences expressing comparisons:

(a) *I danni alla mia màcchina sono stati gravi. Quelli all'altra màcchina sono stati gravìssimi.*
(b) *L'Itàlia è molto montagnosa. La Frància è poco montagnosa.*
(c) *La Frància è molto grande di superfìcie. Non me l'aspettavo.*
(d) *Le òpere sono belle. Anche i concerti sono belli.*
(e) *L'orchestra era buona. I cantanti non èrano molto buoni.*

Exercise 2

Read and write the following fractions:

2/3, 12/20, 4/5, 1/2, 46/100.

Exercise 3

Replace the following approximate numbers with equivalent collective numbers, such as *una decina*:

(a) *C'èrano circa cento persone.*
(b) *Abbiamo visto due, tre o quattro mila uccelli.*
(c) *Ha circa quarant'anni.*
(d) *Ci vògliono sulle dòdici uova.*
(e) *Occòrrono suppergiù ottantamila lire.*

Exercise 4

Write the questions for the following answers:

(a) *È un metro e novanta.*
(b) *Ho quarantadue anni.*
(c) *È a una cinquantina di chilòmetri.*
(d) *Siamo sotto zero.*
(e) *Il quarantadue.*
(f) *Le dòdici e quaranta.*
(g) *Siamo nati lo stesso giorno e mese, ma a distanza di dieci anni l'uno dall'altro.*
(h) *Hai trentanove gradi e tre linee di febbre.*

Exercise 5

Describe your evening at the concert.

LESSON 14

■ UNA DICERIA

Nel milletrecentodue, Dante, il màssimo poeta italiano, dovette andare in esìlio ed abbandonare la sua città di Firenze dove era nato nel milleduecentosessantacinque e nel cui governo aveva servito come uno dei sei priori, nel Partito Bianco.

Passò vari anni a Verona, òspite del signore della città, Cangrande della Scala. Più tardi accettò l'ospitalità del signore di Ravenna, Guido Novello da Polenta, e là morì e fu sepolto nel milletrecentoventuno.

A RUMOUR

Dante, the greatest Italian poet, had to go into exile in 1302 and leave his city of Florence, where he had been born in 1265 and in whose government he had served as one of the six 'priori', in the White party.

He spent several years in Verona, as a guest of the lord of the city, Cangrande della Scala. Later he was given hospitality by the lord of Ravenna, Guido Novello da Polenta, and he died and was buried there in 1321.

*Si racconta che una volta,
mentre a Verona passeggiava
pensieroso in Piazza Erbe,
dove si trovava allora come
oggi un mercato di ortaggi,
alcune donne che lo
frequentàvano si fermàrono a
dargli un'occhiata e poi
mormoràrono tra di loro:
'Dìcono che quell'uomo,
Messer Dante, sia sceso
all'Inferno e sia anche tornato
indietro!'*

It is said that once, while he
was walking thoughtfully in
Market Square in Verona,
where a vegetable market
was situated then as it is now,
some women who frequented
it stopped to glance at him
and then murmured amongst
themselves: 'They say that
this man, Messer Dante,
went down to Hell and even
came back!'

PAST DEFINITE TENSE

The endings are:

-i
-sti
-ò (first conjugation), *-è* (second conj.), *-i* (third conj.)
-mmo
-ste
-rono

For example

First conjugation	Second conjugation	Third conjugation
parlai (I spoke)	*vendei* or *vendetti*	*dormii* (I slept)
parlasti	(I sold)	*dormisti*
parlò	*vendesti*	*dormì*
parlammo	*vendè* or *vendette*	*dormimmo*
parlaste	*vendemmo*	*dormiste*
parlàrono	*vendeste*	*dormìrono*
	vendèrono or	
	vendèttero	

Notice that second conjugation verbs may have two forms in the
first and third persons singular and in the third person plural.

In contrast with the imperfect tense, the past definite tense (*passato remoto*) refers to facts that were concluded in the past and were either very short, almost instantaneous events, or the speaker is not concerned with the duration, but rather whether they actually did or did not take place. The past definite is the typical tense of a report or narrative passage, while the imperfect is more easily associated with a description. The past definite is also the usual tense of historical reports of events. It is often linked to a date, hour, month, year, day, age, or to certain expressions indicating a specific moment, e.g.

a un certo punto, ad un certo momento (at a certain moment)
ad un tratto, improvvisamente, d'improvviso (all of a sudden)
allora (then, at that moment)
una volta, un tempo (once upon a time, at one time)
un giorno (one day)
quando, nell'àttimo in cui, nel momento in cui (when)
per un àttimo (for a second)
in poco tempo (in a short time), *brevemente* (briefly)
per poco, quasi, a momenti (almost).

The past definite is often used with a number of other phrases, when a definite point in time is meant:

stare a (to go on)
èssere sul punto di, èssere lì lì per, fare per, fare l'atto di, trovarsi sul punto di (to be just about to)
tentare, cercare di, provare a (to try)
rischiare di (to risk)
non fare in tempo a (to be late for)
venire da (to be on the point of)
venire fatto di (to chance to)
mancare poco che non (almost)

For example:

Stemmo ad ascoltare ciò che diceva (We listened to what he was saying)
Fui lì lì per andàrmene (I was tempted to leave)
Fece l'atto di alzarsi (He started to stand up)
Cercammo di reagire (We tried to react)
Rischiò di essere investita (She risked being run over)
Non fece in tempo ad alzarsi che la fermàrono (She could hardly stand up, when they stopped her)

Le venne da piàngere (She was about to burst into tears)
Mi venne fatto di dirle che aveva torto (It occurred to me to tell her that she was wrong)
Poco ci mancò che morisse (He almost died)
Quasi vendetti la casa (I almost sold my house)
Fece per dire qualcosa, ma non ci riuscì (He tried to say something, but he was unable to)
Quando fece l'atto di parlare, la gente lo tacitò (When he tried to speak, people silenced him)

PAST PERFECT TENSE

This compound tense (*trapassato remoto*) refers to events which were completed before the events narrated in the past definite. It consists of the past definite of the verbs *avere* or *èssere* followed by the past participle:

ebbi parlato (I had spoken)	*fui arrivato* (I had arrived)
avesti parlato	*fosti arrivato*
ebbe parlato	*fu arrivato*
avemmo parlato	*fummo arrivati*
aveste parlato	*foste arrivati*
èbbero parlato	*fùrono arrivati*

Like the past definite, the past perfect is a typical tense of narration and follows such expressions as:

come, appena, non appena che (as soon as)
dopo che (after)
allorchè, quando (when)
finchè, finchè non, fino a che non, fintanto che (as long as; until)
una volta che (once)
che (that), inserted between the auxiliary verb and the past participle, e.g.

Non ci fècero ripartire finchè non èbbero controllato i passaporti e tutti i bagagli (They did not let us leave until they had checked our passports and all the pieces of luggage)
Partiti che fùrono gli òspiti, tirammo un sospiro di sollievo (After all the guests had left, we sighed with relief)
Dopo che èbbero finito la corsa, si buttàrono sull'erba sfiniti (After

they had finished the race, they flung themselves on the grass, exhausted)

■ **CRONACA CITTADINA, DAL QUOTIDIANO 'IL CORRIERE DELLA SERA': read and translate**

Mini-rapinatore con coltello aggredisce una ragazza ed è bloccato dal padre.

Segue la vìttima fino a casa, la rapina di pochi spìccioli, fugge ma viene arrestato. È accaduto poco dopo la mezzanotte di ieri in Via Pavia, àngolo Corso San Gottardo.

Marisa Bottardi, 21 anni, dopo aver aperto il portone dello stàbile in cui abitava con il padre Alfredo, è salita a piedi fino al quarto piano e ha infilato le chiavi nella serratura per entrare nel suo appartamento.

Dall'ombra è improvvisamente sbucato un giòvane il quale, dopo aver estratto un coltello, ha intimato alla ragazza di consegnargli il portafogli. Dentro c'èrano pochi spìccioli. Credendo che la vìttima abitasse da sola, il rapinatore l'ha costretta a farlo entrare in casa. Il bandito si è trovato faccia a faccia con il padre della rapinata. Ha esitato un àttimo, poi ha preferito ritirarsi, sùbito inseguito da Alfredo Bottardi e da un metronotte incontrato per strada.

Il rapinatore è stato bloccato dopo qualche centinàio di metri: si tratta del diciassettenne M. T. residente nella provìncia di Cosenza, a Milano in casa di parenti. Il coltello e il portafogli rapinato sono stati trovati sotto un'àuto.

'Guardi che ha una gomma a terra'. Il trucco è vècchio ma funziona sempre. Ne ha fatto le spese ieri mattina alle 11.30, in Viale Elvèzia, Alberto Campi, 24 anni, portavalori della ditta Multimax. L'impiegato è sceso dall'àuto per controllare, quando i due giòvani motociclisti che l'avèvano avvertito del guasto hanno estratto le pistole obbligàndolo a consegnare il cappotto che indossava e nelle cui tasche èrano contenuti due milioni.

Exercise 1

Tell a story about an event that happened during your childhood using the past definite.

Exercise 2

Turn the following passage into the past, using the past definite or imperfect as appropriate:

La Resistenza armata contro il fascismo nasce l'8 settembre 1943, nel momento più angoscioso e confuso della nostra stòria. Nasce in Piemonte, a Cùneo, tra un gruppo di uòmini decisi a riscattare la vergogna e il terrore del mondo. Per questo essi sàlgono, soli, sulla montagna. Alle 19.30 di quel giorno la ràdio diffonde l'annùncio dell'armistìzio. Il generale Badòglio legge il comunicato. Sono quarantacìnque giorni che Mussolini è caduto con il colpo del 25 luglio. Dai vari fronti giùngono notìzie disastrose. Le città vèngono bombardate e divèntano cùmuli di macèrie. C'è fame, dolore, misèria. Le divisioni tedesche, comandate da Rommel e Kesselring, sono pronte a liquidare l'alleato italiano.

Exercise 3

Replace the verbs in parentheses with the appropriate forms of the past definite:

(a) *Ad un tratto (arrivare) lei.*
(b) *Per un àttimo noi non (capire) niente.*
(c) *In poche ore loro (finire) tutto il lavoro.*
(d) *Quando ci (guardare), (arrossire).*
(e) *Per poco non mi (investire).*

Exercise 4

Turn the past definite in the following sentences into perfect forms:

(a) *Una volta che finì l'anno scolàstico, andai a lavorare.*
(b) *Finchè non controllàrono tutti i passaporti, non ci lasciàrono passare.*
(c) *Appena passammo la frontiera, ci sentimmo felici.*
(d) *Non ci sentimmo tranquilli, finchè non partìrono tutti i soldati.*
(e) *Andammo in montagna a sciare dopo che aprìrono gli impianti di risalita.*

LESSON 15

■ ESPERIENZE PASSATE

*Dimmi, papà, come ti è
sembrata l'Italia? Che
impressione ti ha fatto, tu che
ci sei vissuto tanti anni?
Vissi a Bologna e a Firenze
dall'autunno millenovecento-
sessantuno alla fine del
millenovecentosettanta, gli
anni sessanta appunto. Il
nonno dovette andarci come
rappresentante della casa
editrice dove lavorava e io vi
trascorsi gli anni della mia
prima gioventù.
Ma ti piacque? Com'era?*

*Beh, èrano altri tempi. Io ci
stetti bene. Ci feci l'abitùdine
agli italiani e alle loro usanze,
compresa quella di mangiare
molto a pranzo e di fare una
lunga sosta nel pomerìggio.
Non mi parèvano nemmeno
così rumorosi.*

PAST EXPERIENCES

Tell me, Daddy, what was
Italy like? What impression
did it make on you, who
lived there so many years?
I lived in Bologna and
Florence from the autumn of
1961 until late in 1970,
indeed throughout the 1960s.
Your grandfather had to go
there as the agent of the
publishers he worked for. I
spent the early years of my
life there.

How did you like it? What
was it like?
Well, things were very
different from now. I was all
right there. I grew
accustomed to the Italians
and their habits, including
that of having the main meal
at midday and having a long
rest in the afternoon. They
did not even seem to me to
be so noisy.

IRREGULAR PAST DEFINITE

The following groups of verbs have different forms of past definite:

Group 1: verb *avere* (to have)

ebbi (I had)	*avemmo*
avesti	*aveste*
ebbe	*ĕbbero*

Group 2: verb *ĕssere* (to be)

fui (I was)	*fummo*
fosti	*foste*
fu	*fúrono*

Group 4 verbs alternate *-c-* and *-cq-*: *tacere* (to keep silent), *dispiacere* (to be sorry; to displease), *piacere* (to like), *giacere* (to lie down), *nuòcere* (to harm), e.g.

tacqui (I kept silent)	*tacemmo*
tacesti	*taceste*
tacque	*tácquero*

Group 5 verbs alternate *-a-* with *-e-*: *fare* (to do, to make), *disfare* (to undo), *soddisfare* (to satisfy), e.g.

feci (I did, made)	*facemmo*
facesti	*faceste*
fece	*fĕcero*

Group 6 verbs alternate *-n-* and *-nn-*: *venire* (to come), *contenere* (to contain), *mantenere* (to keep), *ritenere* (to retain; to believe), e.g.

venni (I came)	*venimmo*
venisti	*veniste*
venne	*vĕnnero*

Group 7 verbs alternate *-l-* or *-g-*, or *-r-* and *-s-*: *valere* (to be worth), *prevalere* (to prevail), e.g. *emĕrgere* (to emerge).

valsi (I was worth)	*valemmo*
valesti	*valeste*
valse	*válsero*

Group 8 verbs alternate *-gli-* and *-l-*: *accògliere* (to welcome), *cògliere* (to pick up), *raccògliere* (to pick up, to collect), *tògliere* (to remove), e.g.

accolsi (I welcomed)   *accogliemmo*
accogliesti   *accoglieste*
accolse   *accòlsero*

Group 10 and 17 verbs alternate -g- or -c and -s-: *aggiùngere* (to add), *attìngere* (to draw), *avvòlgere* (to wind, to wrap), *coinvòlgere* (to involve), *costrìngere* (to compel), *dipìngere* (to paint), *fìngere* (to pretend), *mùngere* (to milk), *piàngere* (to weep, to cry), *rivòlgersi* (to apply to), *tìngere* (to dye), *sconvòlgere* (to upset, to unsettle), *strìngere* (to hug, tighten, clasp), *evòlversi* (to evolve), *vìncere* (to win), e.g.

aggiunsi (I added)   *aggiungemmo*
aggiungesti   *aggiungeste*
aggiunse   *aggiùnsero*

Group 11 verbs alternate -n- and -s-: *comporre* (to compose), *deporre* (to depose), *disporre* (to arrange), *esporre* (to expose, to expound), *porre* (to lay down), *proporre* (to propose), *scomporre* (to separate), *sottoporre* (to submit), *sovrapporre* (to superimpose), *supporre* (to suppose), *rimanere* (to remain), e.g.

composi (I composed)   *componemmo*
componesti   *componeste*
compose   *compòsero*

Group 12 verbs alternate -ae- and -ss-: *attrarre* (to attract), *detrarre* (to deduce), *estrarre* (to extract), *trarre* (to draw), *sottrarre* (to subtract; to purloin), e.g.

attrassi (I attracted)   *attraemmo*
attraesti   *attraeste*
attrasse   *attràssero*

Group 13 verbs alternate -gg and -ss-: *distrùggere* (to destroy), *erìgere* (to erect), *elèggere* (to elect), *frìggere* (to fry), *inflìggere* (to inflict), *lèggere* (to read), *protèggere* (to protect), *sconfìggere* (to defeat), e.g.

distrussi (I destroyed)   *distruggemmo*
distruggesti   *distruggeste*
distrusse   *distrùssero*

Group 14 verbs alternate -bb- and -sc-: conóscere (to know), crëscere (to grow), decrëscere (to decrease), e.g.

conobbi (I knew)	conoscemmo
conoscesti	conosceste
conobbe	conóbbero

Groups 15 and 16 verbs alternate -c- and -ss-: dire (to say, to tell), benedire (to bless), condurre (to lead), dedurre (to deduce), disdire (to cancel), contraddire (to contradict), indire (to summon, to announce), indurre (to cause), maledire (to curse), produrre (to produce), ridurre (to reduce), sedurre (to seduce), e.g.

dissi (I said)	dicemmo
dicesti	diceste
disse	díssero

Group 19. Cuócere (to cook) alternates -uoc- and -oss-:

cossi (I cooked)	cuocemmo
cuocesti	cuoceste
cosse	cóssero

Group 20 verbs alternate -i and -v-: apparire (to appear), comparire (to turn up, show up), parere (to seem), scomparire (to disappear), e.g.

apparvi (I appeared)	apparimmo
apparisti	appariste
apparve	appárvero

Group 21 verbs alternate -ett- or -ied- and -e: dare (to give), stare (to stay), e.g.

detti or diedi (I gave)	demmo
desti	deste
dette or diede	déttero or diédero

Group 22. Bere (to drink) alternates -evv- and -ev-:

bevvi (I drank)	bevemmo
bevesti	beveste
bevve	bévvero

Group 26. Sapere (to know, to know how) alternates -ap- and -epp-:

seppi (I knew)	*sapemmo*
sapesti	*sapeste*
seppe	*sëppero*

Group 30. *Volere* (to want) alternates *-l-* and *-ll-*:

volli (I wanted)	*volemmo*
volesti	*voleste*
volle	*völlero*

Group 31 verbs alternate *-d-* and *-dd-*: *cadere* (to fall), *accadere* (to happen), *decadere* (to decay; to forfeit a right), e.g.

caddi (I fell)	*cademmo*
cadesti	*cadeste*
cadde	*cäddero*

Group 32 verbs alternate *-id-* and *-ed-*: *vedere* (to see), *prevedere* (to forecast), e.g.

vidi (I saw)	*vedemmo*
vedesti	*vedeste*
vide	*vïdero*

Group 33 verbs alternate *-omp-* and *-upp-*: *corrömpere* (to corrupt), *römpere* (to break), *prorömpere* (to burst out), e.g.

corruppi (I corrupted)	*corrompemmo*
corrompesti	*corrompeste*
corruppe	*corrüppero*

Group 34. *Redïgere* (to lay out, to edit) alternates *-ig-* and *-ass-*: *erïgere* (to erect) alternates *-ig-* and *-ess-*,

redassi (I edited)	*redigemmo*
redigesti	*redigeste*
redasse	*redässero*

Group 35 verbs alternate *-ett-* and *-is-*: *ammëttere* (to admit), *compromëttere* (to compromise), *dimëttersi* (to resign), *permëttere* (to permit), *promëttere* (to promise), *mëttere* (to set, to put), *sottomëttere* (to submit; to subdue), e.g.

ammisi (I admitted)	*ammettemmo*
ammettesti	*ammetteste*
ammise	*ammïsero*

Group 36 verbs alternate -ond- and -us-: *confondere* (to confuse), *diffóndere* (to spread), *fóndere* (to smelt, to melt), e.g.

confusi (I confused)	*confondemmo*
confondesti	*confondeste*
confuse	*confúsero*

Group 37. *Espéllere* (to expel) alternates -ell- and -uls-:

espulsi (I expelled)	*espellemmo*
espellesti	*espelleste*
espulse	*espúlsero*

Group 38 verbs alternate -iv- and -iss-: *vívere* (to live), *convívere* (to live together), e.g.

vissi (I lived)	*vivemmo*
vivesti	*viveste*
visse	*víssero*

Group 39: verbs which alternate -nd- or -d- with -s- (pronounced /z/): *attèndere* (to wait), *esclùdere* (to exclude), *chiùdere* (to close), *decídere* (to divide), *comprèndere* (to understand; to comprise), *prèndere* (to take), *difèndere* (to defend), *offèndere* (to offend), *pretèndere* (to demand, to pretend), *tèndere* (to stretch out; to tend).

attesi (I waited)	*attendemmo*
attendesti	*attendeste*
attese	*attèsero*

Group 40: verbs which alternate -d-, -v-, or -t- with -ss-:

concèdere (to grant), *discùtere* (to discuss; to argue), *muòvere* (to move), *commuòvere* (to move emotionally)

concessi (I granted)	*concedemmo*
concedesti	*concedeste*
concesse	*concèssero*

■ **LA DIVINA COMMÈDIA: read and translate**

La 'Commedia', così chiamata dal suo autore, Dante Alighieri (Firenze 1265–Ravenna 1321), è un poema allegòrico di cento canti in terzine, divisi in tre càntiche di trentatrè canti ciascuna, più uno d'introduzione con cui si apre la prima càntica. Non sfugga l'importanza che nella costruzione della 'Commedia' ha il nùmero tre, nùmero mìstico e simbòlico della Trinità.

Il poeta immàgina di trovarsi a trentacìnque anni smarrito in una 'selva selvàggia', che rappresenta simbolicamente la vita viziosa. Gli viene in aiuto Virgìlio che, mandato da Beatrice, mossa a sua volta dalla Misericòrdia divina, lo conduce a salvamento per altra via più lunga e più aspra, cioè attraverso l'Inferno e il Purgatòrio, per arrivare infine al Paradiso.

■ INFERNO, CANTO PRIMO (VERSI 1–12)
INFERNO, CANTO I (LINES 1–12)

Nel mezzo del cammin di nostra vita
Mi ritrovai per una selva oscura,
Che la diritta via era smarrita.
Ah quanto a dir qual era è cosa dura
Questa selva selvàggia ed aspra e forte,
Che nel pensier rinnova la paura!
Tanto è amara, che poco è più morte:
Ma per trattar del ben ch'i' vi trovai,
Dirò dell'altre cose ch'io v'ho scorte.
I' non so ben ridir com'io v'entrai;
Tant'era pien di sonno in su quel punto,
Che la verace via abbandonai.

La Divina Commèdia

Half way on the journey of our life
I found myself in a dark forest,
For the straight path had been lost.
As for saying what it was it is a hard thing to say
This savage forest, rough and stern,
Which in the very thought renews the fear!
So bitter it is that death is little more:
But to deal with the good that I found there,
I shall speak of the other things that I noticed there.
I cannot well repeat how I entered there;
So full of slumber I was at that moment,
When I abandoned the true way.

Dante, *The Divine Comedy*

Che = perchè, poichè (as, since, because)

Ch'i', poetic for *che io*. Similarly, *v'ho = vi ho, v'entrai = vi entrai, tant'era = tanto ero. Era* for *ero* is poetic.

Dropping the final vowel after *n, l* and *r* is common in poetry: *cammin = cammino, dir = dire, qual = quale, pensier = pensiero, trattar = trattare, ben = bene, pien = pieno*.

Exercise 1

Tell in brief what the following Italian historical personages did:

(a) *Dante*.
(b) *Boccaccio*.
(c) *Machiavelli*.
(d) *Christopher Columbus*.
(e) *Marco Polo*.
(f) *Palladio*.
(g) *The Cabot brothers*.
(h) *Galileo*.
(i) *Marconi*.
(j) *Fermi*.

Exercise 2

The following questions are in the perfect tense. Answer them, using the past definite, e.g. *Chi ha dipinto 'La Gioconda'? La dipinse Leonardo.*

(a) *Chi ha inventato il telefono?*
(b) *Chi è successo alla Regina Vittoria?*
(c) *Che cosa ha fatto Churchill?*
(d) *Dove era nato Shakespeare?*
(e) *Chi ha bevuto il veleno?*
(f) *Che cosa ha composto Beethoven?*

Exercise 3

Answer the following questions concerning Italian history, using the past definite:

(a) *Che cosa successe subito dopo la seconda guerra mondiale?*

(b) *Quali furono le capitali dell'Italia del Risorgimento?*
(c) *Che cosa avvenne alla caduta dell'Impero Romano?*
(d) *Perchè furono importanti i Comuni?*
(e) *Quale fu la conseguenza della caduta di Napoleone?*
(f) *Che cosa fece Mussolini?*

LESSON 16

■ **PROGETTI**

PLANS

Io e mia moglie abbiamo deciso di andare ad abitare in Italia, in Toscana. Partiremo domani per firmare il contratto di acquisto di una fattoria e stiamo per completare la vendita della nostra casa qui.
E che cosa farete là?

Finalmente potrò dedicarmi ai miei studi artistici ed archeologici, ora che sono in pensione. Insegnerò anche in una scuola internazionale, ma soprattutto studierò, camminerò per i campi, farò ricerche, viaggerò per l'Italia, mi godrò il sole e parlerò con la gente. A mia moglie è sempre piaciuto dipingere e fare fotografie ed ora potrà realizzare il suo sogno anche lei.

My wife and I have taken the decision of going to live in Italy, in Tuscany. We shall leave tomorrow to sign the contract to purchase a farmhouse and we are about to complete the sale of our house here.
What will you be doing there?
At long last I shall be able to devote myself to my studies of art and archaeology, as I am a pensioner now. I shall do some teaching at an international school too, but above all I'll study, I'll walk in the fields, I shall do research, I shall travel through Italy, I'll enjoy the sun and talk to the people. My wife has always liked painting and taking photographs and she too will now be able to make her dreams come true.

Ma sa che Lei è una persona
simpàtica! Se avrò
l'occasione, verrò a trovarLa.

You know, you are a
pleasant person to talk to! If
I have the chance, I'll come
and see you there.

Venga pure, sarà benvenuto!

Do come, you'll be welcome.

Simpàtico is a very useful and common adjective, meaning 'nice
and pleasant to be with and talk to'.

FUTURE TENSE

Its endings are:

-rò, -rai, -rà, -remo, -rete, -ranno, e.g.

First conjugation	Second conjugation	Third conjugation
parlerò (I shall speak)	*venderò* (I shall sell)	*dormirò* (I shall sleep)
parlerai	*venderai*	*dormirai*
parlerà	*venderà*	*dormirà*
parleremo	*venderemo*	*dormiremo*
parlerete	*venderete*	*dormirete*
parleranno	*venderanno*	*dormiranno*

Notice that the characteristic vowel *-a-* of the first conjugation
becomes *-e-* in the future.

The future tense is used:

(a) to refer to future events, e.g.

Chi vivrà, vedrà (Who will live, will see)
Che sarà, sarà (What will be, will be)
Domattina dormirò fino a tardi (Tomorrow I shall sleep until late)

(b) to indicate supposed or probable facts, e.g.

Chi sarà a quest'ora? (Who can it be at this time?)
Forse saranno i ladri (Perhaps it is the thieves)
Avrà più o meno vent'anni (She may be twenty or so)

(c) after *quando* (when), *se* (if), *appena, non appena che* (as soon
as), *finchè, fintanto che, finchè non* (as long as; until, till), *la
pròssima volta che* (the next time), *la prima volta che* (the first
time), when in English the present is used, e.g.

Ti amerò finchè vivrò (I shall love you as long as I live)
Se avrò bisogno di voi, vi chiamerò (If I need you, I'll send for you)

(d) to indicate an order, a prohibition or a threat, e.g.

Il settimo giorno riposerai (On the seventh day you shall rest)
Stasera resterai in casa! (You will stay at home tonight!)

(e) just because of the added meaning of supposition or uncertainty or cautious statement, it may be used instead of the subjunctive in certain cases, e.g.

Spero che starete bene qui (I hope you are all right here)
Credo proprio che non cambierà niente (I believe that nothing is going to change)
Qualunque cosa succederà, state calmi (Whatever may happen, keep quiet)

(f) as a stylistic device, to narrate historical events, especially in literary and journalistic accounts, e.g.

Napoleone sconfisse i nemici nelle campagne militari, ma perderà le battaglie navali (Napoleon defeated his enemies in the military campaigns, but lost naval battles)

Generally speaking the future tense is not so much used in Italian as it is in English. It is never used in such interrogative sentences as the following:

Apro la finestra? (Shall I open the window?)
Andiamo? (Shall we go?)
Vai in ufficio? (Are you going to the office?)

The present tense indicative is often preferable to the future tense in other sentences.

An alternative form of future consists in using the expressions *stare per* (to be going to), *essere sul punto di* (to be on the point of) followed by the infinitives, e.g.

Sta per entrare in scena la soprano (The soprano is just about to come on stage)
Stavamo per venire da voi (We were going to come to you)

The duration of an action can be expressed by the future tense of *stare* followed by the gerund, or by *stare a* followed by the infinitive, or by *andare* or *venire* followed by the gerund, e.g.

Che cosa andrà cercando? (What may he be looking for?)
Starò a prèndere il sole (I shall be sunbathing)
Starà prendendo il sole (She may be sunbathing)

Compound future tense

This consists of the future tense of the verbs *avere*, or *èssere* followed by the past participle, e.g.

Chi avrà mangiato i cioccolatini? (Who can have eaten the chocolates?)
Quando avrai fatto il còmpito, uscirai (When you have done your homework, you will go out).

■ MILANO CELEBRA LA FESTA DI S. AMBRÒGIO, PERTINI ALLA 'PRIMA' DELLA SCALA: read and translate

(Dal 'Corriere della Sera', quotidiano di Milano, di venerdì 7 dicembre 1979)

Oggi Sandro Pertini è a Milano. Il Presidente della Repùbblica arriva in aèreo nel primo pomeriggio. Viene però in forma privata, come un qualsìasi cittadino.

Alle 19.30 Pertini andrà alla Scala per sentire il 'Boris Godunov' che inàugura la stagione. Ma, secondo il suo stile, vuole andarci 'a titolo personale'. Di certo si sa soltanto questo, nè si pòssono azzardare previsioni sul programma milanese (eventuali altre vìsite) che il 'cittadino' Pertini, uomo imprevedìbile, ha in mente.

Pertini è già stato a Milano il 31 gennàio di quest'anno, in forma pùbblica quella volta, per i funerali in Duomo del giùdice Alessandrini. Allora si trattenne poche ore, andò a pranzare al Bagutta e in giornata ripartì.

La 'lìbera uscita' del presidente si concluderà domattina, quando Pertini ripartirà per Roma.

Fino alla magistratura di Saragat era tradizione che il Capo dello Stato venisse a Milano anche due o tre volte nel corso di un anno;

quasi sempre ai due appuntamenti costituiti dall'apertura della Fiera Campionària internazionale e dell'inaugurazione della stagione scaligera. La tradizione fu bruscamente interrotta dal Presidente Leone che, durante tutto il suo mandato, interrotto per dimissioni nel giugno del 1978, comparve a Milano soltanto una volta: il 14 aprile del 1972, all'inaugurazione della Fiera.

Saragat, presidente dal 28 dicembre del 1964, la prima volta arrivò nell'ottobre del 1965 per visitare i nuovi impianti della Rai-Tv. Poi venne diverse altre volte.

Segni venne a Milano nel 1962, a pochi mesi dall'elezione, per l'inaugurazione della stagione scaligera e per visitare la nuova aerostazione di Linate. Tornò altre volte negli anni successivi o per la Scala o per la Fiera.

Gronchi era milanese d'adozione; raramente mancò a uno dei due appuntamenti annuali, Scala o Fiera, e venne anche in forma privata.

Einàudi, presidente dal 1948, lo stesso anno venne ad inaugurare la Fiera e, anzichè in Prefettura com'è consuetùdine, senza avvertire andò a trascòrrere la notte in casa del figlio, in Corso Matteotti 9, provocando apprensione tra chi doveva vigilare sulla sua sicurezza. Allora, comùnque, èrano tempi tranquilli rispetto ad oggi.

Einàudi venne ancora frequentemente a Milano, e per occasioni anche diverse dai due tradizionali appuntamenti della Scala e della Fiera. Ad esèmpio, nel 1951 presenziò alle manifestazioni per il cinquantenàrio della morte di Verdi, nel 1952 alla celebrazione del mezzo sècolo dell'Università Bocconi, nel 1955 alle celebrazioni per il decennale della Liberazione. De Nicola fu Presidente della Repùbblica (il primo) soltanto per pochi mesi, dal gennàio al màggio del 1948. Ma venne nel 1947 quando era capo provvisòrio dello Stato. Inaugurò la prima edizione della rinata Fiera dopo la guerra.

Se andiamo a ritroso nel tempo, ai sovrani, appena la Lombardia diviene regione del Regno d'Itàlia vediamo arrivare Vittorio Emanuele II che l'8 giugno del 1859 entrò a cavallo a Milano dall'Arco della Pace, insieme a Napoleone III. Andò ad abitare per alcuni giorni nel palazzo Serbelloni.

Vittorio Emanuele II venne ancora altre volte a Milano. Nel febbràio del 1860 si portò appresso Cavour e il figlio Umberto. In quell'occasione accettò tra l'altro di partecipare a un ballo organizzato in suo onore dalla Società del Giardino, e ci andò con

Cavour che tra una danza e l'altra confabulava con il ministro di Frància Talleyrand.

Non parliamo di Umberto I che qui 'montò' casa, nella Villa Reale di Monza, e che qui ebbe pure avventure galanti. Poveretto, qui lasciò anche la pelle.

Meno proclive ai viaggi – e quindi anche alle visite di città – fu invece suo figlio Vittorio Emanuele III che comùnque qualche volta c'era. C'era, ad esèmpio, all'inaugurazione della Fiera del 1928, scampando all'attentato che provocò una strage.

Ma i re arrìvano in pompa magna, attorniati da pattùglie di generali. Più democraticamente i presidenti – ricordiamo specialmente Einàudi – qui sono venuti con disinvolto stile; e per onorare due aspetti della metròpoli: cultura ed arte (la Scala), indùstria e commèrcio (la Fiera). Senza orpelli.

(Glàuco Licata)

Exercise 1

Tell what you will be doing next weekend.

Exercise 2

Turn the following present tenses into future tenses expressing uncertainty or probability:

(a) *Forse sono le tre ormai.*
(b) *Magari non hai ancora vent'anni.*
(c) *Che sia sposata?*
(d) *Chissà se viene?*
(e) *Che stia migliorando la situazione?*

Exercise 3

Rewrite the following passage in the future:

Le previsioni non sono molto buone. L'inflazione e la disoccupazione non diminuìscono. Al contrario la produzione continua a decrèscere. In questa situazione gli investimenti non pòssono èssere soddisfacenti, anche perchè i tassi di interesse rimangono alti. Forse verso la fine dell'anno si comìnciano a vedere i risultati delle attuali misure prese dal governo.

LESSON 17

■ DAL MÈDICO

Buon giorno, dottore.
Buon giorno. Lei non ha il libretto dell'assistenza mutualistica?
No, vengo privatamente.

Mi dica che cosa si sente, quali sono i sìntomi, che cos'ha.
Dunque, ho spesso dei forti mal di testa, digerisco male ed ho dei dolori allo stòmaco, specialmente qui sul fianco destro e dietro la schiena. Mi sento spesso intontito e mi gira la testa.
Si còrichi pure. Facciamo una visitina. Si tolga la camìcia.
Fa male? Si giri. Respiri forte. Le fàccio una ricetta. Sono pastìglie per la digestione. Ma sarebbe mèglio fare una radiografia e delle anàlisi. Vada con questa richiesta all'ospedale.

AT THE DOCTOR'S

Good morning, doctor.
Good morning. Haven't you got a national health booklet?

No, I am here as a private patient.
Tell me, please, what you feel, what the symptoms are, what is the matter with you.
I often have bad headaches, indigestion and stomach-ache, in particular here on the right side and behind my back. I often feel dazed and dizzy.

Please lie down. Let's examine you. Take off your shirt, please. Does it hurt? Please turn around. Breathe deeply. I shall write you a prescription. They are indigestion pills. But you had better be X-rayed and have some tests done. Please go to the hospital with this request.

Dai raggi X risúltano dei	From the X-rays, there
cálcoli alla cistiféllea.	appear to be stones in the
Dovrebbe operarsi. Le fáccio	gall-bladder. You ought to
una richiesta di ricóvero.	have an operation. I shall
	write a note to the hospital.

Andare dal dottore or *dal médico* (To go to the doctor's). *Andare in ospedale* or *all'ospedale* (to go to hospital). *Andare dallo specialista* (to see a consultant), *dal dentista* (a dentist), *dall'oculista* (an eye specialist). *Andare in farmacia* (to go to a chemist's).

Sentirsi (to feel) *bene* (all right, well), *male* (ill), *girare la testa* (dizzy). *Avere mal di testa* or *dolori alla testa* (to have a headache), *mal di stómaco* or *dolori allo stómaco* (stomach-ache), *un dolore* (a pain), *mal di gola* (a sore throat), *mal di denti* (toothache), *mal di mare* (seasickness). *Fare male* (to have a pain): *mi fa male un dente* (I have toothache), *una gamba* (I have a pain in the leg), *la ferita* (my wound smarts).

PRESENT CONDITIONAL TENSE

This tense points to an event which is considered possible in the present or future, conditional upon other factors being realized. Its endings are the following:

-rei, -resti, -rebbe, -remmo, -reste, -rébbero.

As in the case of the future tense, the characteristic vowel *-a-*, as in *parlare* (to speak), changes to *-e-*: *parlerei*, e.g.

First conjugation	Second conjugation	Third conjugation
parlerei (I'd speak)	*venderei* (I'd sell)	*dormirei* (I'd sleep)
parleresti	*venderesti*	*dormiresti*
parlerebbe	*venderebbe*	*dormirebbe*
parleremmo	*venderemmo*	*dormiremmo*
parlereste	*vendereste*	*dormireste*
parlerébbero	*venderébbero*	*dormirébbero*

For example:

Mi comprerei un'Alfa Romeo, ma non ho soldi (I'd buy an Alfa Romeo, but I don't have the money)

Devo andare a lavorare, altrimenti dormirei fino a tardi (I must go to work, otherwise I would sleep until late)

As previously observed, it is also used to express wishes and courteous requests, or cautious statements, e.g.

Cosa desìdera? Vorrei un caffè con panna (What would you like? I'd like a coffee with cream)
Potrei avere un bicchiere? (Could I have a glass?)
Le dispiacerebbe passarmi l'ŏlio e l'aceto? (Would you mind passing me the oil and vinegar?)
Bisognerebbe rifare tutto (It would be necessary to do everything all over again)
Ci vorrĕbbero almeno due giorni (It would take at least two days)
Mi porteresti alla stazione? (Could you drive me to the station?)
Chissà se mi aiuterebbe (I wonder whether he would help me)

The conditional also translates the present tense of the verb 'to wish' followed by the past tense of a verb, expressing yearning for something which is supposed impossible to achieve, e.g.

Vorrei ĕssere giŏvane (I wish I were young)
Come vorrei abitare a Londra! (I wish so much that I could live in London!)

PAST CONDITIONAL TENSE

It consists of the auxiliaries *avrei* (I would have) or *sarei* (I would be) followed by the past participle: *avrei parlato* (I'd have spoken), *avrei venduto* (I'd have sold), *avrei dormito* (I'd have slept).

Contrary to the English use, the past conditional is used when it refers to past events which happened or were supposed to happen after the actual time of the narration or description, i.e. it indicates what is sometimes called a future in the past. This is shown by turning the main clause to a present one, in which case the dependent clause would be expressed in the future tense:

Diceva che si sarebbe operato (He said he would have an operation), resulting from *Dice che si opererà* (He says that he will have an operation)
Ho capito che ti sarebbe piaciuto (I understood that you would like

it), resulting from *Capisco che ti piacerà* (I understand that you will like it). Colloquially, the past conditional is often replaced by the imperfect indicative in this case, e.g. *Diceva che si operava* (He said he would have an operation)

Ho capito che ti piaceva (I understood you would like it)

IRREGULAR FUTURE AND CONDITIONAL

The following groups of verbs have special forms:

(2) *èssere* (to be),

future	conditional
sarò (I shall be)	*sarei* (I'd be)
sarai	*saresti*
sarà	*sarebbe*
saremo	*saremmo*
sarete	*sareste*
saranno	*sarèbbero*

(1), (23), (26), (28) and (29): *avere* (to have), *andare* (to go), *sapere* (to know), *dovere* (to have to), and *potere* (to be able) lose the vowel preceding *-re*, e.g.

avrò (I shall have), etc., *avrei* (I'd have), etc.

(6), (7), (22) and (30): *venire* (to come), *tenere* (to hold, to keep), *contenere* (to contain), *mantenere* (to keep), *rimanere* (to remain), *ritenere* (to retain, to think) change *-n-* to *-rr-*; *valere* (*prevalere*) (to prevail) and *volere* (to want) change *-l-* to *-rr-*; *bere* (to drink) doubles the *-r-*, e.g.

verrò (I shall come), etc., *verrei* (I'd come), etc.

(5): the verb *fare* (to do, to make) does not change *-a-*:

farò (I'll do, I'll make), etc., *farei* (I'd do, I'd make), etc.

■ IN BANCA: read and translate

Vorrei aprire un conto corrente e un conto depòsito. Vorrei anche cambiare delle sterline e dei dòllari. Potrei anche avere la carta di crèdito?

Sul conto corrente diamo normalmente il nove per cento di interesse. Se vuole un conto depòsito vincolato ad un anno l'interesse è dell'ùndici per cento. Prego compili questi mòduli e firmi qui. Le sterline e i dòllari li vuole accreditati in conto o in contanti?

Vorrei mezzo milione di lire in contanti ed il resto in conto, per cortesia.

Bene, signore. Ecco il suo libretto assegni e quello depòsito. La carta di crèdito Le verrà spedita al Suo indirizzo al più presto, al màssimo tra un mese.

Stacco un assegno ora, per avere i contanti?

Sì, per favore. Il costo del libretto di assegni Glielo addebitiamo in conto o lo paga separatamente?

Me lo addèbiti pure.

Si accòmodi alla cassa, prego.

Exercise 1

Replace the verbs between brackets with the appropriate future forms:

(a) *Se mi ferma la polizia, (pagare) la multa.*
(b) *Prima di partire, noi (dovere) controllare i freni.*
(c) *Quando avrò finito, (rimanere) volentieri.*
(d) *(Venire) a trovarvi la pròssima estate.*
(e) *Voi (essere) lìbere sàbato sera?*

Exercise 2

Replace the verbs between brackets with the appropriate present conditional forms:

(a) *Signora, (volere) un caffè?*
(b) *Noi (prendere) tè.*
(c) *Che cosa si (potere) fare?*
(d) *Ah, come (volere) aver finito questo lavoro!*
(e) *(Valere) la pena uscire per fare una passeggiata.*

Exercise 3

Replace the past conditional in the following sentences with the imperfect indicative:

(a) *Diceva che sarebbe venuta, ma non si vede ancora.*
(b) *Non credevamo che ci sareste riusciti.*
(c) *Pensava che ci avrebbe fatto piacere.*
(d) *Chissà se avrei avuto tempo!*
(e) *Non avrebbe avuto per caso una scala* (ladder) *da prestarmi?*

Exercise 4

Tell what a person should know or be able to do before going on a long car journey. Use the following conditionals:

(a) *Occorrerebbe.*
(b) *Sarebbe necessàrio.*
(c) *Sarebbe opportuno.*
(d) *Si dovrebbe.*
(e) *Sarebbe mèglio.*

Exercise 5

Someone does not feel well. Tell him or her what he or she could possibly do.

LESSON 18

■ **L'ABITAZIONE**

HOUSING

Mi sono stancato di stare in pensione. Che ne diresti se affittassi o comperassi un appartamento?
Mi pare una buona idea. Saresti più lìbero e staresti più còmodo se avessi un allòggio tuo. Magari non prenderei una càmera presso una famìglia, perchè saresti

I have grown tired of staying at a guest-house. What would you say if I rented or bought a flat?
It seems a good idea to me. You would be freer and more comfortable if you had your own place. Possibly I wouldn't get a room with a family, as you would be

legato alle loro necessità ed abitŭdini. Piuttosto potresti rivŏlgerti ad una agenzia immobiliare e vedere se hanno un appartamento da affittare, magari nel centro stŏrico, anche ammobigliato.

bound to their needs and habits. Rather you could go to an estate agent and see if they have a flat to rent, possibly in the city centre, even furnished.

Certo sarebbe mĕglio sotto tutti i punti di vista e avrei la possibilità di arredarlo come vŏglio.

It would certainly be better on all accounts and I'd have the opportunity of furnishing it as I like.

La casa (house), *l'appartamento* (flat), *il palazzo* (palace; block of flats), *il piano* (floor; storey), *il palazzo a dieci piani* (ten-storey house), *il seminterrato* (basement), *il pianterreno* (ground floor), *il primo piano* (first floor), *l'ŭltimo piano* (top floor), *l'ascensore* (lift), *il portiere* (doorkeeper), *la casa popolare* or *comunale* (council house).

Affittare una casa, un appartamento (to rent a house, a flat), *comperare* (to buy), *prĕndere in affitto* (to rent), *pagare l'affitto* (to pay the rent), *fare un contratto d'affitto* (to sign a rent agreement) or *firmare un contratto di locazione, avere lo sfratto* or *ĕssere sfrattato* (to be given notice to quit, to be evicted), *chiĕdere un mŭtuo* or *prĕstito* (to ask for a loan).

L'agenzia immobiliare (estate agent's), *l'arredamento* (furnishing), *i mŏbili* (furniture), *pagare l'IVA* (to pay VAT).

IMPERFECT SUBJUNCTIVE

Its endings are: *-ssi, -ssi, -sse, ⁺ssimo, -ste, ⁺ssero*, e.g.

parlassi (that I spoke)	*vendessi* (sold)	*dormissi* (slept)
parlassi	*vendessi*	*dormissi*
parlasse	*vendesse*	*dormisse*
parlăssimo	*vendĕssimo*	*dormĭssimo*
parlaste	*vendeste*	*dormiste*
parlăssero	*vendĕssero*	*dormĭssero*

This tense replaces the imperfect indicative whenever the subjunctive is required. It is also used in the following cases:

(a) to express yearnings, often preceded by *magari* or *ah, se*:

Magari venisse! (I wish he would come!)
Ah, se almeno piovesse! (I wish it would rain)

(b) as the clause of a conditional sentence:

Se fossi in te, non ci penserei due volte (If I were you, I would not give it a second thought)

(c) when 'whether . . . or' is implied:

Fosse la stanchezza, fosse la ràbbia, non ce la facevo pròprio più (Whether it was fatigue or anger, I couldn't go on any longer)

PLUPERFECT SUBJUNCTIVE

This compound tense consists of *avessi* (that I had), *avessi, avesse, avèssimo, aveste, avèssero*, or *fossi* (that I were), *fossi, fosse, fòssimo, foste, fòssero*, followed the past participle, e.g.

Magari l'avessi conosciuta prima! (I wish I had met her earlier)
Avrei casa mia ora se avessi risparmiato di più (I'd have my own house now, if I had saved more)

Colloquially, the pluperfect subjunctive is often replaced by the imperfect indicative, when it is dependent on a conditional clause, e.g.

Se non risparmiavo, non avremmo la casa ora is more colloquial than *Se non avessi risparmiato, non avremmo la casa ora* (If I had not saved money, we would not have a house now)
Se non c'eravate voi, non so come avrei fatto (If it had not been for you, I wonder how I would have managed to make it)

IRREGULAR IMPERFECT SUBJUNCTIVE

The following groups of verbs have special forms of imperfect subjunctive:

(2) *èssere* (to be), imperfect subjunctive

fossi
fossi
fosse
fòssimo
foste
fòssero

(5) and (15) add *-c-*:

fare (to do, to make), imperfect subj., *facessi*, etc.

More verbs:

disfare (to undo)
disfarsi (to melt away; to get rid of)
contraddire (to contradict)
predire (to anticipate, forecast)

soddisfare (to satisfy)
dire (to say, to tell)
benedire (to bless)

(16) change *-rr-* to *-c-*:

tradurre (to translate), imperfect subj. *traducessi*, etc.

More verbs:

condurre (to lead)
indurre (to induce)
ridurre (to reduce)

dedurre (to deduce)
produrre (to produce)
sedurre (to seduce)

(11) change *-rr-* to *-n-*:

porre (to put), imperfect subjunctive *ponessi*, etc.

More verbs:

deporre (to depose)
comporre (to compose)
proporre (to propose)
sovrapporre (to superimpose)

disporre (to have available)
esporre (to expose, to expound)
sottoporre (to submit)
supporre (to suppose)

(12) change *-rr-* to *-e-*:

trarre (to draw), imperfect subjunctive *traessi*, etc.

More verbs:

attrarre (to attract)	*estrarre* (to extract)
detrarre (to deduct)	*sottrarre* (to subtract)

(21) *dare* (to give), imperfect subj. *dessi*, etc.
    stare (to stay, to stand), imperfect subj. *stessi*, etc.

(22) *bere* (to drink), imperfect subj. *bevessi*, etc.

■ IN NEGOZIO: read and translate

In che cosa posso servirLa?
Vorrei una camicia come quella in vetrina. Le dispiace farmi vedere?
Che numero porta?
Porto il quindici e mezzo in Inghilterra.
Allora dev'essere il quaranta.
Questa quanto costa?
Viene venticinquemila lire.
E questa quant'è?
Questa è di seta ed è in svendita. Scontata costa ventinovemila lire.
Se vuole, può provarla.
Le maniche sono un po' troppo lunghe ed è troppo larga in vita.
Non si preoccupi. Gliela faccio stringere e Le faccio accorciare le maniche.
La prendo. Posso pagare con assegno?
Sì, certo. Ha la carta di credito?

Exercise 1

Insert the appropriate imperfect subjunctive forms in the following sentences:

(a) *Che ne direbbe se (tradurre) il Suo libro?*
(b) *Magari ci (dare) la sua macchina per andare in montagna!*
(c) *Almeno (vincere) al totocalcio!*
(d) *Se questo paese (produrre) di più, sarebbe meglio per tutti.*
(e) *Nel caso che non (fare) in tempo, aspettateli.*

Exercise 2

Turn the following sentences into the past:

(a) *Può darsi che non lo sappiate.*
(b) *Speriamo che almeno si decida.*
(c) *Nessuno dùbita che sia la verità.*
(d) *Credi che sia fàcile?*
(e) *Ti sbagli se pensi che ne tragga vantàggio per sè.*

Exercise 3

Turn the following imperfect into pluperfect subjunctives:

(a) *Non che non facesse il suo dovere, ma era un po' pigro.*
(b) *Fosse la tarda ora o bevesse troppo, era insopportàbile.*
(c) *Non passava una volta senza che brontolasse.*
(d) *Qualùnque cosa gli dicessi, lui non si offendeva.*

LESSON 19

■ **UNA TELEFONATA**

A TELEPHONE CALL

Pronto, chi parla?
Parla John. Sei tu, Màrio?
Non sento molto bene. La
lìnea è disturbata. Parla un
po' più forte. Scùsami se
telèfono a quest'ora, ma
volevo avere da te un
consìglio su come farmi
installare il telèfono. Si
diventa matti con questi
gettoni! Pronto . . . mi senti?

Hello, who's speaking?
This is John speaking. Is that
you, Mario? I can't hear very
well. The line is noisy. Speak
a little louder. Sorry to ring
you up at this late time, but I
wanted to have a piece of
advice on how to have a
telephone installed for me.
You become crazy with these
tokens! Hello . . . can you
hear me?

*Accidenti, è caduta la linea
. . . Rifàccio il nùmero . . .*

Oh, dear, the line has been
cut off. . . . Let me re-dial
the number. . . .

*Occupato. . . . Pronto, sono
ancora io!*

Engaged. . . . Hello, it is still
me!

*Ah, bene, quindi, dicevamo.
Devi andare alla SIP,
riempire i mòduli, pagare il
costo dell'installazione e il
canone e aspettare
l'allacciamento.*

Oh, good, well, we were
saying. You must go to the
Telephone Company, fill in
the forms, pay the installation
cost and the standing charge,
and wait for the installation.

Ci vuole molto?

Does it take long?

*In centro non tanto, credo. In
periferia ci mèttono di più.*

Not too long in the town
centre, I believe. It takes
longer in the suburbs.

*Tutto questo aspettare mi fa
venire i nervi.*

All this waiting gets on my
nerves.

Devi prèndertela con la SIP.

You ought to lay the blame
on SIP.

Che c'entro io?

It's not my business.

*Ecco cosa dìcono sempre gli
italiani. Io non c'entro, non
sono affari miei, è colpa del
sistema, degli altri!*

This is what Italians always
say. It's not my business, it's
nothing to do with me, it's
the fault of the system, of
somebody else!

CAUSATIVE SENTENCES

These sentences consist of the verb *fare* followed by an infinitive,
in a wide variety of meanings, such as: 'to let, to allow to', 'to
make', 'to cause to', 'to force to', 'to order', 'to have or get something done', 'to cause something to be done', e.g.

Li fàccia entrare (Let them in)
Hai fatto spedire i bauli? (Did you have the trunks sent off?)
Devi far riparare la màcchina (You must have the car repaired)
Mi fate rìdere (You make me laugh)
Ci hanno fatto stare in piedi (They forced us to stand)
Vi hanno fatto mangiare? (Did they get you something to eat?)
Lo fàccio fare sùbito (I'll have it done straight away)

If the infinitive is followed by a direct object, or a direct object is understood, the third person pronouns to be used are *gli* (to him), *le* (to her) and *a loro* or *loro* (to them). In the case of a noun, this must be preceded by *a*, e.g.

Le fanno lavare i piatti e pulire i pavimenti (They make her wash the dishes and clean the floors)
Glielo insegno io (I'll teach him it)
Faccio registrare le punterie al meccànico (I'll make the mechanic set the tappets)
Ho fatto fare i mòbili ad un bravo falegname (I had my furniture made by a good carpenter)

In most of these sentences it should be possible to replace the infinitive with a sentence consisting of *fare* or *farsi* followed by *che* and the subjunctive, especially if there is an implied idea of achieving something through an effort, e.g.

Fa che siano contenti (Make them feel happy)
Voglio farsi che ritorni (I want to make him come back)

Lasciare (to let, to allow to) follows the same pattern as *fare*, e.g.

Làscialo fare (Let him do it)
Làscialo fare a Giòrgio (Let Giorgio do it)
Lasciate che ascòltino i dischi e bàllino (Let them listen to records and dance)

MODAL VERBS DOVERE, POTERE AND VOLERE

These verbs are either followed by an infinitive or an infinitive is understood, e.g.

Puoi uscire? No, non posso (Can you go out? No, I can't)
Si può fumare? No, mi dispiace non si può (Can I smoke? No, sorry, you may not)
Può piòvere o potrebbe anche fare il sole (It may rain or it might be sunny)
Può darsi che piova, ma potrebbe anche darsi che fosse una bella giornata (Maybe it will rain, but it might possibly be a sunny day)
Può darsi! (Maybe!)

Sapere is used instead of *potere*, when it means 'to be able', 'to be unable', 'to know how', 'not to know how' in general statements not referring to the present moment, e.g.

Non sa fare niente (He is unable to do anything)
Sa giocare al tennis? Sì, ma oggi non posso (Can you play tennis? Yes, but today I can't)
So arrangiarmi (I can make it by myself)

Volete qualcosa da bere o da mangiare? (Would you like something to drink or eat?)
Sì, grazie, vorrei una limonata, se ce l'ha (Yes, thank you, I'd like a lemonade, if you've got one)
Vorrei che fosse vacanza (I wish it was a holiday)
Ti voglio tanto bene (I'm very fond of you)
Vuole accomodarsi, prego? (Would you please yourself?)
Vorrebbe essere così gentile da darmi le Sue generalità? (Would you be so kind as to give me your particulars?)
Volevamo rimborsargli le spese, ma lui non ha voluto (We wanted to reimburse his expenses, but he wouldn't let us do so)
Dobbiamo stare attenti (We must be careful)
Dovreste trattarla meglio (You ought to treat her bettter)
Avresti dovuto dirmelo prima (You should have told me before)
Il dottore non c'è, è dovuto uscire per una visita urgente (The doctor is not in, he had to go out on an urgent call)
Le leggi devono essere osservate scrupolosamente (Laws are to be observed strictly)
La corriera deve arrivare a minuti (The coach is due to arrive in a matter of minutes)
Deve tutto a me (She owes everything to me)
Non mi devi proprio niente (You owe me absolutely nothing)
Sarei dovuto andare a prenderli alla stazione, ma non ho potuto (I was to have gone to fetch them at the station, but I was unable to)

CONTINENTS, COUNTRIES AND REGIONS

These are usually preceded by the definite article, unless they are used in lists, headings or with the prepositions *di* (of), *da* (from), *con* (with), *per* (for):

l'Asia (Asia)
la Danimarca (Denmark)
l'Europa (Europe)
il Canadà (Canada)
la Cina (China)
l'Inghilterra (England)
l'Irlanda (Ireland)
la Bretagna (Brittany)
l'Italia (Italy)
gli Stati Uniti (the US)
gli USA (the USA)
la Svizzera (Switzerland)

l'América (America)
la Fráncia (France)
l'África (Africa)
il Bélgio (Belgium)
la Gran Bretagna (Britain)
il Galles (Wales)
la Norvègia (Norway)
l'Unione Soviètica (the Soviet Union)
l'URSS (the USSR)
la Rússia (Russia)

Nationality nouns and adjectives have the following endings:

(a) *-ese*, plural *-esi* (or *-e*, plural *-i*), e.g.

danese (Danish, Dane)
cinese (Chinese)
francese (French, Frenchman)
olandese (Dutch, Dutchman)
canadese (Canadian)
scozzese (Scottish, Scot)
statunitense (US)
piemontese (from Piedmont)
laziale (from Latium)
torinese (from Turin)
veronese (from Verona)
senese (from Siena)
londinese (Londoner)
dublinese (Dubliner)

inglese (English, Englishman)
irlandese (Irish, Irishman)
giapponese (Japanese)
norvegese (Norwegian)
gallese (Welsh, Welshman)
portoghese (Portuguese)
svedese (Swedish, Swede)
abruzzese (from Abruzzo)
milanese (from Milan)
genovese (from Genoa)
bolognese (from Bologna)
ferrarese (from Ferrara)
viennese (from Vienna)
marsigliese (from Marseilles)

(b) *-o*, *-a*, *-i*, *-e* (or *-anno*, *-ana*, *-ani*, *-ane*), e.g.

austríaco, austríaca, austríaci, austríache (Austrian)
polacco, polacca, polacchi, polacche (Polish, Pole)
turco, turca, turchi, turche (Turkish, Turk)
soviètico, soviètica, soviètici, soviètiche (Soviet)
greco, greca, greci, greche (Greek)
australiano (Australian)

umbro (from Umbria)
napoletano (Neapolitan)
palermitano (from Palermo)

americano (American)
jugoslavo (Yugoslav)
israeliano (Israeli)
spagnolo (Spanish, Spaniard)
siciliano (Sicilian)
mantovano (from Mantua)
padovano (from Padua)
lombardo (Lombard)
friulano (from Friuli)
romagnolo (from Romagna)
marchigiano (from the Marches)

russo (Russian)
corso (Corsican)
sardo (Sardinian)
trentino (from Trento)
svìzzero (Swiss)
bresciano (from Brescia)
triestino (from Trieste)
veneziano (from Venice)
veneto (from Veneto)
emiliano (from Emilia)
toscano (Tuscan)
romano (Roman)
parigino (from Paris)

(c) *-a* in the masculine and feminine singular, *-i* in the masculine plural, and *-e* in the feminine plural, e.g.

cipriota (Cypriot)

■ **CORRISPONDENZA AMOROSA. LÈTTERA AD UNA RAGAZZA: read and translate**

Firenze, 18/9/1982

Carìssima Anna,
   come vorrei ⁺èssere vicino a te ora. Ti vòglio tanto bene. Ti amo tanto da morire. Mi sei piaciuta fin dal primo momento che t'ho vista e mi piaci sempre di più. Non vedo l'ora di rivederti, di abbracciarti, di strìngerti forte forte e di baciarti. Ah, come vorrei dirti tante cose, ma non è fàcile per lèttera.
   Mi ami anche tu, vero? Senti la mia mancanza? Tu mi manchi tanto. Non faccio che pensare a te. Mi sembra di rivedere i tuoi capelli biondi, i tuoi occhi blu, il tuo dolce sorriso.
   Scrìvimi presto, amore mio, e dimmi che mi ami. Un bacione grosso grosso.

Tuo,
Pietro

Exercise 1

Combine the following pairs of sentences, e.g.

Devo fare/ Faccio il visto = Devo far fare il visto.

(a) *La polizia di frontiera fa/ Noi dichiariamo la valuta.*
(b) *Dobbiamo fare/Ci facciamo la carta verde.*
(c) *Noi facciamo/Ci prenotiamo l'albergo all'agenzia.*
(d) *L'agenzia fa/Noi troviamo i migliori alberghi.*
(e) *Tu fai/Io faccio una brutta figura.*

Exercise 2

Turn the following sentences consisting of *fare* or *lasciare* followed by *che* and subjunctive into equivalent ones consisting of *fare* or *lasciare* followed by the infinitive, e.g.

Non fate sì che arrivino in ritardo = Non fateli arrivare in ritardo.

(a) *Non fate sì che si arrabbino.*
(b) *Lasciate che ci pensi io.*
(c) *Non fatevi prendere per il naso* (make fun of you).
(d) *Bisogna che si faccia riempire questi moduli.*
(e) *Non occorreva che lasciaste che mi venissero a prendere.*
(f) *Faccio che imbianchino la stanza.*
(g) *Lascia che ti taglino i capelli corti.*

Exercise 3

The following sentences express something that subjects do or make themselves. Turn them into ones in which the subjects have or get it done by somebody else, or order, cause or persuade somebody to do it, e.g.

Vado a otturarmi un dente (fill a cavity) *= Vado a farmi otturare un dente.*

(a) *Io faccio sempre le riparazioni di casa.*
(b) *Io e mio figlio sostituiamo le grondaie vecchie.*
(c) *L'idraulico è venuto ieri da noi.*
(d) *Aggiungi l'acqua alla batteria?*

(f) *Sara mèglio che cambi le candele* (sparking-plugs).

(g) *Pulisce il carburatore.*

(h) *Règolano le punterie.*

(i) *Contròllano l'accensione, i freni e la frizione.*

Exercise 4

In the following sentences, choose between the use of the verbs *potere* and *sapere*:

(a) *Stasera non (potete* or *sapete) uscire.*

(b) *Non ha mai (potuto* or *saputo) andare all'università.*

(c) *Meglio chiamare l'idràulico; tanto non (potrebbe* or *saprebbe) riparare il guasto da solo.*

(d) *Ma che cosa (puoi* or *sai) fare?*

(e) *Non (potresti* or *sapresti) dirmi come si fa?*

(f) *Speriamo che àbbiano (potuto* or *saputo) entrare senza aver prenotato.*

(g) *(Potrò* or *saprò) guidare la màcchina quando avrò la patente o il fòglio rosa* (learner's provisional driving licence)

Exercise 5

Use appropriate forms of *volere* to translate the following sentences:

(a) What can I do for you, sir?

(b) Would you like to see our clothing department?

(c) Would you mind opening the window?

(d) Follow me, will you?

(e) Shut the door, would you?

(f) She wishes he would love her.

(g) I wish he could be here now.

(h) We wanted to pay for it, but he would not let us.

(i) He would not accept; he bluntly refused.

Exercise 6

Use appropriate forms of *dovere* to translate the following sentences:

(a) Do I owe you anything?

(b) One should be more careful.

(c) Ought you not to help her?

(d) You shall not go.

(e) I was to have met him at eleven.

(f) You have got to go now.

(g) The train is expected now.

(h) The bus is to leave from here.

(i) They were supposed to be waiting for us.

Exercise 7

Name the nationalities of Europe, together with the respective countries.

LESSON 20

■ AL DISTRIBUTORE DI BENZINA

AT THE PETROL STATION

Sono quasi a secco. La spia della benzina è accesa. Devo fermarmi a far benzina al pròssimo distributore.
Mi fa il pieno di super, per favore?
Àcqua, òlio, gomme a posto?

Mi controlli l'acqua della batteria e del raffreddamento e mi aggiunga anche mezzo litro di òlio, per favore. Controlliamo anche la pressione delle gomme.

I'm running out of petrol. The red light is on. I must stop and fill the petrol tank at the next petrol station.
Will you fill it up with 'super' petrol, please.
Are water, oil and tyres all right?
Can you check the battery water and the cooling water and can you also add half a litre of oil? Let's check the tyre pressure, too.

Le gomme anteriori sono un po' consumate da un lato, signore. Se la polizia La ferma sono guai.	The front tyres are worn on one side, sir. If the police stop you, you'll be in trouble.
Bisognerebbe almeno ruotare i pneumàtici e fare la convergenza e l'equilibratura. Forse tanto vale che cambi le gomme davanti.	You should at least rotate the tyres and do the balancing and the convergence. Perhaps I might as well change the front tyres.
Bene, si parte! Tutti in vettura! Tutti a bordo! A tutta velocità!	Good, we can leave now! Everyone in the car! All on board! At full speed!
John, ricòrdati di fermarti al casello dell'autostrada per ritirare lo scontrino del pedàggio che devi pagare all'arrivo. Da noi le autostrade non sono mica gratis. Non dimenticarti che è vietato fare àutostop e trasportare autostoppisti lungo l'autostrada. E speriamo di non avere guasti al motore, gomme che scòppiano, incidenti e scontri.	John, remember to stop at the motorway gate to collect the ticket for the toll you have to pay on arrival. Here motorways are not free. Don't forget that it is forbidden to hitch-hike and to carry hitch-hikers along a motorway. And let's hope that we shan't have a broken engine, burst tyres, accidents and crashes.

Petrol can either be *normale* (low-octane) or *super* (high-octane). You ask for *il pieno* (fill it up), or so many *litri* (litres) or thousands of lire.

VERBS FOLLOWED BY AN INFINITIVE

Some verbs can be followed by a simple infinitive, e.g.

dovere (to have to)	*sentire* (to hear, to feel, to smell)
potere (to be able)	
volere (to want)	*desiderare* (to wish)
osare (to dare)	*bisognare* (to be necessary)
sapere (to know how)	*occòrrere* (to be necessary)
udire (to hear)	*preferire* (to prefer)

ascoltare (to listen)
vedere (to see)
notare (to notice)

lasciare (to let)
bastare (to be sufficient)
osservare (to observe)
fare (to make, to have)

Devi fare qualcosa? (Must you do something?)
Non osavo parlare (I did not dare speak)
Non sa decidersi (He cannot make up his mind)
Hai sentito suonare il campanello? (Did you hear someone ringing the bell?)
Non occorre pagare sùbito (We need not pay at once)

Some verbs are followed by *a* and the infinitive, e.g.

andare (to go)
aiutare (to help)
cominciare (to begin)
còrrere (to run, to rush)
continuare (to continue)
costrìngere (to compel)
imparare (to learn)
invitare (to invite)

insegnare (to teach)
mandare (to send)
mèttersi (to start)
ritornare or *tornare* (to go back)
riuscire (to succeed)
salire (to go up)
servire (to be used for)
venire (to come)

Non riusciamo a capire (We cannot understand)
A che serve? Serve a tagliare la carta (What's the use of it? It's used to cut paper)
Manda a chiamare qualcuno (Send for somebody)
L'ho invitata a ballare (I asked her to dance)

Other verbs are followed by *di* and the infinitive, e.g.

pensare (to think)
crèdere (to believe)
chièdere or *domandare* (to ask)
pregare (to beg, to request)
finire or *terminare* (to end, to stop)
dimenticare or *dimenticarsi* (to forget)

evitare (to avoid)
impedire (to prevent)
ricordare or *ricordarsi* (to remember)
permèttersi (to take the liberty)
ordinare (to order)
permèttere (to allow)
vantarsi (to boast)

Pensi di prènderti le vacanze ora? (Are you thinking of taking your holiday now?)
Non mi ricordo di averLa mai vista prima (I can't remember having seen you earlier)

Verbs may be followed by *per*, or, more emphatically, by *allo scopo di, al fine di, onde* (in order to, with a view to), e.g.

Per aprire prèmere e tirare (Press and pull to open)
Sono venuto per vederLa (I've come with the purpose of seeing you)
Si prega di non fumare, onde evitare reclami (You are requested not to smoke, in order to avoid complaints)

Infinitives can also be preceded by such prepositions as *prima di* (before), *dopo (di)* (after – plus past infinitive), *col, collo, coll'* (by), *nell', nel, nello* (in, on), *invece di* (instead of), *senza* (without), e.g.

Prima di entrare, pulìtevi le scarpe sullo zerbino (Before coming in, clean your shoes on the mat)
Dopo aver speso tutto sarai contento (After spending everything you'll be satisfied)
Coll'andar del tempo il dolore non si sente più (As time passes, the pain is not felt any more)
Nel mèttere in moto, mi sono accorto che la frizione slittava (In starting the car, I noticed that the clutch was slipping)
Invece di lamentarvi, fate qualcosa (Instead of complaining, do something)
Come fa a vìvere senza lavorare? (How does he manage to live without working?)

PREPOSITIONS

Di is used:

(a) to indicate specification; time; measurement; possession; origin; matter, e.g.

Le pàgine del libro (The pages of the book)
Gli abitanti di Milano (The people of Milan)
Una vacanza di due settimane (A two-week holiday)
Alla distanza di tre chilòmetri (At three kilometres' distance)

La casa dei miei genitori (My parents' house)
È una poltrona di pelle vera (It is a real leather armchair)
Ha il cuore di ghiàccio (She has a heart of ice)

(b) after such verbs and phrases as:

èssere (to be from), *èssere originàrio* (to come from)
morire (to die from), *parlare* (to speak)
raccontare (to tell), *soffrire* (to suffer)
èssere contento (to be pleased with), *ringraziare* (to thank for)
èssere soddisfatto (to be satisfied with), *fidarsi* (to trust with)
èssere malcontento (to be unhappy with), *dire* (to tell of)
èssere insoddisfatto (to be unsatisfied with)
accontentarsi (to be contented with), *godere* (to enjoy)

(c) after certain nouns, such as:

amore di (love of)
bisogno di (need for)
felicità di (happiness for)
orìgine di (origin of)

desidèrio di (wish for)
necessità di (necessity for)
soddisfazione di (satisfaction with)
gràzie di (thanks for)

(d) after such adjectives as:

felice (happy for)
contento (happy with)

pieno (full of)

Da is used to indicate origin; destination or use; 'at somebody's house'; 'to somebody's house'; a quality, e.g.

Da giugno a settembre è vacanza (It is a holiday from June until September)
L'aèreo parte da Londra (The plane leaves London)
Attrezzi da lavoro (Tools for work)
Bottìglia da liquore (Liqueur bottle)
Tazza da tè (Teacup)
Una persona da non sottovalutare (A person not to be underestimated)
Un film da non dimenticare (An unforgettable film)
Vengo da te? No, devo andare dal dottore (Shall I come to your house? No, I must go to the doctor's)

Per indicates aim; cause; going through or across; time, e.g.

Tutto per te (All for you)
Non l'ho fatto per pigrizia (I didn't do it because of laziness)
Quando passi per Roma, vieni a trovarmi (When you happen to be in Rome, come and see me)
Ho vissuto a Londra per cinque anni (I lived in London five years)

A indicates staying or going somewhere, e.g.

Resto a casa (I'll stay at home)
Vieni a casa mia (Come to my house)
Vado a Firenze tutti gli anni (I go to Florence every year)
Ho abitato a Milano (I lived in Milan)

In indicates staying or going somewhere; precise time (months, seasons and years); number of persons, e.g.

Mi piace andare in città (I like going into town)
Nel millenovecentoquarantacinque finì la guerra (The war ended in 1945)
Siamo in tre (There are three of us)
In quanti siete? (How many are there of you?)

Fra or *tra* means 'in' or 'within' followed by time; 'between' or 'among', e.g.

Fra due ore è tutto finito (Everything's over in two hours)
Fra noi tutto è finito (It's all over between us)

Fuori or *fuori di* or *fuori da* (out of), e.g.
Fuori di prigione (Out of prison)

Dentro or *dentro a* (in, inside), e.g.

Dentro all'ospedale (Inside the hospital) but *Dentro di me* (Inside me)

Davanti a (before), *di fronte a* (opposite), e.g.

Davanti alla legge (Before the law)
Di fronte a casa mia c'è la questura (Opposite my house there is the police station)

Prima di (before), e.g.

Prima della partenza (Before the departure)

Dietro a (behind), e.g.

Dietro la scena (Behind the scenes)

Con (with), *insieme con* (together with), e.g.

Allegro, con brio (Lively, with brio)

Contro (against), e.g.

Chi non è con me è contro di me (Who is not with me is against me)

Addosso a (on the back of), e.g.

Mi viene addosso (It's running against me)

Attorno a (around), e.g.

Tutt'attorno alla città ci sono parchi (There are parks all around the city)

Entro (within) followed by time, e.g.

Entro stasera avrò deciso (I'll have taken a decision by tonight)

Via da (away from), *lontano da* (far from), e.g.

Siamo lontani da tutto (We are far away from everything)

Fino a (as far as; until, till), e.g.

Aspetta fino a domani (Wait until tomorrow)
Camminiamo fino alla spiaggia (Let's walk as far as the beach)

Attraverso or *attraverso a* (through, across), e.g.

Attraverso i secoli l'Italia ha avuto molte invasioni (Italy experienced many invasions in the course of centuries)

Su (on), *sopra, al di sopra di* (over, above), e.g.

Gli aerei volano bassi sopra questo quartiere (Planes fly low over this district)

Sotto a, al di sotto di (under, underneath, beneath, below), e.g.

Una galleria sotto la Manica (A tunnel under the Channel)

Per mezzo di or *con* (by means of), e.g.

Si pulisce l'argento con un preparato speciale (You polish silver with a special preparation)

Con il denaro si fa molto (You can do much if you have money)

I rapinatori sono entrati nella banca per mezzo di un trucco (The robbers entered the bank by means of a trick)

A braccetto con or *a braccetto di* (arm in arm with), e.g.

A braccetto di una bella ragazza per il corso (Arm in arm with a beautiful girl along the high street)

Appeso a (hanging on), *attaccato a* (hanging from), e.g.

Un quadro appeso alla parete (A picture hanging on the wall)
Un lampadàrio appeso al soffitto (A chandelier hanging from the ceiling)

Oltre a (besides; beyond), *in aggiunta a* (in addition to), e.g.

Oltre al fiume e tra gli àlberi (Beyond the river and among the trees)

Di fianco a, di lato a (by the side of, beside). *accanto a* (next to), e.g.

Di fianco a noi àbita uno scrittore (A writer lives next to us)

Vicino a (near, close to), *nelle vicinanze di* (in the vicinity of), e.g.

Fièsole è vicinìssima a Firenze (Fiesole is very near Florence)

DIMINUTIVES AND AUGMENTATIVES

Such features as being big (*grande, grosso*), small or little (*pìccolo*), pretty, pleasant, nice (*grazioso, carino, simpàtico*), dear, affectionate (*caro*), bad, ugly, nasty (*cattivo, brutto*), may be expressed by adding special endings to the nouns. It is not always predictable which ending is most appropriate. Therefore, the student of Italian should only use those nouns as modified which he or she knows about, e.g.

(a) ending *-one* (big):

un omone (a big, stocky man)
una donnona or *un donnone* (a big woman)

un casone or *una casona* (a big, rather unpleasant house)
una macchinona or *un macchinone* (a big car)
un testone (a big head: a blockhead; a stubborn man)
una testona (a big head; a female blockhead; a stubborn woman)
Notice that feminine nouns tend to be used in the masculine when the new ending is added, unless misunderstanding is likely.

(b) ending *-ino*, *-etto*, *-cino*, *-ŭccio* (small, little, pretty):

un casino (a shooting lodge; a brothel; a great mess or muddle)
una casina (a little house)
un gattino (a kitten)
un omino (a little man)
un formaggino (a little segment of creamy cheese)
un libriccino (a little book)
una cittadina (a small town)
un cuoricino (a little heart)
un canino or *cagnolino* or *cagnetto* (a little dog)
una vecchina (a nice, little, old woman)
poverino (poor fellow)
stupidino (a rather silly person)
una porticina (a tiny door)
un uccellino (a little bird)
che caldŭccio! (how nice and warm!)
una cosŭccia (a trivial matter, trifle)

(c) ending *-ello*, *-ella* (little):

un bambinello (a tiny baby)
una signorinella (a young girl posing as a young lady)
stupidello, stupidella (silly boy, silly girl)

(d) ending *-ăccio*, *-ăccione* (bad, ugly, unpleasant, nasty):

un omaccione (a big, not very good-looking man)
una donnăccia (a bad woman)
sporcaccione, sporcacciona (filthy pig!)
un poverăccio (a poor, unlucky man)
cartăccia (waste paper)
un librăccio (a bad book)
che robăccia! (what rubbish, trash!)

un cagnàccio (a bad, ugly dog)
un gattàccio (bad, unpleasant cat)
una vitàccia (an unpleasant life)
che tempaccio! (what nasty weather!)

(e) ending *-astro*, *-astra* (bad, or step-):

un giovinastro (a rather bad young man)
un fratellastro (a step-brother)
una sorellastra (a step-sister)
bluastro (bluish)
verdastro (greenish)
rossastro (reddish)
nerastro (blackish)

EMERGENCY KIT

Divieto di sosta (No parking)
Permanente Continua (24-hour no parking)
Senso ùnico (One-way street)
Divieto di svolta (No right/left turn)
La pòlizza di assicurazione (the insurance policy)
Basta! (Stop it)
Ancora! (Go on; some more; again)
Viva! (Long live!)
Mi lasci stare! (Leave me alone!)
Mi hanno rubato (They have stolen my) *la borsetta* (handbag)

Attenzione! (Attention!, Caution!, Careful!)
Aiuto! (Help!)
Capisce? (Do you understand?) *l'inglese?* (English)
Non capisco (I don't understand)
Sono inglese (I'm English)
Non parlo l'italiano (I do not speak Italian)
Ho perduto (I have lost) *la borsa* (handbag), *il portafoglio* (wallet), *la valigia* (suitcase)

■ COME SI VIVE NEL CUORE DEL MEZZOGIORNO: read and translate

Chi non fugge si rinchiude nel paese dei fantasmi.
  Nel profondo Sud, tra le montagne della Basilicata, c'è un paese

che riproduce, nel suo microcosmo, tutti i mali del Mezzogiorno, tutte le promesse non mantenute. È Sasso di Castalda, con i suoi milletrecento abitanti, con il dominio assoluto della civiltà dei muli, che soltanto da qualche anno conosce le strade asfaltate, la televisione, la macchina delle fotocopie. Tutto il resto deve ancora arrivare: non ci sono le sezioni dei partiti, nè quelle dei sindacati, manca il cinema come la gioia di vivere. Ci sono invece, come un retaggio secolare che pesa sulle spalle dei vecchi e dei giovani, gli antichi tabù, la fatica di strappare pochi frutti ad una terra ingrata, la rabbia della segregazione. La natura, quasi per uno spietato paradosso, ha però elargito quei beni incommensurabili, invidiati dai cittadini delle metropoli, il silenzio dei boschi, la mancanza di semafori, di code di macchine, di inquinamento, l'acqua delle sorgenti.

Questo non basta: Sasso, che poggia su un pianoro dominato da un grande macigno grigio, un tempo parte di un esteso latifondo dei conti Gaetani d'Aragona, ora è l'immagine della morte lenta. Negli ultimi mesi si sono registrati tre suicidi: quello di un quattordicenne che dall'alba al tramonto pascolava le capre in un terrificante isolamento tra le montagne, quello di due donne, vittime della più profonda solitudine familiare. Nel paese sono rimasti i vecchi, i bambini e quei pochi giovani che non sono ancora emigrati (. . .)
A. Baglivo, 'Il Corriere della Sera', venerdì 7 dicembre 1979

Exercise 1

Fill the gaps with the appropriate prepositions, if required:

(a) *Che cosa pensate . . . fare?*
(b) *Devo ricordarmi . . . passare dalla posta.*
(c) *Prima . . . uscire, prendi l'ombrello.*
(d) *Sperano . . . farcela.*
(e) *Mi avete visto . . . intervistare alla televisione?*
(f) *A che serve . . . lavorare tanto?*
(g) *Non riesci . . . organizzarti?*
(h) *Invece . . . lamentarvi, aiutate.*
(i) *Qui si muore . . . noia*
(j) *Di qui si gode . . . un magnifico panorama.*
(k) *Non crede . . . nessuno.*

(l) *Abitiamo vicino . . . voi.*
(m) *Crede . . . convìncermi.*

Exercise 2

Replace the English expressions between brackets with the appropriate Italian prepositions:

(a) *È una commèdia* (to) *non dimenticare.*
(b) *Camminava* (arm in arm with) *una bella ragazza.*
(c) *Il dittatore fu* (hanging from) *un àlbero.*
(d) *Dobbiamo finire* (by) *dicembre.*
(e) *Non andremo mai via* (from) *questa città.*
(f) *Vivi troppo* (far away from) *città.*
(g) *La mia casa è* (by the side of) *municìpio.*
(h) (In addition to) *còmpere, devi ricordarti di andare dal mèdico.*
(i) *L'ho vista* (amidst) *folla.*
(j) *Le fognature* (underneath) *marciapiede* (in front of) *casa mia sono scoppiate.*
(k) *Aspetteremo* (until) *domani.*
(l) (Contrary to) *aspettative, non è una persona di cui fidarsi.*
(m) *Tu sei un bravo ragazzo,* (unlike) *tuo fratello.*
(n) *Il pallone volava* (above) *le case più alte.*

Exercise 3

Turn the following modified nouns into diminutives or augmentatives, as appropriate:

(a) *Che bella casa piccina!*
(b) *Mi piàcciono i gatti e i cani piccini!*
(c) *Lei ha una bocca pìccola pìccola.*
(d) *Si entra per una porta piccolìssima.*
(e) *I marciapiedi sono sparsi di carta vècchia.*
(f) *Come si sta bene qui con questo bel caldo!*
(g) *Non fare lo stùpido.*
(h) *Che pòvero uomo disgraziato!*
(i) *Che razza di orrìbile libro è questo?*
(j) *Brutto gatto spelacchiato!*

(k) *È una ragazza giòvane, ma vuol fare la signorina.*
(l) *È una cosa da niente!*
(m) *Che uomo grande, grosso e flàccido!*
(n) *Sei uno sporco, lurido indivìduo!*

Exercise 4

Explain what you are supposed to do when you start travelling by car in Italy.

KEY TO EXERCISES

LESSON ONE

Exercise 1

(a) Ciao, Marisa. (b) Piacere, professore. (c) Molto lieto, signorina.

Exercise 2

(a) Ingegner (b) Signora (c) la signorina (d) dottore (e) il Signor

Exercise 3

(a) No, grazie. (b) Grazie. (c) Buon giorno, dottore. (d) Tenga pure il resto. (e) Un cappuccino e una brioche, per favore.

Exercise 4

(a) Questa è la Signorina Marisa Bianchi. (b) Come sta, Dottor Conti? (c) Prego, desidera? (d) Ecco il resto. (e) Ciao, Carla, come stai?

Exercise 5

(a) per (b) da (c) pure (d) quant' (e) La

Exercise 6

(a) giorno, Dottor Conti, come (b) un caffè e una brioche, (c) Signor Rossi, come (d) grazie. Arrivederci (e) è la sua sorellina,

LESSON TWO

Exercise 1

(a) Ci sono dei tavoli liberi? (b) Questi formaggi sono buoni ma troppo cari. (c) Sono un po' ubriachi. (d) Abbiamo vini bianchi casalinghi. (e) Ecco gli zii.

Exercise 2

(a) nel (b) alla (c) del (d) della (e) sul

Exercise 3

(a) sant' (b) grande (c) Sant' (d) buon; bell' (e) bell'; buon

Exercise 4

(a) Ha fretta? (b) È ubriaca? (c) Quanti sono Loro? (d) Loro sono psicanalisti? (e) Come sta, signore?

LESSON THREE

Exercise 2

(a) Lei è proprio scozzese. (b) Ormai puoi darmi del tu. (c) Parliamo spesso in italiano. (d) Conosciamo bene John. (e) Parlano sempre di Lei.

Exercise 3

(a) la (b) la (c) in (d) in (e) —

Exercise 4

(a) Ci viviamo. (b) Ne hanno due. (c) Gliene trova una. (d) Glielo diciamo. (e) Le hanno a ghigliottina.

Exercise 5

(a) Che te ne sembra? (b) Te la riscaldo. (c) Me la dici? (d) Si parla molto di voi. (e) Gielo passo.

Exercise 6

a) Non andiamo più in Italia da . . . mesi/È da . . . mesi che non andiamo più in Italia. (b) Non abbiamo più rivisto Roma dal 19. . ./È dal 19. . che non abbiamo più rivisto Roma. (c) È ammalata da . . . giorni/ È da . . . giorni che è ammalata. (d) Restiamo in Italia per. . . settimane. (e) È da . . . anni che faccio il professore/ Faccio il professore da . . . anni.

Exercise 7

(a) Sono anni ormai che abito a Firenze. (b) È molto tempo che c'è il terrorismo. (c) È da giovedì scorso che studiamo a Perugia. (d) È una settimana che l'ascensore non funziona. (e) È da luglio che sono in vacanza.

LESSON FOUR

Exercise 1

(a) Mi place andare al ristorante purchè la cucina sia casalinga. (b) Che non abbiano più pesce? (c) È necessario che stiate zitti. (d) Benchè sia una casa vecchia, è comoda. (e) Qualsiasi cosa succeda, non rispondere al telefono/Non voglio che tu risponda al telefono, qualsiasi cosa succeda.

Exercise 2

(a) tu faccia (b) abbia/abbiamo/abbiate/abbiano (c) spaventino (d) rapinino (e) finisca

Exercise 3

(a) dia (b) accomodino (c) prenda (d) faccia (e) stiano

Exercise 5

Oggi non dobbiamo fare un mucchio di cose perchè il tempo non è bello. Non abbiamo denaro e non possiamo permetterci di comperare tutto quello che vogliamo. Non possiamo andare nei migliori negozi, che oggi non sono aperti.

LESSON FIVE

Exercise 2

(a) Vendimelo! (b) Diteglielo! (c) Chiediamoglieli subito! (d) Daccene un po'! (e) Fatemici sedere su questa poltrona!

Exercise 3

(a) No, non aprite/aprano le finestre! (b) No, non prendere un po' di dolce. (c) No, non si può fumare qui. (d) No, non rimanere/rimanga ancora un po'. (e) No, non dire/dica tutto.

Exercise 4

(a) Mi dica che cosa vuole. (b) Traduca questo, per favore. (c) Non muoia! (d) Non se ne vada! (e) Esca da qui immediatamente.

LESSON SIX

Exercise 1

(a) Non voglio acqua minerale. (b) Non abbiamo testi/alcun testo di chimica. (c) No, non ne abbiamo molti. (d) Non cerchiamo alcuna/nessuna persona che voglia collaborare. (e) Non ci sono cioccolatini e caramelle.

Exercise 2

(a) Penso a tutto io. (b) Non sono loro i colpevoli. (c) Aiutatevi

gli uni gli altri. (d) Telefonami quando arrivi, eh? (e) Lo amo
molto davvero.

Exercise 4

(a) Scherzi, non è vero? (b) Chi, io? (c) Penso che tu stia
scherzando. (d) Non lo pensi, vero? (e) Non è troppo stanca, vero?

Exercise 5

(a) Fatevelo dire sempre due volte. (b) Vattene. (c) Aspettatela
da uno come lui. (d) Fregatene di tutto. (e) Svigniamocela subito.

LESSON SEVEN

Exercise 1

(a) Oggi non ho fatto niente di speciale. (b) Poco fa ho venduto
la casa. (c) Ha mangiato proprio ora. (d) Quest'inverno ho sciato
molto. (e) Che cosa è accaduto?

Exercise 2

(a) Speriamo che non se ne sia dimenticato. (b) Credi che sia
partito? (c) Non lo so se ci sia voluto andare. (d) È importante
che siate venuti/venute anche voi. (e) È una città pericolosa
nonostante ti sia potuta sembrare tranquilla.

Exercise 3

(a) lavata (b) lavate (c) morti (d) scomparsa (e) aiutati (f) venduta
(g) visti/ viste (h) fuggita

LESSON NINE

Exercise 1

(a) No, a mia moglie non piace l'opera lirica. (b) No, nemmeno
a me piace. (c) No, ai miei figli non piace. (d) No, credo che a
Lei non piaccia. (e) No, neanche i concerti ci piacciono.

Exercise 2

Agli stranieri di solito piace molto la Toscana. A loro piacciono
il Chianti, le dolci colline e le storiche città. Forse a loro piace
(di) più delle altre regioni italiane perchè a loro piacciono l'arte
e il Rinascimento. Naturalmente a loro piacciono anche molto
Venezia, Roma e le altre città e regioni storiche d'Italia. Al mio
amico piace di più la Sicilia, per la sua mistura di greco, romano,
arabo, normanno e spagnolo, oltre che per le sue bellezze naturali.
A me piacciono anche l'Umbria, il Veneto e tanti altri posti. E
a te quali regioni o città piacciono di più? Non è sempre facile
dire quale piace di più perchè veramente la scelta è troppo grande.

Exercise 4

(a) Le dispiace riempire questi moduli? (b) Le dispiace uscire?
(c) Ci dispiace comunicarLe che la sua domanda non è accettata.
(d) È con vivo dispiacere che ho appreso la notizia. (e) Mi dispiace
disturbarvi. (f) Le dispiace darmi una birra? (g) Le dispiace
passarmi il pepe?

LESSON TEN

Exercise 1

In Italia si telefona dalle cabine pubbliche, dai telefoni pubblici
nei bar e ristoranti e dagli uffici della SIP. Negli apparecchi a
gettoni, questi si inseriscono nelle apposite feritoie. I gettoni si
vendono negli* uffici della SIP e in* certi bar e tabaccherie o si
distribuiscono con* macchinette. Per fare telefonate interurbane
si deve prima fare il prefisso di teleselezione. L'elenco dei prefissi
si trova all'inizio dell'elenco telefonico. Nel caso di telefonate
internazionali, o si fa il prefisso oppure, se non si riesce ad avere
il collegamento, si chiede la linea al centralino.

Exercise 2

Stamattina, quando mi sono alzato/alzata, c'era un po' di nebbia.

* Note how the preposition has to change.

Ma, poi se c'è nebbia nelle prime ore del mattino, di solito si rasserena più tardi durante il giorno. Infatti, è diventato bello (è uscito il sole), come la nebbia è sparita. È stata una giornata molto tranquilla; non c'è stato affatto vento, nè ci sono state nuvole. È stato anche mite. Ha fatto buio molto tardi e la giornata ci è piaciuta molto.

Exercise 3

(a) È evidente che tu non stia/stai bene. (b) È ora che andiamo a teatro. (c) È evidente che non si ricordi/ricorda più di me. (d) Va da sè che debba/devo comprarle un regalo. (e) Spetta a me dover andare in ufficio sabato. (f) Va bene che prenda la tua macchina. (g) Tocca a te pagare. (h) È ora che finalmente mi abbiano riparato l'auto.

Exercise 4

(a) A qualcuno piace caldo. (b) Lassù alcuni mi amano. (c) Tutti hanno il loro posto. (d) Tutte le settimane ho ricevuto inviti. (e) Altri hanno fatto come me.

Exercise 5

(a) In Italia il sale viene venduto nelle tabaccherie. (b) Molti progressi sono stati fatti, ma non ancora abbastanza. (c) Il traffico in centro è stato migliorato. (d) Le pareti sono state dipinte di rosa (da noi). (e) Delle cose stupende sono state prodotte dagli studenti.

LESSON ELEVEN

Exercise 1

(a) L'Italia è ricca di tesori d'arte, la quale/che è stata creata nel corso di molti secoli. (b) Una conseguenza di ciò, di cui mi dispiace, è che è stata spesso invasa. (c) Alcune importanti città, di cui mi ricordo i nomi, sono Firenze, Venezia, Roma, Torino, Milano, Napoli e Palermo. (d) La ragazza con la quale/cui ti ho visto uscire è bellissima. (e) Quel tipo, la cui macchina ti piace, è un mio amico.

Exercise 2

(a) Sai, il signore a cui ho fatto lezione d'italiano è andato in Italia. (b) Il mio fidanzato, di cui non so più niente da mesi, si è trovato qualcun'altra. (c) La Signora Tedeschi, della cui eleganza non fate altro che parlare, è una miliardaria. (d) Alcuni, fra cui tuo cugino, sono stati arrestati dopo la dimostrazione. (e) La galleria del Monte Bianco, attraverso cui si arriva in Italia dalla Francia, è la più lunga galleria autostradale del mondo.

Exercise 3

(a) Sta arrivando qualcuno. (b) Stai pranzando? (c) Che cosa stai facendo? (d) Silenzio! Sta dormendo. (e) Aspettate un po', ci stiamo preparando.

Exercise 4

(a) Nel cadere/quando sono caduto, mi sono rotto un braccio (b) Se ti comperi la casa, risolvi i tuoi problemi (c) Dopo che l'ho conosciuto, mi piace di più. (d) Stai attento nell'attraversare /mentre attraversi la strada. (e) Se si abita a Firenze, si è quasi al centro d'Italia.

Exercise 5

(a) Sono stanco/stanca d'aspettare. (b) Non vediamo l'ora d'arrivare al mare (c) Dopo essere uscito/uscita, non ho fatto niente. (d) Le piace camminare e guardare le vetrine. (e) Parcheggiare non è facile in questa città.

LESSON TWELVE

Exercise 1

Viveva; è trasferito; era /è stata; pagavano; risparmiavano; lavoravano; hanno potuto; piaceva; è piaciuta; era; era; era; veniva; viaggiava; aveva.

Exercise 2

La luna illuminava tutto a giorno. I due uomini mangiavano seduti l'uno di fronte all'altro e, dopo, Guglielmo ha offerto una sigaretta all'altro. Ma questi ha preferito accendere la pipa. Fino a questo momento avevano scambiato solo poche parole. Ma ora Guglielmo gli ha chiesto quanti anni erano che faceva quel mestiere. 'Quaranta', ha risposto l'uomo. 'Ho cominciato ad andare con mio padre quando avevo quindici anni.' Quel mestiere se lo trasmettevano di padre in figlio.

Exercise 3

(a) L'estate stava finendo lentamente. (2) La sigaretta si andava spegnendo. (c) Il traffico stava diventando sempre più forte. (d) Col passare delle ore del giorno, il caldo andava aumentando in modo insopportabile. (e) Dopo quella dura giornata, stavo sentendo la stanchezza cadermi addosso.

LESSON THIRTEEN

Exercise 1

(a) I danni alla mia macchina sono stati meno gravi di quelli all'altra macchina. (b) L'Italia è più montagnosa della Francia. (c) La Francia ha una superficie più grande di quanto mi aspettasi. (d) Le opere sono belle (tanto) quanto i concerti. (e) L'orchestra era migliore dei cantanti.

Exercise 2

Dur terzi; dodici ventesimi; quattro quinti; un mezzo/una metà; quarantasei centesimi.

Exercise 3

(a) C'erano/c'era un centinaio di persone. (b) Abbiamo visto alcune migliaia/qualche migliaio di uccelli. (c) Ha una quarantina d'anni. (d) Ci vogliono/ci vuole una dozzina d'uova. (e) Occorrono/occorre un'ottantina di migliaia di lire.

Exercise 4

(a) Quanto è alto? (b) Quanti anni ha? (c) A che distanza è / È lontano/lontana? (d) Quanti gradi ci sono? (e) Che numero (vuole/porta)? (f) Che ora è? (g) Quando siete nati? (h) Quanto ho di febbre?

LESSON FOURTEEN

Exercise 2

La resistenza armata contro il fascismo nacque l'8 settembre 1943, nel momento più angoscioso e confuso della nostra storia. Nacque in Piemonte, a Cuneo, tra un gruppo di uomini decisi a riscattare la vergogna e il terrore del mondo. Per questo essi salirono, soli, sulla montagna. Alle 19.30 di quel giorno la radio diffuse l'annuncio dell'armistizio. Il generale Badoglio lesse il comunicato. Erano quarantacinque giorni che Mussolini era caduto con il colpo del 25 luglio. Dai vari fronti giungevano notizie disastrose. Le città venivano bombardate e diventavano cumuli di macerie. C'era fame, dolore, miseria. Le divisioni tedesche, comandate da Rommel e Kesselring, erano pronte a liquidare l'alleato italiano.

Exercise 3

(a) arrivò (b) capimmo (c) finirono (d) guardasti/guardò/ guardaste/guardarono, arrossimmo (e) investisti/investì/ investiste/investirono

Exercise 4

(a) Una volta che fu finito l'anno scolastico, andai a lavorare. (b) Finchè non ebbero controllato tutti i passaporti, non ci lasciarono passare. (c) Appena avemmo passato la frontiera, ci sentimmo felici. (d) Non ci sentimmo tranquilli, finchè non furono partiti tutti i soldati. (e) Andammo in montagna a sciare dopo che ebbero aperto gli impianti di risalita.

LESSON FIFTEEN

Exercise 2

(a) Lo inventò Alessandro Graham Bell. (b) Le successe Edoardo VII (settimo). (c) Vinse la guerra contro la Germania e l'Italia. (d) Nacque a Stratford-upon-Avon. (e) Lo bevve Socrate. (f) Compose nove sinfonie e altra musica.

LESSON SIXTEEN

Exercise 2

(a) Forse saranno le tre ormai. (b) Magari non avrai ancora vent'anni. (c) Sarà sposata? (d) Verrà? (e) Starà migliorando la situazione?

Exercise 3

Le previsioni non sono molto buone. L'inflazione e la disoccupazione non diminuiranno. Al contrario la produzione continuerà a decrescere. In questa situazione gli investimenti non potranno essere soddisfacenti, anche perchè i tassi di interesse rimarranno alti. Forse verso la fine dell'anno si cominceranno a vedere i risultati delle attuali misure prese dal governo.

LESSON SEVENTEEN

Exercise 1

(a) pagherò (b) dovremo (c) rimarrò (d) verrò/verrà/verremo/verranno (e) sarete.

Exercise 2

(a) vorrebbe (b) prenderemmo (c) potrebbe (d) vorrei (e) Varrebbe

Exercise 3

(a) Diceva che veniva, ma non si vede ancora. (b) Non credevamo che ci riuscivate. (c) Pensava che ci faceva piacere. (d) Chissà se avevo tempo! (e) Non aveva per caso una scala da prestarmi?

LESSON EIGHTEEN

Exercise 1

(a) traducessi/traducesse/traducessimo/traducessero (b) desse (c) vincessi (d) producesse (e) facessero.

Exercise 2

(a) Poteva darsi che non lo sapeste. (b) Speravamo che almeno si decidesse. (c) Nessuno dubitava che fosse la verità. (d) Credevi che fosse facile? (e) Ti sbagliavi se pensavi che ne traesse vantaggio per sè.

Exercise 3

(a) Non che non avesse fatto il suo dovere, ma era un po' pigro. (b) Fosse stata la tarda ora o avesse bevuto troppo, era insopportabile. (c) Non passava una volta senza che avesse brontolato. (d) Qualunque cosa gli avessi detto, lui non si offendeva.

LESSON NINETEEN

Exercise 1

(a) La polizia di frontiera ci fa dichiarare la valuta. (b) Dobbiamo farci fare la carta verde. (c) Noi ci facciamo prenotare l'albergo dall'* agenzia. (d) L'agenzia ci fa trovare i migliori alberghi. (e) Tu mi fai fare una brutta figura.

Exercise 2

(a) Non fateli arrabbiare. (b) Lasciatemici. (c) Non fate sì che vi prendano per il naso. (d) Bisogna fargli far riempire questi moduli. (e) Non occorreva lasciarli venire a prendermi. (f) Faccio imbiancare la stanza. (g) Lasciati tagliare i capelli corti (da loro).

Exercise 3

(a) Io faccio fare sempre le riparazioni di casa. (b) Io e mio figlio facciamo sostituire le grondaie vecchie. (c) Abbiamo fatto venire l'idraulico ieri da noi. (d) Fai aggiungere l'acqua alla batteria? (f) Sarà meglio che faccia cambiare le candele. (g) Fa pulire il carburatore. (h) Fanno regolare le punterie. (i) Fanno controllare l'accensione, i freni e la frizione.

* Note how the preposition has to change.

Exercise 4

(a) potete (b) potuto (c) saprebbe (d) sai (e) potresti (f) potuto
(g) potrò.

Exercise 5

(a) Che cosa vuole che faccia per Lei, signore? (b) Vorrebbe
vedere il nostro reparto abbigliamento? (c) Vorresti/vuoi aprire
la finestra? (d) Vuoi seguirmi? (e) Vorresti/vuoi chiudere la porta?
(f) Vorrebbe che lui l'amasse. (g) Vorrei che lui fosse qui adesso.
(h) Volevamo pagare, ma lui non ha voluto. (i) Non ha voluto
accettare; ha rifiutato fermamente.

Exercise 6

(a) Ti devo qualcosa? (b) Uno dovrebbe essere/stare più attento.
(c) Non dovresti aiutarla? (d) Non devi andare via. (e) Avrei
dovuto incontrarlo alle undici. (f) Devi/deve/dovete/devono
andare ora. (g) Il treno deve arrivare ora. (h) L'autobus deve
partire da qui. (i) Dovevano aspettarci.

Exercise 7

Belgio, belga; Danimarca, danese; Francia, francese; Gran
Bretagna, britannico; Galles, gallese; Inghilterra, inglese;
Irlanda, irlandese; Italia, italiano; Norvegia, norvegese; Svizzera,
svizzero.

LESSON TWENTY

Exercise 1

(a) di (b) di (c) di (d) di (e) — (f) — (g) a (h) di (i) di (j) — (k)
a (l) a (m) di

Exercise 2

(a) da (b) a braccetto con (c) appeso a (d) entro (e) da (f) lontano
dalla (g) di fianco al (h) in aggiunta alle (i) tra la (j) sotto al, di
fronte a (k) fino a (l) contrariamente alle (m) diversamente da
(n) al di sopra delle/sopra le

Exercise 3

(a) Che bella casina! (b) Mi piacciono i gattini e i cagnolini! (c) Lei ha una boccuccia (d) Si entra per una porticina (e) I marciapiedi sono sparsi di cartaccia (f) Come si sta bene qui con questo calduccio! (g) Non fare lo stupidino (h) Che poveraccio! (i) Che razza di libraccio è questo? (j) Brutto gattaccio! (k) È una signorinella, ma vuol fare la signorina. (l) È una cosuccia! (m) Che omaccione! (n) Sei uno sporcaccione!

ITALIAN-ENGLISH
VOCABULARY

a at; in; to; per, a, an, every

abbagliante m. main headlight

abbandonare to abandon

abbasso down with

abbastanza enough

abbigliamento m. clothing

abbondanza f. plenty

abbracciare to embrace

abitante m. & f. inhabitant

abitare to live, to inhabit

abitazione f. dwelling, housing

abitudine f. habit

abolire to abolish (Group 3)

accademia f. academy

accadere to happen (Group 31)

accanto by the side of (+ *a*)

accarezzare to caress, to fondle

accendere to light, to switch on (Group 39)

accento m. accent, word (poetic)

acceso adj. switched on (light or engine)

accettare to accept

accidenti! damnation!

accogliere to welcome (Group 8)

accomodarsi to take a seat

accompagnare to accompany

accontentare to satisfy

accorciare to shorten

accordarsi to come to a settlement, a compromise

accordo m. agreement

accorgersi to realize, to notice (Group 17)

accorrere to rush to (Group 10)

accreditare to credit

accusare to accuse, to acknowledge

acerbo adj. sour

aceto m. vinegar

àcqua f. water

acquistare to buy, to get, to acquire

acquisto m. purchase

ad (+ vowel) = *a*

adattarsi to make do; to suit (+ *a*)

adatto adj. suitable

addebitare to debit

addensarsi to thicken

addio m. good-bye, farewell

addizione f. addition

addolorare to grieve

addormentarsi to fall asleep

addosso on one's back, close to the body, on top of oneself

aderire to adhere, to stick (Group 3)

adesso now, at the present moment

adottare to adopt

adozione f. adoption

aèreo m. aeroplane; adj. air

aerostazione f. airport terminal

affanno m. breathlessness

affare m. piece of business; bargain; affair

affatto at all, altogether

affermare to state, to affirm

affermazione f. statement; affirmation

affetto m. affection; adj. afflicted with (+ *da*)

affiatato adj. getting on well together

affidare to entrust

affittacàmere m.&f. landlord, landlady

affittare to rent, to let

affitto m. rent

affliggere to afflict (Group 13)

affogare to drown

agenzia f. agency

aggiùngere to add (Group 10)

aggiunta f. addition

aggredire to attack, to assail (Group 3)

àgile adj. nimble

agire to act (Group 3)

agosto m. August

agrìcolo adj. agricultural

agricoltura f. agriculture

ah! oh!

ahi! ouch!

ahimè! alas!

aiutare to help

ala f., pl. *ali*, wing

alba f. dawn

alberello m. little tree

albergo m. hotel

albero m. tree

alcoòlico m. spirit (drink); adj. alcoholic

alcoolizzato m. alcoholic

alcuno adj. sing. no; pl. some, a few; none

alga f. seaweed

alimentare m. & adj. food

aliscafo m. hydrofoil

alleato m. ally, allied

allacciamento m. connection

allegare to enclose

allegro adj. merry, lively

allegòrico adj. allegoric

allestire to prepare, to equip (Group 3)

all'incirca about, approximately

alloggiare to lodge, to put up; to stay overnight

allòggio m. lodging, accommodation

allontanarsi to go away (+ *da* + noun)

allora then; at that time

allorchè when

allùdere to hint at (+ *a*)

allungato adj. elongated; diluted

almeno at least

Alpi f. pl. Alps

Alpini m. pl. (mountain troops)

alquanto somewhat

alto adj. high; tall

Alto Àdige m. South Tyrol

altoatesino adj. from South Tyrol

altrimenti otherwise

altro adj. other

alzarsi to stand up; to get up

amàbile adj. amiable

amare to love

amaro adj. bitter

amica f. female friend

amicìzia f. friendship

amico m. male friend

ammaccato adj. dented

ammalato adj. sick, ill

ammèttere to admit (Group 35)

amministrare to administer, to rule

ammobigliato adj. furnished

ammontare m. amount; to amount

amore m. love

amoroso adj. love

anabbagliante m. headlight

anàlisi f. analysis

anche also, too

ancora still; yet; more

àncora f. anchor

andare to go (Group 23)

andàrsene to go away

andata f. outward journey

andata e ritorno m. return trip

àngolo m. corner

angoscioso adj. painful

animato adj. animated; *cartoni animati* m. pl. cartoons

anniversàrio m. anniversary

anno m. year

annoiare to bore

annuale adj. yearly

annuàrio m. annuary

annullare to cancel

annùncio m. announcement

anònimo adj. anonymous

ansare to gasp

ansietà f. anxiety

anteriore adj. frontal; earlier

antichità f. old time, antiquity; pl. antiques

anticipato adj. in advance

antìcipo m. advance

antico adj. ancient

antipasto m. hors-d'oeuvres

antiquariato m. antique trade

antiquàrio m. antique dealer

anzi more than that
anziano adj. elderly
anzichè instead of
aperto adj. open; opened
apertura f. opening
apòstrofo m. apostrophe
appaiato adj. paired, coupled
apparire to appear (Group 20)
appartamento m. flat
appartenere to belong (Group 6)
appena hardly, as soon as, no sooner . . . than
appèndere to hang (Group 31)
appeso a adj. hanging from
appòsito adj. suitable, appropriate
apprèndere to learn (Group 39)
apprensione f. apprehension
appresso near; with oneself
approfittare to take advantage of, to profit by
appuntamento m. appointment, date
appunto just, indeed, exactly
approssimativamente roughly
aprile m. April
aprire to open (Group 20)
àrabo adj. Arab, Arabic
arància f. orange
aràncio or *arancione* orange (colour)
architetto m. architect
architettura f. architecture
arco m. arch
àrdere to burn (Group 10)

ardire to dare (Group 3)
argento m. silver
ària f. air
arma f., pl. *armi*, arm, weapon
armato adj. armed
armistìzio m. armistice
armonia f. harmony
arrabbiarsi to get angry
arrangiarsi to make do, to manage, to get along
arredamento m. furnishing
arredare to furnish
arrestare to arrest
arrestarsi to stop
arresto m. arrest
arrivare to arrive
arrivederci good-bye until we meet again
arrivo m. arrival
arroccato adj. nestled
arrossire to blush (Group 3)
arrosto m. or adj. roast
arte f. art
artìcolo m. article
artista m. & f. artist
artìstico adj. artistic
ascensore m. lift
asciugamano m. towel
asciugare to dry up
ascoltare to listen to
asfaltato adj. tarred
asfalto m. tar
asiàtico adj. Asian, Asiatic
aspettare to wait
aspettàrsela to expect
aspettarsi to expect
aspettativa f. expectation; leave of absence

aspetto m. aspect
aspirina f. aspirin
aspro adj. harsh, rough
assai very much
assalto m. assault
assegnare to allot, to assign
assegno m. cheque
assente adj. absent
assenza f. absence
assicurare to assure; to ensure; to insure
assicurarsi to make sure, to secure
assicurazione f. assurance; insurance
assistenza f. assistance
assistente m. & f. assistant
associato adj. associated
assoluto adj. absolute
asterisco m. asterisk
attaccare to attack
attaccato adj. attached, tied hanging
attèndere to wait for (Group 39)
attenersi to stick to (Group 6)
attentato m. terrorist action
attento adj. attentive, careful
atterrato adj. crushed; landed
attesa f. wait; expectation
àttimo m. moment
attìngere to draw (Group 10)
attirare to attract
attivo adj. active
atto m. act, action
attore m. actor
attorniato adj. surrounded
attorno a around
attrarre to attract (Group 12)

attraversare to cross
attraverso across; through
attrezzo m. tool
attrezzatura f. equipment
attribuire to attribute (Group 5)
attrice f. actress
attuale adj. present-day
audace adj. daring
augurare to wish
augùrio m. wish
austerità f. austerity
autista m. & f. professional driver
àuto f. motor-car
autoarticolato m. trailer lorry
àutobus m. bus
autocarro m. lorry
automòbile or *àuto* f. motor-car
automobilista m. & f. motorist
automobilìstico adj. motor-car
autònomo adj. autonomous, self-governing
autore m. author
autorità f. authority
autorizzare to authorize
àutostop m. & f. hitch-hiking
autostrada f. motorway
autostradale adj. motorway
autunno m. autumn
avanti forward; come on; come in; fast
avena f. oats
avere to have (Group 1)
avèrcela to have it in for somebody (+ *con*)
avèrsene a male to take umbrage, to take offence

(+ *con*)

avidità f. greed

avvenimento m. event

avvenire to happen (Group 6); m. future

avventura f. adventure

avvertire to warn

avvicinarsi to get nearer, to approach (+ *a*)

avvìncere to thrill (Group 11)

avvisare to inform; to warn

avvòlgere to wind (Group 10)

azienda f. firm, corporation

azione f. action; (company's) share

azzardare to risk

babbo m. daddy

bacchetta f. rod, stick, baton

bàcio m. kiss

bacione m. big kiss

badare a to look after, to mind

baffo m. moustache

bagàglio m. luggage

bagnato adj. wet

bagnino m. bathing-attendant

bagno m. bath; bathing; swim

balena f. whale

baleno m. jiffy; lightning

balia f., *in balia di* at the mercy of

ballare to dance

ballo m. dance, ball; dancing

bambina f., *bambino* m. baby; child

banca f. bank

bancàrio adj. banking; m. bank-clerk

banco m. patch

bandiera f. flag, banner

bandito m. bandit, gangster

bar m. café, bar, coffee-bar

barba f. beard

bàrbaro adj. barbarian, barbaric

barbiere m. barber

barca f. boat

barista m. & f. bar-tender

basso adj. low, short (stature); m. bass

basta that's enough; it is enough

bastare to be sufficient

battàglia f. battle

bàttere to beat; to wink

bàttere a màcchina to type

batteria f. battery

bàttersela to slip away

battuto adj. routed; wrought

baule m. trunk

beige beige

belga adj. Belgian

Bèlgio m. Belgium

bellezza f. beauty

bello adj. fine, beautiful

bene well, good; *benìssimo* very well

bene m. good; right

benedire to bless (Group 15)

benvenuto adj. welcome

benzina f. petrol

bere to drink (Group 22)

bergamasco adj. from Bergamo

bianco adj. white

bìblico adj. Biblical

Bìbbia f. Bible

bicchiere m. glass

bicchierino m. liqueur glass

bicicletta f. bicycle

bigliettàrio m. ticket collector, ticket inspector

biglietteria f. ticket-counter, box-office

biglietto m. ticket

bilància f. scales; balance

binàrio m. track; adj. binary

biondo adj. blond, fair-haired

bisestile adj. leap (-year)

bisogno m. need (+ *di*)

bistecca f. steak

bloccare to block

bocca f. mouth

boccàccia f. grimace

bollare to stamp

bolletta f. bill

bollire to boil (Group 3)

bollo m. stamp

bombardare to bomb

bordo m. board; *a bordo* on board

borsa f. bag; *borsetta* f. handbag

bosco m. wood

botta f. blow

botteghino m. box-office

bottìglia f. bottle

bottone m. button

braccetto m., *a braccetto di* arm in arm with

bracciante m. farm-hand

bràccio m., pl. *bràccia* f., arm

bravo adj. good, clever, bravo

bravura f. cleverness

breve adj. short, brief

brevemente shortly, briefly

brioche (pron. bree'osh) f. croissant

brodo m. chicken or meat soup

brontolare to grumble

bruciare to burn

bruno adj. brown; dark-haired

bruscamente abruptly

brusco adj. sharp, rough

bruto m. brute

brutto adj. ugly

bue m., pl. *buoi*, ox

buio adj. dark; m. darkness

busta f. envelope

buttare to throw, to fling

cabina f. cabin; (telephone) booth

cacciare to hunt, to shoot, to chase away

cadere to fall (Group 31); to be cut off (telephone line)

caduta f. fall

caffè m. coffee; café

caffelatte m. coffee and milk

calamita f. magnet

calare to lower

calcàreo adj. chalky

calce f. lime

càlcolo m. calculation; stone

caldamente warmly

caldo adj. warm, hot

calmo adj. calm

calzature f. footwear

calze f. pl. stockings

calzoni m. pl. trousers

calzini m. pl. socks

cambiare to change; to exchange

càmbio m. change; exchange

càmera f. bedroom; chamber

cameriera f. waitress

cameriere m. waiter

camicetta f. blouse

camìcia f. shirt

camion m. lorry, truck

camminare to walk

cammino m. walking journey

campagna f. countryside; campaign

campana f. bell

campanello m. doorbell

campeggiare to camp

campèggio m. camping

campionàrio m. set of samples; pattern book; *fiera campionària* trade fair

campo m. field

camposanto m. churchyard

cancellazione f. cancellation

candela f. candle; sparking-plug

candeliere m. candlestick

cane m. dog

cannonata f. cannon-shot; smasher

cànone m. rent

canònico m. canon

canoro adj. singing

cantante m. & f. singer

cantare to sing

càntica f. long narrative poem

canto m. song; canto; singing

capitale f. capital city; m. capital

canzone f. song

caos m. chaos

capace adj. capable

capacità f. capability

capanna f. hut, cabin

capello m. hair

capigliatura f. hair

capire to understand (Group 3)

capo m. head; chief

caporale m. corporal

caporeparto m. & f. foreman

capostazione m. & f. stationmaster

capovòlgere to capsize, to overturn (Group 10)

cappello m. hat

cappotto m. coat, overcoat

cappuccino m. coffee with creamy milk

capra f. goat

capriccioso adj. capricious, whimsical

capuffìcio m. head of office, manager

carabiniere m. (territorial) policeman

caraffa f. carafe

caramella f. toffee, sweet

caràttere m. character

carbonara f. spaghetti with egg and bacon

carbone m. coal

carburatore m. carburettor

carburazione f. carburettor

cardinale adj. cardinal

carezza f. caress

cariato adj. decayed (tooth)

caricare to load (+ *di*)

càrico adj. loaded (+ *di*)

càrie f. caries, tooth decay

carino adj. pretty

carnale adj. carnal

carne f. flesh; meat

carnevale m. carnival

caro adj. dear; expensive

carro m. cart

carrozza f. coach, carriage

carta f. paper; card; *carta di crèdito* credit card *carta bollata* stamped paper

cartello m. sign

cartòccio m. parcel

cartolina f. postcard

cartone m. cardboard

cartone animato m. cartoon

casa f. house

casalingo adj. domestic, home-made

cascare to fall

cascata f. waterfall

casello m. motorway barrier

casino m. brothel; mess, muddle

casinò m. casino

caso m. case; chance; *per caso* by chance

cassa f. case; crate; cashier's desk

castano adj. brown

castello m. castle

cattivo adj. bad, nasty

causa f. cause; *a causa di* because of

càuto adj. wary

cavallo m. horse

cavàrsela to make do, to scrape along

càvolo m. cabbage; damn

cèdere to give up; to yield

celebrare to celebrate

celebrazione f. celebration

cemento m. cement

cemento armato m. concrete

cena f. dinner, supper

cenare to have supper

centìgrado m. centigrade

centinàio m., pl. f. *centinàia*, a hundred

centralinista m. & f. switchboard operator

centralino m. switchboard

centralizzato adj. centralized

centro m. centre

cera f. wax; look

cercare to try; to look for

cèrchio m. circle

cerotto m. sticking plaster

certezza f. certainty

certificato m. certificate

certo adj. certain; certainly

cesso m. (vulgar) lavatory

che that; what; which; who

chi who; which of

chiàcchiera f. chat

chiacchierare to chat

chiamare to call

chiamata f. call; ring

chiaramente clearly

chiave f. key

chièdere to ask (Group 11)

chilo or *chilogrammo* m. kilo

chilòmetro m. kilometre

chìmica f. chemistry

chìmico adj. chemical; m. (research) chemist

chissà who knows?, I wonder

chiùdere to close (Group 39)

chiusura f. closing; shutting down

chiusura lampo m. zip fastener

ci us; to us; here; there

ciao hello; good-bye

ciascuno adj. each

cibo m. food

ciclista m. & f. cyclist

cielo m. heaven; sky

ciglio m., pl. *ciglia* f., eyelashes

ciglio m. edge, brink, brim

cimitero m. churchyard

cinema m. cinema

cinquantenario m. fiftieth anniversary

cinquantina f. about fifty

cintura f. belt

cioccolata f. cocoa; bar of chocolate; chocolate

cioccolatino m. chocolate

cioè that is, i.e.

cipolla f. onion

circa about

circondare to surround

circostante m. person around; onlooker

circostanza f. circumstance

circuito m. circuit

cistifellea f. gall bladder

città f. city, town

cittadino m. citizen; adj. city, town

ciuffo m. tuft of hair, forelock

civile adj. civil, civic; civilized

civilizzare to civilize

civiltà f. civilization

clacson m. vehicle horn

clima m. climate, weather

clinica f. clinic, nursing-home

coda f. tail; queue, line

coetaneo m. contemporary, person of the same age

cognata f. sister-in-law

cognato m. brother-in-law

coinvolgere to involve (Group 10)

colazione f. breakfast; lunch

collana f. necklace

colle m. hill

collegamento m. connection

collezione f. collection

collina f. hillock

collinare adj. hilly, standing on a hill

collo m. neck

colonna f. column

colpa f. guilt, fault

colpevole m. & f. guilty, culprit, offender

colpire to hit (Group 3)

colpo m. hit, strike, blow; coup

coltello m. knife

coltivare to grow, to cultivate

coltivatore m. farmer

comandare to lead

comando m. command, order; commando

combinare to combine

combinazione f. combination; coincidence; matching colours

come how; as; like

come mai how come

commedia f. comedy, play

commediografo m. playwright

commèrcio m. commerce, trade

commovente adj. moving

commozione f. commotion, emotion

commozione cerebrale f. concussion

comodità f. comfort

còmodo adj. comfortable

compagnia f. company

compagno m. companion, mate; comrade

compare m. godfather

comparire to turn up (Group 20)

compartimento m. railway zone headquarters

compensare to make good for; to offset; to compensate

compensazione f. clearing, counterbalancing

compenso m. remuneration, pay, fee

còmpera f. purchase

comperare to buy

competenza f. competence, ability

compètere to compete

compiacere to please (Group 4)

compiàngere to be sorry for (Group 10)

còmpiere to fulfil; to complete

compilare to fill in

compire to complete

còmpito m. task, duty; homework

compleanno m. birthday

completo adj. complete; full up

comporre to compose (Group 11)

comportamento m. behaviour

comportarsi to behave

composto adj. consisting of; m. composition, compound

comprèndere to understand; to include (Group 39)

comprensione f. comprehension

compreso adj. included, including, inclusive

compromesso m. compromise

compromèttere to compromise (Group 35)

comunale adj. municipal

comune m. municipality; adj. common, mutual

comunicato m. communiqué

comunista m. & f. Communist

comunità f. community

comùnque anyway, however, yet

concèdere to grant (Group 40)

concerto m. concert; concerto

concessione f. concession, grant

concetto m. concept, idea

conclùdere to conclude (Group 39)

concordare to agree upon

concorso m. state competition

condizione f. condition

condurre to conduct, to lead (Group 16)

conduttore m. conductor (train)

confabulare to talk in a secretive way

conferma f. confirmation

confessare to confess

confezione f. manufacture; article of clothing

confidenza f. trust; intimacy

confine m. boundary

confondere to confuse (Group 36)

confortare to comfort

confrontare to compare

confuso adj. confused

congegno m. device

congelare to freeze

congelatore m. freezer

congiuntivo m. subjunctive

congratulazione f. congratulation

congresso m. congress, conference

coniuge m. & f. spouse

conoscenza f. knowledge

conoscere to know, to come to know, to meet, to get acquainted with (Group 14)

conquistare to conquer

consegnare to hand over; to deliver

conseguenza f. consequence

conserva f. preserve

conservatore m. conservative

considerato considering

consigliare to advise

consigliere m. councillor; counsellor; adviser

consiglio m. piece of advice;

Consiglio dei Ministri Cabinet

consistenza f. importance

consistere di to consist of (Group 41)

consuetudine f. custom

consulente m. & f. consultant

consultare to consult

consumare to consume

consumato adj. worn out

consumatore m. consumer

consumo m. consumption

contabile m. & f. bookkeeper

contabilità f. book-keeping

contachilometri m. speedometer

contadino m. peasant, farmer

contagiri m. rev-counter

contanti cash;

in contanti for cash

contare to count, to calculate

contatore m. meter

contatto m. contact

conte m. count

contea f. county

contenere to contain (Group 6)

contento di adj. happy, satisfied with

contenuto m. contents

continuare to continue

continuo adj. continuous

conto m. account

contorno m. side-dish

contraccambiare to reciprocate

contraddire to contradict (Group 15)

contrário adj. contrary

contrattare to bargain over

contratto m. agreement

contravvenzione f. fine

contribuente m. taxpayer

contribuire to contribute
  (Group 3)

contributo m. contribution

contro against

controllare to control, to
  check

controllo m. check; test

controllore m. ticket-inspector

controverso adj. debatable

convegno m. meeting,
  congress, conference

convenire to suit (Group 6)

convergenza f. convergence

convincere to convince
  (Group 17)

convocare to summon

convóglio m. train; convoy

copérchio m. lid

coperta f. blanket

copertina f. book-jacket

coperto adj. cover; covered;
  overcast; covert

cópia f. copy

cóppia f. couple

coprire to cover (Group 20)

corággio m. courage

corda f. rope

coricarsi to lie down, to go to
  bed

cornice f. frame

corno m., pl. corna f., horn

coro m. chorus; choir

corona f. crown

corpo m. body

corréggere to correct (Group
  13)

corrente f. stream; (electric)
  power; adj. current

córrere to run (Group 10)

corretto adj. correct

corridóio m. corridor

corriera f. coach

corrispondenza f.
  correspondence

corrispóndere to correspond
  (Group 11)

corrómpere to corrupt
  (Group 33)

corruzione f. corruption

corsa f. run; race

corsia f. hospital ward

corso m. course; high street

corto adj. short

cosa f. thing

così so, thus; such

cosicchè so that

costa f. coast

costante adj. constant

costare to cost

costata f. chop

costituire to consist; to
  constitute (Group 3)

costituzione f. constitution

costo m. cost

costríngere to compel (Group
  10)

costruire to build (Group 3)

costruzione f. construction

costume m. custom; costume;
  costume da bagno m.
  bathing-costume

cotone m. cotton

cotta f. infatuation, crush

cotto adj. cooked
cottura f. cooking, baking
cravatta f. tie, neck-tie
creare to create
credere to believe
credito m. credit
crescere to grow (up) (Group 14)
crescione m. water-cress
crescita f. growth
criminale adj. criminal
crimine m. serious crime
crisi f. crisis
cristiano adj. Christian
Cristo m. Christ
critica f. criticism; critique
criticare to criticize
critico adj. critical
croce f. cross
crociera f. cruise
crollare to collapse
crollo m. collapse
cronaca f. chronicle
cronista m. & f. reporter
crudo adj. raw, underdone
cubico adj. cubic
cucchiaiata f. spoonful
cucchiaino m. tea or coffee spoon
cucchiaio m. spoon
cucina f. kitchen; cuisine, cookery
cucire to sew
cucitura f. seam
cuffia f. cap, bonnet
cugina f. female cousin
cugino m. cousin
cui whom; whose; to whom
cullare to rock, to cradle

cumulo m. heap
cuoca f. cook
cuocere to cook (Group 19)
cuoco m. cook
cuoio m. leather, hide
cuore m. heart
cupola f. dome
cura f. cure, care
curioso adj. curious
curva f. curve
curvare to bend
curvarsi to stoop
cuscino m. cushion; pillow
custode m. & f. keeper, janitor, custodian, porter

da from, at, to
dai come on
d'altronde on the other hand
danneggiare to damage
danno m. damage
danza f. dance
dappertutto everywhere
dare to give (Group 31); *darsi del tu* to call each other *tu* (familiar form)
data f. date
dattilografa f. typist
dattilografare, *dattiloscrivere* to type
davanti a in front of
davvero really, is that so?, indeed
debitamente duly
debito m. debt
decina about ten
decennale adj. decennial; m. tenth anniversary
decennio m. decade, ten

years' time

decenza f. decency

decidere to decide (Group 39)

decidersi to make up one's mind

decisione f. decision

deciso adj. resolute, firm, decisive

decomporre to decompose (Group 11)

dedurre to deduce, to deduct (Group 16)

deficit m. deficit

delinquenza f. delinquency, crime

delitto m. crime

deluso adj. disappointed

democratico adj. democratic

denaro m. money

dente m. tooth

dentista m. & f. dentist

denuncia f. accusation; tax return

deporre to depose (Group 11)

deposito m. deposit

deputato m. & f. deputy, member of the Chamber of Deputies

derivare to derive, to come from

desiderare to wish

destino m. fate

destro adj. right hand; *a destra* on the right

detenere to detain (Group 6)

detrarre to deduct (Group 12)

di of, from

diabolico adj. devilish

dialetto m. dialect

diamante m. diamond

diceria f. rumour

diciassettenne m. & f. 17-year-old person

dieta f. diet

dietro behind

difetto m. defect

diffondere to spread; to broadcast (Group 36)

digerire to digest (Group 3)

dignità f. dignity

dignitoso adj. dignified

diluviare to rain heavily

diluvio m. deluge, heavy rain

dimensione f. dimension, size

dimenticare, *dimenticarsi* (*di*) to forget

dimettersi to resign (Group 35)

diminuire to decrease (Group 3)

dimissioni f. pl. resignation

dimostrare to prove, to demonstrate

dimostrazione f. demonstration

dinamica f. dynamics

dinanzi a in front of

dintorni m. pl. vicinity, proximity

dio m. god pl. *gli dei*

dipingere to paint (Group 10)

diplomatico m. diplomat; adj. diplomatic

diplomato adj. holding a secondary school final diploma

diramarsi to branch off

dire to say, to tell (Group 15)

diretto adj. direct

direzione f. direction

diritto m. right; adj. straight

dirotto, a dirotto in torrents, heavily

disapprovazione f. disapproval

disastroso adj. disastrous

disco m. record; disc

discorso m. talk, speech

discussione f. discussion, debate

discùtere to discuss, to debate (Group 40)

disdire to cancel (Group 15)

disfare to undo (Group 5)

disfarsi to do away with (+ *di*)

disinvolto adj. easy-going

disoccupato m. unemployed

disoccupazione f. unemployment

disparte, in disparte aside

disperato adj. desperate, despairing

disperazione f. despair

dispiacere m. displeasure; to displease, to dislike, to be sorry, to regret (Group 4)

disporre to arrange; to have at one's disposal (Group 11)

disposizione f. disposal; disposition

distare to be distant

distanza f. distance

disteso adj. lying down

distògliere to distract (Group 8)

distributore m. petrol station; distributor

disturbare to disturb, to bother, to annoy

disturbato adj. noisy

ditta f. firm, company

dittatore m. dictator

dittatura f. dictatorship

divenire to become (Group 6)

diverso adj. different; various

divertimento m. amusement, fun

divertirsi m. to enjoy oneself, to have a good time

divìdere to divide (Group 39)

divieto m. prohibition

divino adj. divine

divisione f. division

dòccia f. shower; *fare la dòccia* to have a shower

documento m. document

dogana f. customs

doganiere m. customs-officer

dolce adj. sweet; cake, dessert

dolcezza f. sweetness

dolente adj. painful; full of sorrow; sorry

dòllaro m. dollar

dolore m. pain, grief, sorrow, ache

doloroso adj. painful, aching

domènica f. Sunday

domèstico adj. domestic, home; m. servant

dominare to dominate, to domineer; to overhang

domìnio m. dominion

donna f. woman; lady

dopoguerra m. post-war period

doppio adj. double
dormire to sleep
dormiveglia m. doze
dosaggio m. dosage
dotato adj. endowed (+ *di*)
dote f. dowry; endowment
dottore m. doctor
dottoressa f. female doctor
dottrina f. doctrine
dove where
dovere to have to, must, to
be to, to be due at or on,
should, ought to (Group
28); m. duty
dramma m. drama
drammàtico adj. dramatic
dozzina f. dozen

e and
ebràico adj. Jewish
ebreo adj. Jewish; m. Jew
eccessivo adj. excessive
eccesso m. excess, surplus
eccetera (*ecc.*) etcetera
eccetto except for
eccezione f. exception
eccitare to excite, to incite
ecco here, there it is
eco f. echo; pl. m. *echi*
economia f. economy, thrift;
economics
economista m. & f. economist
edifìcio m. building
edilìzia f. building trade
editore m. publisher
editrice, *casa editrice* f.
publishing house
educare to educate, to train
educazione f. education,

upbringing, training
effettivo adj. actual
effetto m. effect
effettuare to make, to effect
efficàcia f. efficacy,
effectiveness
efficienza f. efficiency
egli he
egoista m. & f. egoist
ehi hello
eh what? Pardon?
elargire to lavish
eleganza f. elegance
eleggere to elect (Group 13)
elementare adj. elementary
elemento m. element
elencare to list
elenco m. list;
elenco telefònico m.
telephone directory
elettivo adj. elective
eletto adj. elected
elettràuto m. car electrician,
car electrical repairs
elettricità f. electricity, power
elèttrico adj. electrical
elezione f. election
eliminare to get rid of
ella she; you (very formal)
emèrgere to emerge
(Group 7)
emèttere to issue (Group 35)
emigrare to emigrate
emigrato or *emigrante* m.
emigrant
emissione f. issue
emozionante adj. exciting
emozionare to excite
emozione f. excitement

energètico adj. energetic; referring to energy

energia f. energy

enèrgico adj. energetic, full of energy

enorme adj. enormous

ente m. state authority, corporation

entrambi adj. pl. both

entrarci to be one's business

entrare to enter, to come, go in

entrata f. entrance, way in

entro within, in

entusiasmante adj. exciting

èpico adj. epic

època f. era

eppure and yet, nevertheless

equilibratura f. balancing

equilìbrio m. balance

equipaggiamento m. equipment

equipàggio m. crew

equivalere a to be equivalent to (Group 7)

èquo adj. fair, equitable

erba f. grass

erbàccia f. weed

erboso adj. covered with grass

erede m. heir

ereditare to inherit

erètico adj. heretical

eretto adj. standing, erect

ergàstolo m. life sentence

erìgere to erect (Group 34)

eròtico adj. erotic

esagerare to exaggerate

esame m. examination

esaminare to examine

esatto adj. exact

esaurimento nervoso m. nervous breakdown

esaurire to exhaust (Group 3)

esaurito adj. exhausted; sold out; out of stock

esclamativo adj. exclamatory

esclùdere to exclude (Group 39)

escluso adj. excluded

esecutivo adj. executive

eseguire to execute

esèmpio m. example; *ad* (or *per*) *esèmpio* for example

esercitare to practise

esercitarsi to get some practice

esercìzio m. exercise

esigenza f. requirement

esìgere to demand (Group 10)

esiliato adj. exiled, banished

esìlio m. exile

esistente adj. existing

esìstere to exist (Group 41)

esitare to hesitate

èsito m. result, outcome

èsodo m. exodus

espatriare to leave the country

espèllere to eject (Group 37)

esperienza f. experience

esperimento m. experiment

esperto adj. expert

esplorare to explore

esporre to expound (Group 11)

esportare to export

esportazione f. export

esposizione f. exhibition

espresso m. express; espresso coffee

esprìmere to express (Group 34)

essa she; *esse* f. they

èssere to be (Group 21); m. human being

essi m. they; *esso* m. he, it

estate f. summer

estèndere to extend (Group 39)

estèndersi to spread out, to extend

estensione f. extent, extension

esterno adj. external

èstero, all'èstero abroad

esteso adj. wide, extensive

estìnguere to extinguish (Group 10)

estivo adj. of the summer

estrarre to extract (Group 12)

estratto m. extract, excerpt

estremista m. & f. extremist

età f. age

eterno adj. eternal

ètica f. ethics

ètico adj. ethical

èttaro m. hectare

etto m. a hundred grammes

eufòrico adj. elated, buoyant

europeista m. & f. supporter of European unity

evàdere to evade, to escape (Group 39)

eventuale adj. possible

eventualità f. possibility

evidentemente evidently, obviously

evitare to avoid

evoluto adj. developed

evòlversi to evolve (Group 10)

ex ex, former

fàbbrica f. factory

fàccia f. face

facchino m. porter

fàcile adj. easy

facoltà f. faculty

fagiolo m. bean

falegname m. joiner, carpenter

fallire to go bankrupt; to fail (Group 3)

fallito m. bankrupt; unsuccessful

falso adj. false

fama f. fame, renown

fame f. hunger

famìglia f. family

familiare adj. family

fanale m. lamp;
 fanale anteriore m. headlight;
 fanale di posizione m. parking light
 fanalino di coda m. rearlight

fanàtico adj. fanatical

fanciulla f. girl

fanciullo m. young boy

fango m. mud

fantascienza f. science-fiction

fantasia f. imagination

fantasma m. ghost

fàrcela to make it, to make do

fare to do, to make (Group 5); to dial

farfalla f. butterfly
farina f. flour
farmacia f. pharmacy, chemist's
farmacista m. & f. chemist
faro m. lighthouse
fascia f. band
fascio m. bundle
fascismo m. Fascism
fascista m. & f. fascist
fastidio m. nuisance
fatica f. toil
faticoso adj. exhausting
fatto m. fact
fattoria f. farm; farmhouse
fattura f. making, manufacture; invoice
fatturato m. proceeds of sales
favore m. favour
favorire to favour (Group 3)
fazzoletto m. handkerchief
febbre f. temperature (of the body)
febbràio m. February
fede f. faith
fedele adj. faithful
fegato m. liver
felice adj. happy
felicità f. happiness
femminile adj. feminine, womanly
ferie f. pl. holidays, furlough
ferire to wound (Group 3)
ferita f. wound
fermare, fermarsi to stop
fermata f. stop
fermo adj. firm; still
ferragosto m. mid-August holiday

ferro m. iron
ferrovia f. railway
ferroviàrio adj. railway
ferroviere m. railwayman
fesso adj. foolish
festa f. feast-day; holiday
festeggiare to celebrate
festivo adj. holiday
fetta f. slice
fiamma f. flame
fiammìfero m. match
fianco m. side
fiasco m. flask; fiasco
fiato m. breath
fibbia f. buckle
fibra f. fibre
fidanzata f. fiancée
fidanzato m. fiancé
fiducia f. confidence
fiducioso adj. confident
fieno m. hay
fiera f. fair
figlio m. son
figlia f. daughter
figlioletto m. little child, son
figura f. figure
fila f. queue, line
filàrsela to take French leave
filastrocca f. rhyme
filettatura f. threading, screw-thread
film m. film, movie picture
filmare to shoot a film
filo m. thread, yarn, warp, woof
filòsofo m. philosopher
filovia f. trolley-bus
filtrare to filter
filtro m. filter

finanziàrio adj. financial
finchè until, till, as long as
finestra f. window
finestrino m. train, car window
fingere to simulate (Group 10)
finire to end, to finish (Group 3)
fino a until, till, up to, as far as
finòcchio m. fennel; homosexual, gay
fintanto che as long as; till, until
fiocchi d'avena m. pl. cornflakes
fiore m. flower
fiorentino adj. Florentine
fiorire to blossom (Group 3)
fiorista m. & f. florist
Firenze f. Florence
firma f. signature
firmare to sign
fiscale adj. fiscal
fisco m. Inland Revenue
fìsica f. physics
fìsico m. physicist; physique; adj. physical
fissare to fix
fisso adj. fixed
fitto adj. thick
fiume m. river
flessìbile adj. flexible
fòglia f. leaf
fòglio m. sheet, piece of paper; *fòglio rosa* m. provisional driving-licence
fogna f. sewer

fognatura f. sewerage
folla f. crowd
fondamento m. foundation; *le fondamenta* f. pl. building foundations
fondare to found
fòndere to melt, to smelt (Group 36)
fondo m. bottom; end; fund
fontana f. fountain
forare to pierce
fòrbici f. pl. scissors
forchetta f. fork
foresta f. forest
forestiero m. stranger
forma f. form, shape
formàggio m. cheese
formare to form
formica f. ant
formidàbile adj. tremendous, terrific
fornire di to supply with (Group 3)
fornitore m. supplier
forno m. oven
forse perhaps
forte adj. strong; loud, loudly; tightly
fortuna f. fortune, luck
fortunato adj. lucky, fortunate
forza f. force, strength
fotocòpia f. photocopy
fotografare to photograph
fotografia f. photograph; photography
fotògrafo m. photographer
fra or *tra* among, between; in, within (time); amidst

francese adj. French
Frància f. France
franco adj. frank
frase f. phrase, sentence
fratello m. brother
fratellastro m. half-brother,
   step-brother
frazione f. fraction
freddo adj. cold
fregare to cheat, to swindle,
   to trick, to fool (vulgar)
fregàrsene not to care at all
   (vulgar)
fregatura f. swindle (vulgar)
frenare to brake
freno m. brake
frequentare to attend, to
   frequent
frequente adj. frequent
fresco adj. cool; fresh
fretta f. hurry, haste
frìggere to fry (Group 13)
frigorìfero or *frigo* m.
   refrigerator
frittata f. omelet
fritto adj. fried
frizione f. rubbing, friction;
   clutch
frizzante adj. fizzy
fronte f. forehead; m. front
fronteggiare to front, to
   confront, to face up
frontiera f. frontier, border
frugare to rummage
frullare to whip up
frumento m. wheat
frutto m., pl. *frutta* f., fruit
fu late, deceased
fucile m. rifle

fuga f. escape
fuggire to escape, to flee
   (Group 13)
fùlmine m. thunderstorm,
   flash of lightning
fumare to smoke
fumatore m. smoker
fumetto m. comic-strip
fumo m. smoke; smoking
fune f. rope, cable
funerale m., or *funerali* m. pl.
   funeral
fungo m. mushroom
funivia f. cable way
funzionare to function, to
   work
funzionàrio m. official, officer
funzione f. function;
   in funzione working
fuoco m. fire
fuori outside
fuoribordo m. outboard
   motor boat
furbo adj. wily, cunning
fùria f. fury
furore m. fury, rage, frenzy
furto m. theft, larceny
fusìbile m. fuse

gabinetto m. cabinet; lavatory
galleggiare to float
galleria f. gallery; tunnel
Galles m. Wales
gallese adj. Welsh; m.
   Welshman; f. Welshwoman
gallina f. hen
gallo m. cock, rooster
gamba f. leg
gàmbero m. crayfish

gàncio m. hook
gara f. competition
garantire to guarantee (Group 3)
garanzia f. guarantee
garòfano m. carnation
gas m. gas
gassato adj. fizzy
gatta f. she-cat
gattino m. kitten
gatto cat
gelare to freeze
gelatàio m. ice-cream man
gelateria f. ice-cream shop
gelatina f. jelly
gelato m. ice-cream; adj. icy, frozen
gèlido adj. ice-cold, frozen, icy
gelo m. frost
gelosia f. jealousy
gemello m. twin
gemma f. gem
gènere m. kind, sort
gènero m. son-in-law
generoso adj. generous
gengiva f. gum
genitore m. parent
gennaio m. January
gente f. people
gentile adj. kind to (+ *con*)
gentilezza f. kindness
genuino adj. genuine
geografia f. geography
geòlogo m. geologist
geòmetra m. & f. land and building surveyor
gergo m. slang, jargon
germe m. germ

germòglio m. sprout, bud
gerùndio m. gerund
gesso m. chalk
gestione f. management
gestire to manage (Group 3)
gesto m. gesture
gestore m. superintendent, administrator
Gesù Jesus
gettare to throw
gettone m. (telephone) token
ghiacciare to ice over
ghiàccio m. ice
ghiacciolo m. icicle, ice lolly
ghiàia f. gravel, pebbles, shingle
già already
giacca f. jacket
giacere to lie down (Group 4)
giacimento m. mineral deposit
giallo adj. yellow
giandùia f. soft chocolate
giardinàggio m. gardening
giardiniere m. gardener
giardino m. garden
gìglio m. lily
ginnàstica f. gymnastics
ginòcchio m. knee, pl. *ginòcchia* f.
giocare to play
giocatore m. player
giocàttolo m. toy
gioco m. toy
giòia f. joy
gioielleria f. jewellery
gioiello m. jewel
giornalàio m. newsagent
giornale m. newspaper
giornaliero adj. daily

giornata f. day

giorno m. day

giostra f. merry-go-round

giòvane adj. young; m. & f. youth

giovare to be useful, to be of use

giovedì m. Thursday

gioventù f. youth; young age

giovinastro m. hooligan

giradischi m. record-player

girare to turn, to go round

giro m. turn, trip, drive, ride

giù down

giudicare to judge

giùdice m. judge

giudiziàrio adj. judicial

giudìzio m. judgment

giugno m. June

giùngere to arrive (Group 10)

giunta f. (local authority government)

giurare to swear

giuria f. jury

giustificare to justify

giustìzia f. justice

giusto adj. just, right

gli m. pl. (before vowel and s + consonant, ps, gn, z) the

gli m. to him; to them (familiar)

gliela her, or it, to him, to her, to you

gliele them, to him, to her, to you

glielo it to him, to her, to you

glieli them to him, to her, to you

gnocchi m. pl. (type of potato noodles)

gòccia f. drop

godere to enjoy

gola f. throat

golf m. jumper, sweater, cardigan; golf

gòmito m. elbow

gomma f. rubber; tyre; chewing-gum

gonfiare to blow up

gònfio adj. swollen

gonna f. skirt

governo m. government

gradire to appreciate, to like (Group 3)

grado m. degree

gràffio m. scratch

grafia f. writing, spelling

grammàtica f. grammar

grammo m. gramme

grana m. Parmesan cheese; (slang) money

grànchio m. crab

grande adj. great, large

grandinare to hail

gràndine f. hail

grandioso adj. grand

grano m. wheat

gràppolo m. bunch

grasso adj. fat

gratis free of charge

grato adj. grateful

grattacielo m. skyscraper

grattare to scratch

gratuito adj. free of charge

grave adj. serious, grave, hard

gravità f. seriousness

gràzia f. grace; Grace

grazie f. pl. thank you

grazioso adj. pretty

gregge m. flock

gridare to shout, to cry

grigio adj. grey

gronda f. or *grondaia* eaves, gutter

grosso adj. big, large

grotta f. cave

gru f. crane

gruppo m. group

guadagno m. earnings

guaio m. difficulty, trouble

guancia f. cheek

guanciale m. pillow

guanto m. glove

guardare to look at, to watch

guardiano m. keeper

guarigione f. recovery

guarire to recover (Group 3)

guastare to spoil, to mar

guasto adj. out of work m. breakdown

guerra f. war

guerriglia f. guerrilla warfare

guerrigliero m. guerrilla

guida m. & f. guide; f. guidebook; guidance, direction; driving; riding

guidare to guide; to drive (vehicles); to ride (motorcycles); to lead

guinzaglio m. leash, lead; *al guinzaglio* on the leash

guscio m. shell

gustare to taste

gusto m. taste

gustoso adj. tasty

hostess f. air-hostess, stewardess

i m. pl. (before consonant) the

idea f. idea

idiota m. & f. idiot; idiotic

idraulico adj. hydraulic; m. plumber

idrofilo, *cottone idrofilo* m. cotton-wool

idrogeno m. hydrogen

ieri yesterday

igiene f. hygiene

ignorare to ignore

ignoto adj. unknown; *Milite Ignoto* m. Unknown Warrior

il m. (before consonant) the

illecito adj. illicit

illeso adj. unharmed

illimitato adj. unlimited

illudere to delude (Group 39)

illuminare to light up, to lighten

illuminazione f. lighting; illumination

illusione f. delusion, illusion

illustrare to illustrate, to expound

illustre adj. distinguished

imballaggio m. packing, packaging

imballare to pack (up)

imbarazzare to embarrass

imbarazzo m. embarrassment

imbarcare to take aboard

imbarcazione f. boat, craft

imbattersi (*in*) to run into

imbiancare to whiten, to bleach, to whitewash, to paint white

imbianchino m. house-painter

imbottito adj. padded, stuffed

imbrogliare to muddle, to cheat

imbròglio m. muddle, cheat

imburrato adj. buttered

imbuto m. funnel

imitare to imitate

immaginare to imagine

immaginàrio adj. imaginary

immàgine f. image; picture

immediato adj. immediate

immenso adj. huge

immèrgere to dip (Group 7)

immigrazione f. immigration

immòbile adj. immovable, stationary

immobiliare adj. estate, property

immondizia f. refuse, garbage

immutàbile adj. unchangeable

impallidire to turn pale (Group 3)

imparare to learn

impaurire to frighten, to scare (Group 3)

impazzire to become insane (Group 3)

impedimento m. obstacle, hindrance

impedire to prevent (+ *di* + inf.) (Group 3)

impegnarsi to undertake, to commit oneself (+ *a*)

impegnativo adj. binding

impegnato adj. engaged, pledged, busy, committed

imperatore m. emperor

imperatrice f. empress

imperfetto adj. imperfect

impero m. empire

impianto m. installation, plant, equipment

impiccare to hang by the neck

impiegare to employ, to use

impiegato adj. used; m. clerk

impiego m. job

implicare to involve

imporre to impose (Group 11)

importanza f. importance

importare to matter, to care; to import

importazione f. import

impossìbile adj. impossible

imposta f. tax, duty

impostare to post

impresa f. enterprise, undertaking

impresàrio m. contractor; impresario

impressionare to impress; to shock

impressione f. impression

imprevedìbile adj. unpredictable

imprevisto adj. unforeseen

imprigionare to imprison, to put in prison

improvviso adj. unexpected; *d'improvviso* suddenly

imprudenza f. imprudence

impulsivo adj. impulsive

in in, into, to, at, inside

inadatto adj. unsuitable

inaugurare to inaugurate, to open

incapace adj. incapable

incapacità f. inability

incaricare to entrust; to appoint

incàrico m. task, job, appointment

incassare to cash

incèndio m. fire, flare-up

incertezza f. uncertainty

incerto adj. uncertain

inchiesta f. investigation, enquiry

inchiostro m. ink

incidente m. accident; incident

incinta f. pregnant

incitare to spur

inclinazione f. slant, tendency

inclùdere to include (Group 39)

incluso adj. inclusive, including

incollare to glue, to paste, to stick

incolore adj. colourless

incommensuràbile adj. immeasurable

incomparàbile adj. matchless

incongruente adj. inconsistent

incontrare to meet

incontrarsi con to meet

incontro m. meeting, encounter; adv. towards

inconveniente m. inconvenience

incòrrere in to incur (Group 7)

incriminare to indict

incrociare to cross

incubo m. nightmare

indàgine f. investigation

indebitarsi to get into debt

indebolire to weaken

indeciso adj. undecided

indegno di adj. unworthy of

indennizzare to indemnify

indennizzo m. indemnity; *domanda d'indennizzo* f. claim for damages

indicare to indicate

indice m. index

indicizzato adj. index-linked

indietro back, behind, backwards

indigesto adj. heavy (food)

indignato adj. indignant, angry

indire to summon, to announce (Group 15)

indirizzare to address

indirizzo m. address

indiscreto adj. indiscreet

indiscutìbile adj. indisputable

indivìduo m. individual, fellow, bloke

indossare to put on, to wear

indossatrice f. model, mannequin

indosso on (clothing)

indovinare to guess

indovinello m. riddle

indurre to induce (Group 16)

indùstria f. industry

industriale adj. industrial; m. industrialist

inesatto adj. inaccurate

infantile adj. childish
infànzia f. childhood
infarto m. coronary
 thrombosis
infatti in fact, as a matter of
 fact
infelice adj. unhappy
infelicità f. unhappiness
infermiera f. female nurse
infermiere m. male nurse
inferno m. hell
infilare to thread; to insert
infine finally, at last, after all;
 eventually
infisso m. fixture, casing
inflazione f. inflation
infliggere to inflict (Group 13)
influenza f. influence;
 influenza
informare to inform
informazione f. piece of
 information
inganno m. deception, deceit
ingegnere m. engineer
ingegneria f. engineering
ingiustìzia f. injustice
ingiusto adj. unfair
inglese adj. English; m. & f.
 Englishman, Englishwoman
ingrandire to enlarge, to blow
 up (Group 3)
ingrato adj. ungrateful
ingresso m. entrance
ingrosso, all'ingrosso
 wholesale
iniziativa f. initiative
inìzio m. beginning
innalzare to raise
innamorato adj. in love

innocente adj. innocent, not
 guilty
inondare to flood
inondazione f. flood
inquilino m. tenant, lodger
inquinamento m. pollution
insalata f. salad; lettuce
insegna f. sign
insegnamento m. teaching
insegnante m. & f. teacher
insegnare to teach
inseguire to pursue
inserire to insert (Group 3)
insieme (a) together (with)
insistente adj. persistent,
 incessant
insìstere to insist (Group 41)
insoddisfatto adj. unsatisfied
 (+ *di*)
insòlito adj. unusual
insomma in short
insònnia f. sleeplessness
insopportàbile adj. intolerable
instàbile adj. unstable
installare to install
installazione f. installation
insuccesso m. failure
insulto m. insult
intanto meanwhile
intelletto m. intellect, brain
interessante adj. interesting
interessare to interest
interessarsi di to be interested
 in
interesse m. interest
interferire to interfere (Group
 3)
intermèdio adj. intermediate

internazionale adj. international

intèrprete m. & f. interpreter

interrogare to interrogate

interròmpere to interrupt (Group 33)

interruttore m. switch

interurbana f. trunk call; long-distance telephone call

intervallo m. interval

intervenire to intervene (Group 6)

intervento m. intervention

intervenuto adj. a person of those present

intervistare to interview

intimare to order

intontito adj. dazed

intorno around

introdurre to introduce

introduzione f. introduction

intuizione f. perception

inùtile adj. useless

invàdere to invade (Group 39)

invano in vain

invece (*di*) instead (of)

invernale adj. wintry

inverno m. winter

investimento m. investment; collision, crash

investire to invest; to collide with

inviare to send

invìdia f. envy

invito m. invitation

ipoteca f. mortgage

ipòtesi f. hypothesis

ira f. anger, fury

irreale adj. unreal

irregolare adj. irregular

irrigare to irrigate

irritare to irritate

iscritto m. subscriber; member; enrolled

ìsola f. island

isolamento m. isolation

isolato adj. isolated; m. block

ispettore m. inspector

ispezione f. inspection

ispirare to inspire

istante m. instant, second

istituire to set up (Group 3)

istituto m. institute

istruire to instruct (Group 3)

istruito adj. educated

istruzione f. instruction, education

IVA f. VAT

la f., pl. *le*, the

là there

labbro m., pl. *labbra* f. lip

laboratòrio m. laboratory

laburista m. & f. labour

làccio m. string

làcrima f. tear

lacrimoso adj. tearful, tear-jerking

ladro m. thief

laggiù down there, over there

lago m. lake

làico adj. secular, lay

lama f. blade

lamentarsi (*di*) to complain (about)

lamentela f. complaint

lamento m. moan
lamiera f. plate, sheet
lămpada f. light, lamp
lampadărio m. chandelier
lampadina f. electric bulb
lampeggiare to flash
lampione m. lamp-post
lampo m. flash of lightning
lampone m. raspberry
lana f. wool
lancetta f. watch, clock hand
lanciare to throw, to hurl
lanterna f. lantern
lardo m. lard, bacon fat
larghezza f. breadth, width
largo adj. broad, wide
lărice m. larch
lasciare to let, to leave
lassù up there
latifondo m. large estate
lato m. side
latta f. tin
lattăio m. milkman
latte m. milk
latteria f. milk-shop
latticini m. pl. milk-products
lattuga f. lettuce
lăurea f. university degree
laureato adj. university
   graduate
lavare to wash
lavastovĭglie f. dish-washer
lavello m. wash-basin
lavorare to work
lavoratore m. worker
lavoratrice f. female worker
lavoro m. work; job
Lăzio m. Latium
leale adj. loyal, fair (+ *con*)

legare to tie up
legge f. law
leggenda f. legend
lĕggere to read (Group 13)
leggero adj. light
legno m. wood;
   di legno wooden
lei she; *Lei* you (formal); her
lente f. lens
lento adj. slow
lenzuolo m., pl. *lenzuola* f.
   bed-sheet
leone m. lion
lepre f. hare
lesso adj. boiled;
   manzo lesso boiled beef
lĕttera f. letter
letterale adj. literal
letterărio adj. literary
letteratura f. literature
letto m. bed
lettura f. reading
leva f. conscription, draft
lezione f. lesson
li m. pl. them
lì there
libbra f. pound (weight)
liberare to free, to liberate
liberarsi (*di*) to get rid of
liberazione f. liberation
lĭbero adj. free
libreria f. bookshop
libretto m. booklet; libretto
libro m. book
licenza f. licence
liceo m. (classical secondary
   school)
lido m. shore, beach
lieto adj. glad, happy

lima f. file

limitarsi a to confine oneself to

limite m. limit

limonata f. lemonade; lemon drink

limone m. lemon

limpido adj. crystal-clear

linea f. line; tenth of degree centigrade

lineetta f. dash; hyphen

lingua f. tongue; language

linguaggio m. language, speech

linguista m. & f. linguist

liquidare to eliminate, to wipe out

liquido adj. liquid

liquore m. liqueur

lira f. Italian lira (currency)

lirico adj. lyrical; operatic

liscio adj. smooth

lista f. list

listino m. shop list, tariff

lite f. or *litigio* m. quarrel

litigare to quarrel

litro m. litre

livello m. level;
    passaggio a livello m. level crossing

lo m. (before nouns starting with s + consonant, z, gn, ps) the; him, it

locale adj. local; m. room

locatario m. tenant

locazione f. lease, tenancy

locomotiva f. or *locomotore* m. locomotive

lodare to praise

lode f. praise

logica f. logic

logico adj. logical, consistent

Lombardia f. Lombardy

lombardo adj. Lombard

logoro adj. worn

londinese adj. from London

Londra f. London

lontano adj. far away

loro adj. their, theirs; *Loro*, your, yours (formal)

loro m. & f. they; them, to them

lotta f. struggle

lottare to struggle

lozione f. lotion

luccicare to glitter

lucente adj. shining

lucidare to polish

lucido adj. polished, shiny; m. shoe polish

lui m. he; him

luminoso adj. bright

luna f. moon

luna-park m. fun-fair, amusement park

lunatico adj. moody

lunedì m. Monday

lunghezza f. length

lungo adj. long; along

lungomare m. seaside, shore

luogo m. place

lupo m. wolf

lupara f. sawn-off shotgun

luppolo m. hops

lusingare to flatter

lusso m. luxury

lussuoso adj. luxurious

lussuria f. lechery, lust

lutto m. mourning

ma but
macabro adj. macabre
màcchia f. strain, smear;
  scrub, bush
màcchina f. machine; motor-
  car;
  màcchina del caffè coffee
  percolator;
  màcchina da scrìvere
  typewriter
macchinetta f. slot machine
macchinista m. & f. engine-
  driver
macellàio m. butcher
macèrie f. pl. rubble, ruins
macigno m. rock, stone
macinare to grind
Madonna f. Our Lady
madre f. mother
maestà f. majesty
maestro m. school-master;
  maestro
magari perhaps; would to
  God; I wish
magazzino m. warehouse;
  grande magazzino
  department store
màggio m. May
maggioranza f. majority
maggiore adj. greater; elder,
  eldest; m. major
maggiorenne adj. of age
magistrato m. magistrate
magistratura f. magistracy;
  term of office
magnìfico adj. magnificent
magro adj. thin, slim

mai never, ever
maiale m. pig; pork
maiùscola f. capital letter
malato adj. sick, ill
malattia f. illness
malavita f. gangsterism,
  underworld
malcontento adj. unsatisfied
male m. evil, ill, wrong,
  harm; badly;
  fare male to hurt
maledetto adj. cursed
maledire to curse (Group 15)
maledizione f. curse; damn it!
maleducato adj. rude,
  impolite
malgrado in spite of
malinteso m.
  misunderstanding
maltrattare to abuse, to ill-
  treat
mamma f. mummy, mother
mancanza f. lack, want,
  shortage, absence
mancare to be lacking, to be
  needed; to be absent
mància f. tip
mancino adj. left-handed
mandare to send
mandato m. term of office
màndorla f. almond
maneggiare to handle
mangiare to eat
mànica f. sleeve; the Channel
mànico m. handle
maniera f. manner, way
manifestare to manifest
manifestazione f. celebration;
  demonstration

manifesto m. poster, bill, notice

mano f. hand

manomèttere to tamper with (Group 35)

manoscritto m. manuscript

manovra f. manoeuvre

mantenere to keep (Group 6)

manuale adj. manual; m. handbook

manutenzione f. maintenance, upkeep

marca f. mark, brand; stamp

marciapiede m. pavement

marciare to march

marcire to rot (Group 3)

mare m. sea, seaside

margarina f. margarine

margherita f. daisy

màrgine m. margin

marionetta f. puppet

marito m. husband

marmellata f. jam, marmalade

marmo m. marble

marrone brown

martello m. hammer

maschile adj. masculine

màschio m. male

massa f. mass

massìccio adj. massive

màssimo adj. greatest;
al *màssimo* at the most, at the latest

masticare to chew

màstice m. putty; adhesive

matemàtica f. mathematics

materasso m. mattress

matèria f. matter, subject, topic

maternità f. maternity; motherhood

matita f. pencil

matrigna f. step-mother

matrimònio m. marriage

mattina f. or *mattino* m. morning

maturare to mature, to ripen

maturità f. maturity; final secondary school diploma

mazzo m. bunch

me me, myself

meccànica f. mechanics

meccànico adj. mechanical; m. mechanic, garage

mèdia f. average, mean;
in *mèdia* on an average

mediante through, by means of

mèdico m. doctor, physician; adj. medical

mèdio adj. average

medioevo m. Middle Ages

mediterràneo Mediterranean

mèglio better

mela f. apple

membro m. member; limb

memòria f. memory; recollection; memoir

meno less; fewer; minus

mensa f. canteen; mess

mensile adj. monthly

mente f. mind

mentre while

meravigliarsi to wonder

mercato m. market

mercoledì m. Wednesday

meridionale adj. southern; m. southern Italian

meridione m. South Italy

meritare to deserve

mescolare to mix

mese m. month

messa f. Mass;
   messa in piega f. hairset

mestiere m. trade, job;
   fare un mestiere to have a job

metà f. half

metallo m. metal

metodo m. method

metro m. metre

metronotte m. night-watchman

metròpoli f. metropolis

metropolitana f. underground railway

mettere to put, to set, to lay, to arrange (Group 35)

mettersi to set to, to start; to put on

mezzanotte f. midnight

mezzo adj. half

mezzogiorno m. noon; southern Italy

mi me, to me, myself, to myself; E (music)

mica in the least

micio m. or *micino* m. kitten, pussy-cat

microcosmo m. microcosm

micròfono m. microphone

miele m. honey

migliàio m., pl. *migliàia* f. one thousand; about a thousand

miglio m., pl. *miglia* f. mile

migliorare to improve

migliore adj. better

miliardàrio m. multi-millionaire

miliardo m. a thousand million

milionario m. millionaire

milione m. million

militare adj. military; m. military; v. to serve in

minestra f. soup

minestrone m. thick vegetable soup

minimo adj. least, smallest

ministero m. ministry

ministro m. minister, secretary of state

minore adj. lesser, smaller, minor

minorenne m. & f. under age

minùscolo adj. tiny;
   lèttera minùscola f. small letter

minuto m. minute

mio adj. my, mine

miscela f. mixture, mix

misèria f. extreme poverty, misery

misericòrdia f. mercy

mìstico adj. mystical

mistura f. mixture

misura f. measure, measurement; size

mòbile adj. movable; moving; fickle; m. piece of furniture

moda f. fashion;
   alla moda fashionable

modella f. model

modello m. model, pattern; mould

moderatore m. moderator; chairman of a meeting

modificare to modify

modo m. way, manner, mode

mòdulo m. form; module

mòglie f. wife

molla f. spring

moltiplicare to multiply

moltiplicazione f. multiplication

molto adj. much, a lot, very

momento m. moment, instant, time

Mònaco f. Monaco; Munich

monaco m. monk

mondiale adj. world-wide

mondo m. world

monello m. mischievous boy, naughty boy

moneta f. coin; currency

monetàrio adj. monetary

monopòlio m. monopoly

monòtono adj. monotonous

montàggio m. assembly; fitting up; (cinema) splicing

montagna f. mountain; *in montagna* in, to the mountains

montagnoso adj. mountainous

montare to assemble

monte m. mountain, mount

morale adj. moral; f. morals, morality

mòrbido adj. soft, tender, mellow

morboso adj. morbid

mòrdere to bite (Group 7)

morire to die (Group 20)

mormorare to mutter

moro m. moor; *testa di moro* 'cap of mast' (colour)

morte f. death

mortificare to humble

morto adj. dead; m. dead person

mosca f. fly

moscato adj. muscat (wine, grapes)

mostrare to show, to prove, to demonstrate

motivo m. motive, reason, motif

moto m. motion

motocicletta or *moto* f. motorcycle

motociclista m. & f. motorcycle-rider

motore m. engine

movimento m. movement, motion

mozzicone m. stub, butt, stump

mùcchio m. heap; *un mùcchio* a lot

mulino m. mill

multa f. fine, penalty

mùngere to milk (Group 10)

municìpio m. town-hall

muòvere to move (Group 40)

muòversi to hurry, to stir

muro m. wall; pl. *mura* f. town-walls

mùscolo m. muscle

museo m. museum

mùsica f. music

musicista m. & f. musician

mutande f. pl. underpants, knickers

muto adj. dumb, mute

mutualistico adj. health insurance

mŭtuo adj. mutual, reciprocal; m. loan; mortgage loan;
fare un mŭtuo to borrow from a bank

nafta f. naphtha, diesel oil

nanna (child language) sleep;
fare la nanna to sleep

nasale adj. nasal

nǎscere to be born (Group 4)

nǎscita f. birth

nascŏndere to hide, to conceal (Group 39)

naso m. nose;
prĕndere per il naso to pull one's leg

nastro m. ribbon

natale adj. birth; m. Christmas;
Buon Natale Happy Christmas

natalità f. birth-rate

natalĭzio adj. Christmas

nato adj. born

natura f. nature

nǎusea f. nausea, sickness;
sentire nǎusea to feel sick

navale adj. naval

navata f. nave, aisle

nave f. ship

navigare to sail

nazione f. nation

nazista m. & f. Nazi

ne from there, from here; of it, of him, of her; some, any; (poetic) us, to us

nè neither, nor; *nè . . . nè* neither . . . nor

neanche not even; nor

nĕbbia f. fog;
ĕsserci nĕbbia to be foggy

necessità f. necessity, need

negare to deny

negoziante m. shop-keeper, dealer

negoziare to negotiate

negŏzio m. shop

negra f. black woman

negro m. black man

nemico m. enemy

nero adj. black

nervo m. nerve

nervoso adj. nervous;
esaurimento nervoso m. nervous breakdown

nessuno adj. no; m. no one, nobody, none

Nettezza Urbana f. Street Cleaning Dept

nĕutro adj. neutral

neve f. snow

nevĭschio m. sleet

nevoso adj. snowy

nido m. nest;
nido d'infănzia crèche

niente nothing

nipote m. nephew; grandson; f. niece; granddaughter

no no

nobĭle adj. noble

nocciola f. hazelnut

noce f. walnut

nocivo adj. harmful

nodo m. knot

noi we, us

nòia f. boredom, tediousness

noioso adj. boring

noleggiare to hire, to charter

nolèggio m. hire;
  a nolèggio for hire

nome m. name

nòmina f. appointment,
  nomination

nominare to name, to appoint

nonna f. grandmother

nonno m. grandfather

nonnina f. grandma, granny

nonnino m. grandpa,
  granddad

nord m. north

nòrdico adj. northern
  European, Nordic

normanno adj. Norman;
  le Ìsole Normanne the
  Channel Islands

nostalgia f. nostalgia;
  avere nostalgia to be
  homesick

nostro adj. our, ours

nota f. note

notàio m. notary public

notare to note, to notice

notìzia f. piece of news

notiziàrio m. news bulletin

noto adj. well-known

notte or *nottata* f. night

novantina f. about ninety

novella f. tale, short story

novembre m. November

novità novelty

nozze f. pl. wedding;
  viàggio di nozze
  honeymoon

nùbile adj. unmarried
  (woman)

nudità f. nakedness; nudity

nudo adj. naked; nude

nulla m. nothing

nulla osta m. authorization,
  permit

nullo adj. null and void

numerare to number

numerazione f. numbering,
  numbers, numeration

nùmero m. number

nuòcere to be bad for, to
  harm (Group 4)

nuotare to swim

nuotata f. swim

nuotatore m. swimmer

nuotatrice f. female swimmer

nuoto m. swimming

nuovo adj. new

nutrire to nourish

nùvola f. cloud

nuvoloso adj. cloudy

oh or *o* oh

o, or *od* (before vowel), or

obbedire to obey (Group 3)

obbligare to force

òbbligo m. obligation

obiettivo m. objective

obiezione f. objection

oca f. goose

occasione f. opportunity,
  occasion

occhiali m. pl. glasses

occhiata f. glance;
  dare un'occhiata to take a
  glance at
òcchio m. eye
occidentale adj. western
occidente m. west
occòrrere to need (Group 7)
occupare to occupy
occupato adj. busy, engaged,
  taken, occupied
occupazione f. occupation
oculista m. & f. oculist
odiare to hate
òdio m. hate
odorare to smell
odore m. smell
offendersi to take offence
  (Group 39)
offerta f. offer
offesa f. offence
offeso adj. offended
officina f. workshop;
  officina meccanica garage
offrire to offer (Group 20)
oggetto m. object
oggi today
ogni each, every
ognuno m. everyone
oleodotto m. oil-pipeline
oleoso adj. oil, greasy
òlio m. oil
oliva f. olive
olivo m. olive-tree
olmo m. elm
oltre beyond, over and above,
  besides
oltremare m. overseas
omàggio m. homage
ombra f. shadow, shade

ombrello m. umbrella
ombroso adj. shadowy, shady
omèttere to omit (Group 35)
òncia f. ounce
onda f. or *ondata* f. wave
ondulato adj. wavy;
  corrugated
onestà f. honesty
onorare to honour
onorèvole adj. honourable
  (deputies)
òpera f. work; opera; action;
  òpera lìrica opera;
  òpera d'arte work of art
operàia f. worker (female)
operàio m. worker (male)
operare to operate
opporre, opporsi a to oppose
  (Group 11)
opportuno adj. opportune
oppositore m. adversary,
  opponent
opposto adj. opposed;
  opposite
opprimente adj. oppressive
opprìmere to oppress (Group
  34)
opùscolo m. booklet,
  pamphlet
ora f. hour, time; now;
  non vedere l'ora di to look
  forward to
oràrio m. schedule, timetable
orchestra f. orchestra
orchestrale m. & f. musician
ordinamento m. organization
ordinare to order
ordinàrio adj. ordinary

ordinato adj. tidy, neat;
   orderly
ordinazione f. (commerce)
   order
orecchio m., pl. *orecchie* f.,
   ear
orecchioni m. pl. mumps
orefice m. goldsmith, jeweller
orfano m. orphan
organo m. organ
organizzare to organize
organismo m. organism, body
orgoglio m. pride
orgoglioso adj. proud
orientale adj. eastern
orientarsi to see one's way
oriente m. east
originario adj. native, original
origine f. origin
orina f. urine
orinare to urinate
orizzontale adj. horizontal
orizzonte m. horizon
orlo m. rim
ormai by now
ornare to adorn
oro m. gold
orologiaio m. watchmaker
orologio m. watch; clock
orpello m. tinsel
orribile adj. horrible
orso m. bear
ortaggi m. pl. vegetables
orto m. kitchen-garden, back
   garden
ortografia f. correct spelling
orzo m. barley
osare to dare
osceno adj. obscene

oscillare to swing
oscurarsi to get dark; to
   cloud over
oscuro adj. dark
ospedale m. hospital
ospitale adj. hospitable
ospite m. guest, host
osservazione f. observation,
   remark
osso m., pl. *ossa* f. bone
ostacolare to obstruct
ostacolo m. obstacle
ostaggio m. hostage
oste m. publican, inn-keeper
ostello m. hostel
ostessa f. female inn-keeper
ostile adj. hostile
ostinato adj. stubborn
ostinazione f. doggedness
ostruire to obstruct (Group 3)
ottantenne m. & f. eighty-
   year-old person
ottantina f. about eighty
ottenere to obtain (Group 6)
ottico adj. optic; m. optician
ottimo adj. excellent, very
   good
ottobre m. October
otturare to fill a cavity
ovest m. west
ovunque everywhere
ovvio adj. obvious
ozio m. idleness, sloth

pacchetto m. packet
pacco m. parcel, package
pace f. peace
padella f. frying-pan

padre m. father

padrino m. godfather

padrone m. master, boss, owner

paesaggio m. landscape

paese m. village; country

paga f. pay

pagamento m. payment

pagare to pay

pagina f. page

paio m. pl. *paia* f. pair

palazzo m. palace; block of flats

palco m. theatre-box

palestra f. gymnasium

palla f. ball

pallido adj. pale

pallone m. football, ball

panca f. or *panchina* f. bench

pancia f. belly

pane m. bread

panificio m. bakery

panino m. small loaf; *panino imbottito* stuffed bread

panna f. cream

panorama m. panorama

pantaloni m. pl. trousers

pantofola f. slipper

papa m. pope

papà m. daddy

paradiso m. paradise, heaven

paradosso m. paradox

parafulmine m. lightning conductor

paragonare to compare

paragone m. comparison; *in paragone con* in comparison with

parcheggiare to park

parcheggio m. car-park; parking

parchimetro m. parking meter

parco m. park

parecchio adj. a lot

parente m. relative, kinsman

parere to seem (Group 20)

parete f. wall

pari adj. even (number); equal

parlamento m. parliament

parlare to speak

parola f. word

parolaccia f. swearword

parte f. part

partecipare to take part in (+ *a*)

partenza f. departure

particolare adj. particular; m. detail

partire to leave

partita f. lot, parcel, consignment

partito m. party (political)

parto m. childbirth

pascolare to tend sheep

Pasqua f. Easter

passaggio m. passage, crossing

passaporto m. passport

passare to pass; to spend; to call at

passatempo m. pastime

passato adj. past; m. past

passeggero m. passenger

passeggiare to walk, to take a walk

passeggiata f. walk, stroll

pàssero m. sparrow

passivo adj. passive; liabilities

passo m. step

pasta f. pasta; (fancy) cake

pasticceria f. confectionery

pasto m. meal

patata f. potato

patente f. driving-licence

patètico adj. touching;
  sentimental; pathetic

pàtria f. native country

patriòttico adj. patriotic

patrono m. patron

pattùglia f. patrol

paura f. fear;
  avere paura to be afraid

pavimento m. floor, flooring

paziente adj. patient

pazzo adj. crazy; mad

peccato m. sin; pity, shame

pècora f. sheep

pedaggio m. toll

pèggio worse

peggiore adj. worse

pelare to skin, to peel

pelle f. skin, hide, leather;
  lasciarci la pelle to die

pellìccia f. fur

pelo m. hair

pena f., *valere la pena* to be
  worthwhile

pendenza f. slope, slant

pèndere to hang down

pèndolo m. pendulum

penna f. pen; feather; plume

pennello m. brush; paint-
  brush

pensare (+ *a* + noun, + *di* or
  che + verb) to think

pensiero m. thought

pensieroso adj. thoughtful

pensione f. board and
  lodging; boarding-house;
  retirement; pension

pentirsi to repent

pèntola f. pot

penùltimo adj. last but one

pepe m. pepper

peperone m. pepper; chilli

per for; through; across; in
  order to; by, within (time)

percentuale f. per cent

perchè why, because, as,
  since

perciò therefore,
  consequently

percòrrere to run along; to
  scour (Group 7)

percorso m. route, way

pèrdere to lose (Group 7)

pèrdita f. loss; waste

perdono m. forgiveness;
  pardon

perfetto adj. perfect

perfino or *persino* even

perìcolo m. danger

pericoloso adj. dangerous

periferia f. outskirts; suburbs

periòdico adj. periodical

perìodo m. period

perito m. expert; engineer

perla f. pearl

permanente f. perm (hair)

permesso m. permission

permèttere to permit, to allow
  (Group 35)

perno m. pivot; pin; gudgeon;
  stud; journal

pernottare to stay overnight
però but, however
perquisire to search (Group 3)
perseguitare to persecute
persiana f. blind, window-shutter
persona f. person
personàggio m. personage; character
persuadere to persuade (Group 39)
pervàdere to pervade (Group 39)
pesante adj. heavy
pesare to weigh
pesca f. peach; fishing
pesce f. fish
peso m. weight
pèssimo adj. very bad, wretched
petroliera f. oil-tanker
pettinarsi to comb one's hair
pèttine m. comb
petto m. chest, breast; bosom
pezzo m. piece, bit
piacere to like, to please (Group 4); m. pleasure;
  fare piacere to please
  fare un piacere to do a favour
piaga f. wound
piàngere to cry, to weep (Group 10)
pianista m. & f. pianist
piano adj. flat; m. piano; floor, storey
pianoro m. plateau
pianta f. plant; tree

pianterreno m. ground floor
piattaforma f. platform
piatto adj. flat; m. plate, dish
piazza f. or *piazzale* m. square
piccante adj. spicy, hot; saucy
picchiare to beat, to hit, to thrash
piccino adj. tiny
piccolo adj. little, small; short
piede m. foot;
  in piedi on foot, standing; walking
piegare to fold up
Piemonte m. Piedmont
pieno adj. full, filled (+ *di*)
pietà f. pity, compassion
pietra f. stone
pinza f. pliers; pincers
piòggia f. rain
piombo m. lead
piòvere to rain (Group 22)
piovigginoso adj. drizzly
piovoso adj. rainy
pipa f. pipe
pisello m. pea
pistàcchio m. pistachio
pistola f. pistol, gun
pittore m. painter
pittura f. painting
più more
piuma f. feather, down, plume
piuttosto rather; fairly; sooner
pizza f. pizza
pizzeria f. pizzeria
pizzicare to pinch
plàstica f. plastics
platea f. stalls (theatre)

pneumàtico adj. pneumatic;
  m. tyre
poco adj. little, a little
poema m. long descriptive
  poem
poesia f. poetry; poem
poeta m. poet
poetessa f. poetess
poètico adj. poetical
poggiare to lie on
poi then, afterwards
poichè because, since, as
politica f. politics
politico adj. political; m.
  politician
polizia f. police
pòlizza f. policy
pollo m. chicken
polmone m. lung
polso m. wrist
poltrona f. arm-chair
poltroncina f. stalls seat
pòlvere f. dust
pomeriggio m. afternoon
pomodoro m. tomato
pompa f. pump; pomp;
  pompa magna pomp and
  circumstance
ponente m. west
ponte m. bridge; chain of
  days off work
pontèfice m. pontiff, pope
pontificio adj. pontifical
popolare adj. popular; of the
  people;
  casa popolare f. council
  house
popolazione f. population
pòpolo m. people, folk,

nation
porcheria f. filth, indecency;
  indecent thing; trash,
  rubbish
pòrgere to hand, to pass
  (Group 10)
porre to place, to put (Group
  11)
porta f. door
portacènere m. ash-tray
portafòglio m. wallet
portalèttere m. postman
portare to bring, to carry, to
  take, to fetch, to wear, to
  bring about
portata f. course of a meal;
  tonnage
portavalori m. money van
  attendant
portiera f. car-door; female
  doorkeeper
portiere m. doorkeeper,
  concierge; goalkeeper
porto m. harbour, port
portone m. gate
porzione f. portion; helping
posare to lay down
posata f. knife or fork or
  spoon cover; pl. cutlery
positivo adj. positive,
  practical
possedere to possess (Group
  27)
possibilità f. possibility
posta f. post; mail
posteriore adj. back
posto m. place; job; seat;
  a posto in order
potente adj. powerful

potere to be able, to know how, to be possible (Group 29)

pòvero adj. poor

pranzare to have lunch, dinner

pranzo m. dinner, lunch, mid-day meal

pràtica f. practice

prato m. meadow, lawn

preavviso m. advance notice

precedente adj. preceding

preciso adj. precise

prèdica f. sermon; lecture

preferire to prefer (Group 3)

prefettura f. office of provincial representative of the government

prefisso m. telephone area code number

pregare to pray

pregiato adj. valued

pregiudìzio m. prejudice, bias

prego please; pardon?

prèmere to press, to squeeze

premessa f. premise

premèttere to premise (Group 35)

prèmio m. prize

prèndere to take, to catch (Group 39)

prèndersela to worry; to complain

prenotare to reserve, to book

prenotazione f. reservation, booking

preoccupare to preoccupy, to worry;

preoccuparsi to worry

preoccupazione f. worry

preparare to prepare

presentare to present, to introduce

presentazione f. presentation, introduction

presenziare to be present, to participate

prèside m. headmaster

presidente m. president; chairman; premier

pressione f. pressure

presso near, by, close to; with

prestare to lend

prèstito m. loan

presùmere to presume (Group 10)

prete m. priest

pretèndere to claim, to pretend (Group 39)

pretesto m. pretext

prevalere to prevail (Group 7)

prevedere to foresee (Group 32)

prevenire to prevent (Group 6)

previsione f. forecast

prezioso adj. precious

prezzo m. price

prigione f. prison

prima before; earlier; f. première, first night

primavera f. spring

primo adj. first

prìncipe m. prince

principessa f. princess

princìpio m. beginning; principle

privare to deprive

privato adj. private

privilègio m. privilege

privo di adj. deprived of

probàbile adj. probable

problema m. problem

procedimento m. or
  procedura f. procedure

processare to try in court

processo m. trial in court

proclive adj. inclined

prodotto m. product; produce

produrre to produce (Group
  16)

produttore m. producer

professore m. teacher;
  professor

professoressa f. lady teacher,
  professor

profitto m. profit

profondo adj. profound; deep

profumato adj. sweet-smelling

profumo m. perfume, scent,
  sweet smell

progettare to plan

progetto m. plan, project

programma m. programme

progresso m. progress

proibire to forbid (Group 3)

promessa f. promise

promèttere to promise (Group
  35)

promuòvere to promote
  (Group 40)

pronto adj. ready; hello (on
  the telephone)

pronùncia f. pronunciation

proporre to propose (Group
  11)

proposta f. proposal

proprietà f. property

proprietàrio m. owner

pròprio adj. own; just,
  exactly

prorogare to postpone

prosa f. prose

prosciutto m. ham

pròssimo adj. next, following

protagonista m. & f.
  protagonist; main character

protèggere to protect (Group
  13)

protesta f. protest

prova f. trial, experiment

provare to try, to taste, to try
  on

provenire to come from
  (Group 6)

provèrbio m. proverb

provìncia f. province

provocare to provoke

provvedere to provide, to
  supply (Group 32)

provvedimento m. provision

provveditore agli studi m.
  provincial superintendent
  of education

provvigione f. commission

provvisòrio adj. provisional

prugna f. plum

prurito m. itching, itch

pseudònimo m. pen-name

psicòlogo m. psychologist

psichiatra m. & f. psychiatrist

pubblicare to publish

pubblicità f. advertising;
  publicity; advertisement

pùbblico adj. & m. public

Pùglia f. Apulia

pulire to clean (Group 3)

pulire a secco to dry-clean
pulito adj. clean
pulitura f. cleaning; *pulitura a secco* f. dry-cleaning
pulizia f. cleaning
pŭngere to sting (Group 10)
punire to punish (Group 3)
punto m. point; spot, place
punteria f. tappet
puntina da disegno f. drawing-pin
puntino m. dot, spot
punto m. point; full stop;
puntuale adj. punctual
purchè provided that, on condition that, as long as
pure too, also
purè m. potato mash
purgante m. purgative
purgatòrio m. purgatory
puro adj. pure
purtroppo unfortunately
puzza f. stench, stink

qua here
quaderno m. exercise book; copy book
quadrato adj. square
quadro m. painting, picture
quàdruplo m. quadruple
qualche adj. sing. some, a few
qualcosa something
qualcuno m. somebody, someone, some of
qualìfica f. capacity, qualification, title
qualità f. quality
qualora in case

qualsìasi or *qualŭnque* any, whatever
quando when
quantità f. quantity
quanto adj. how much; as regards
quarantina f. about forty
quartiere m. town quarter, district
quarto m. fourth; quarter
quasi almost, nearly
quattordicenne a fourteen-year-old person
quello adj. that
quĕrcia f. oak
querela f. lawsuit
querelare to sue at law
questionàrio m. questionnaire
questione f. issue, matter
questo adj. this
questura f. police headquarters
qui here
quiete f. quietness
quieto adj. quiet
quindi therefore,
quindicina f. about fifteen
quinquennale five-yearly
quintale m. a hundred kilos
quotidiano adj. daily; m. daily newspaper

ràbbia f. anger; rabies
rabbuiarsi to become dark
raccŏgliere to pick up (Group 8)
raccolta f. picking, harvesting
raccolto adj. collected; m. crop

raccomandare to recommend

raccontare to tell, to give an account

racconto m. story

raddoppiare to double

rădersi to shave (Group 39)

radiatore m. radiator

radice f. root

radio f. radio

radiografia f. x-ray

răffica f. gust of wind; volley

raffinato adj. refined

raffineria f. refinery

rafforzare to strengthen

raffreddamento m. cooling system

raffreddarsi to cool; to catch a cold

raffreddato adj. having a cold

raffreddore m. cold

ragazza f. girl

ragazzo m. boy

răggio m. ray

raggiŭngere to reach (Group 10)

raggruppare to group

ragionamento m. reasoning

ragione f. reason

ragionĕvole adj. reasonable

ragioniere m. accountant

RAI–TV f. radio & TV corporation

rallentare to slow down

rame m. copper

ramo m. branch, bough

rana f. frog

rancore m. grudge

rannuvolarsi to become overcast

rapa f. turnip

rapidità f. swiftness

răpido adj. rapid

rapina f. robbery, plunder

rapinare to rob

rapinatore m. robber

rapire to abduct (Group 3)

rapitore m. kidnapper

rapporto m. report; ratio; rapport

rappresentante m. & f. representative, agent

rappresentanza f. representation

rappresentare to represent

rappresentazione f. performance; representation

raramente seldom

raro adj. rare, unusual

rasato adj. clipped, mown, trimmed; shaven

rasatura f. trimming, clipping, mowing, shave

rasentare to skim along

rasŏio m. razor

rassegna f. review, muster

rassegnato adj. resigned

rasserenarsi to clear up

rassicurare to reassure

rassomiglianza f. resemblance

rassomigliare (a) to resemble, to look like

rastrellamento m. raking; mopping up

rastrelliera f. rack

rastrello m. rake

rata f. instalment

rateale adj. by instalments

răuco adj. hoarse

razionale adj. rational

razza f. race

razzo m. rocket

re m. king

reagire to react (Group 3)

reale adj. royal; regal; real; actual

realizzare to fulfil, to carry out

realtà f. reality

reato m. offence

reazione f. reaction

recipiente m. container

recitare to recite

reclamare to claim; to protest, to complain

reclamo m. claim, complaint

redattore m. editor

reddito m. income

redigere to draw up (Group 34)

referenza f. testimonial; reference

regalare to give a present

regalo m. present, gift

reggere to hold upright, to support (Group 13)

reggiseno m. bra

regia f. cinema direction

regina f. queen

regione f. region; district

regista m. & f. film director

registrare to record; to adjust

registratore m. tape-recorder

registrazione f. record, recording

registro m. register

regnare to reign

regno m. reign, kingdom

regola f. rule, regulation

regolamento m. regulation; settlement

regolare adj. regular; to adjust, to set

relativo adj. relative, relevant

relazione f. report; relation

remo m. oar

remoto adj. distant, remote

rendere to give back (Group 39)

rendersi conto to realize

rendiconto m. statement of account

reparto m. department (store), ward

reprimere to suppress (Group 40)

repubblica f. republic

requisito m. requirement

resa f. surrender; yield

residente m. & f. resident

residenza f. residence

resistenza f. resistance

resistere to resist (Group 41)

resoconto m. account of facts; report

respingere to repel, to drive back (Group 10)

respirare to breathe

respiro m. breathing, breath

responsabile adj. responsible; m & f. head

responsabilità f. responsibility

ressa f. rush, crush

restare to remain, to stay; *restare al telefono* to hold on, to hold the line

restaurare to restore

restituire to give back (Group 3)

resto m. remainder, rest; change, balance

restrìngere to tighten, to narrow (Group 10)

retàggio m. heritage

rete f. net

retribuzione f. recompense, salary, pay

retro m. behind

retromàrcia f. reverse gear

rettore m. chancellor, president of a university

revisione f. overhaul; review

rèvoca f. repeal

rialzo m. rise, increase

ribassare to lower, to reduce

ribasso m. rebate

ribelle m. & f. rebel

ricaduta f. relapse

ricalcare to transfer, to trace

ricambiare to reciprocate

ricamo m. embroidery

ricavo m. proceeds

ricchezza f. riches, wealth

ricco adj. rich

ricerca f. research; search

ricercato adj. sought after; much in demand; wanted by the police

ricetta f. recipe; prescription

ricèvere to receive

ricevimento m. reception

ricevitore m. telephone receiver

ricevuta f. receipt

richièdere to request (Group 11)

richiesta f. request

ricompensa f. reward

riconòscere to recognize (Group 14)

riconoscimento m. recognition

ricordare to remember; to remind

ricordarsi to remember

ricordo m. memory, remembrance

ricorso m. petition, claim, appeal

ricotta f. curd cheese

ricoverare to shelter; to admit to hospital

ricòvero m. shelter; admission to hospital; old people's house

ricuperare to retrieve; to reclaim

rìdere to laugh (Group 39)

ridìcolo adj. ridiculous; m. ridicule

ridotto adj. reduced

ridurre to reduce (Group 16)

riduzione f. reduction

riempire to fill up

riferimento m. reference

riferire to report (Group 3)

rifiutare to refuse

rifiuto m. refusal

riflessivo adj. thoughtful

riflèttere to reflect

riformare to reform

rifornimento m. filling up; supply

rifornire to supply, to provide (Group 3)

rifùgio m. refuge

riga f. line

riguardo m. regard, consideration

rilasciare to release

rilassarsi to relax

rilegare to bind (a book)

rilevamento m. survey

rilievo m. relief

rima f. rhyme

rimanere to remain (Group 6)

rimborsare to reimburse

rimborso m. repayment

rimediare to remedy, to make up for

rimèdio m. remedy

rimessa f. remittance

rimèttersi to recover one's health (Group 35)

rimòrchio m. tow, trailer

rimorso m. remorse

rimpasto m. reshuffle; rekneading

rimpianto m. regret

rimproverare to rebuke

rinascimentale adj. of the Renaissance

Rinascimento m. Renaissance

rinato adj. reborn

rinchiùdere to lock up (Group 39)

rincrèscersi to be sorry, to regret

rincrescimento m. regret

rinforzare to strengthen

rinfrescare to refresh

ringraziamento m. thanks

ringraziare to thank

rinnovare to renew

rinnovo m. renewal

rinùncia f. waiver, renunciation

rinviare to put off

riparare to repair, to mend

riparazione f. repair

riparo m. shelter

ripartire to leave

ripètere to repeat

rìpido adj. steep

riposare to rest

riposo m. rest

riprodurre to reproduce (Group 16)

risalita f. ascent; *impianto di risalita* m. ski lifts and cableways

risarcire to indemnify (Group 3)

riscaldamento m. heating

riscaldare to heat

riscattare to ransom, to redeem

riscatto m. ransom, redemption

rischiararsi to become clear

rischiare to risk

rìschio m. risk

risciacquare to rinse

riscuòtere to cash (Group 34)

riserva f. reserve, stock

riservare to reserve

riservato adj. reserved, restrained

risièdere to reside, to dwell

riso m. laughter; rice

risòlvere to resolve (Group 10)

risòrgere to rise again (Group 10)

Risorgimento m. (Italian 19th century political movement)

risotto m. dish of rice

risparmiare to save

rispàrmio m. saving, thrift; *cassa di rispàrmio* f. savings-bank

rispettare to respect

rispetto m. respect; *rispetto a* in comparison with

rispettoso adj. respectful

rispòndere to answer (Group 11)

risposta f. answer, reply

rissa f. brawl

ristagno m. stagnation

ristampa f. reprint

ristorante m. restaurant

ristoro m. comfort, relief, solace

risultare to result

risultato m. result, outcome

ritardare to delay

ritardo m. delay; *in ritardo* late

ritenere to retain; to believe (Group 6)

ritirare to withdraw

ritmo m. rhythm

ritornare to return

ritorno m. return

ritratto m. portrait

ritroso, a ritroso backwards

riunione f. meeting

riuscire to succeed (+ *a*) (Group 24)

riuscita f. success, result

riva f. shore

rivedere to check (Group 32)

rivelare to reveal

rivenditore m. shopkeeper; second-hand dealer

rivestimento m. coating, lining

rivestire di to coat with; to line

rivòlgersi (a) to turn, to address oneself (to) (Group 10)

rivolta f. rebellion

rivoluzionàrio adj. revolutionary; m. revolutionary

roba f. stuff; goods

robusto adj. sturdy

ròccia f. rock

ròdere to gnaw, to nibble (Group 39)

romànico adj. Romanesque

romanticismo m. romanticism

romàntico adj. romantic

romanza f. aria

romanzo m. novel

ròmpere to break (Group 33)

ròndine f. swallow

rosa f. rose; adj. pink

ròseo adj. rosy, ruby

roso adj. corroded, eaten up

rosso adj. red

rosticceria f. fried fish shop & restaurant

rotàia f. rail

ròtolo m. roll

rotondo adj. round

rotta f. ship's or plane's course

rottura f. breakage, breach

rovesciare to upset, to overturn
rovesciarsi to capsize
rovina f. collapse, fall, ruin
rozzo adj. rough, coarse
rubare to steal
rubinetto m. tap
rubino m. ruby
rude adj. rude, impolite, rough
ruga f. wrinkle
rŭggine f. rust
rugiada f. dew
rullo m. roller, roll
rumore m. noise
rumoroso adj. noisy
ruolo m. list, roll; *di ruolo* with tenure, permanent
ruota f. wheel
ruotare to rotate
ruspa f. scraper; bulldozer
ruttare to belch
rŭvido adj. rough, bristly
ruzzolare to tumble

săbato m. Saturday
săbbia f. sand
sacco m. sack, bag; a lot, a long time
sacrifĭcio m. sacrifice
săggio adj. wise
sala f. hall, room
salărio m. wages, pay
salato adj. salty; costly
sale m. salt
sălice m. willow
salire to climb, to go up (Group 7)
salita f. climb, ascent

salsa f. sauce
salsĭccia f. sausage
saltare to jump, to hop, to leap
salutare to greet; to salute; to say hello; to say good-bye
salute f. health; cheers!
saluto m. greeting, salutation
salvagente m. life-belt
salvare to save, to salvage
salvatăggio m. rescue
salvo adj. safe, secure
săndalo m. sandal
săngue m. blood
sanitărio adj. health, medical
sano adj. healthy
santità f. holiness; sanctity
santo adj. saint, holy
sapere to know, to know how to, to be aware (Group 26)
sapone m. soap
saponetta f. cake of soap
sapore m. taste, flavour
saporito adj. savoury
saracinesca f. rolling shutter
Sardegna f. Sardinia
sarto m. tailor
sarta f. dressmaker
sasso m. stone
sătira f. satire
sbagliare to make a mistake
sbagliarsi to be mistaken
sbăglio m. mistake
sbarcare to disembark
sbarco m. landing
sbăttere to slam
sbiadito adj. faded
sbŏrnia f. booze
sbrigarsi to hurry

sbucare to spring out
scacchi m. pl. chess
scadenza f. maturity
scadere to fall due
scaffale m. shelf
scala f. stairs, ladder
scaldare to warm
scalino m. step, stair
scalo m. port of call, intermediate stop
scalzo adj. barefoot
scàmbio m. exchange, barter
scappare to escape, to flee
scaricare to unload
scarpa f. shoe
scarpone m. boot
scarso adj. scarce
scàtola f. box
scavo m. excavation, dig
scègliere to choose (Group 8)
scelta f. choice
scena f. scene, stage
scèndere to descend (Group 39)
scheda f. card; *scheda perforata* punch card
schèdario m. filing-cabinet
schermo m. screen
scherzare to joke, to jest
scherzo to joke
schiacciare to crush
schiaffo m. slap
schiarirsi to become clean
schiavo m. slave
schiena f. back
schifoso adj. filthy, disgusting
schiuma f. foam
sci m. ski; skiing
sciare to ski

scienza f. science
scienziato m. scientist
scintilla f. spark
sciocco adj. silly
sciògliere to loosen (Group 8)
sciòpero m. strike; *in sciòpero* on strike
scippo m. bag-snatching
scivolare to slide, to skid, to slip
scocciare to annoy
scodella f. bowl
scòglio m. cliff
scolaro m. school-boy
scolàstico adj. scholastic, school
scollato adj. low-necked
scolpire to engrave
scommèttere to bet (Group 35)
scomparire to disappear (Group 20)
scomparsa f. disappearance
scompartimento m. train compartment
scomporre to decompose (Group 11)
sconfiggere to defeat (Group 13)
sconforto m. dejection
sconsigliare di to dissuade from
scontare to sell with a discount
sconto m. discount
scontrino m. ticket, tally
scontro m. crash
sconvòlgere to upset (Group 10)

scopa f. besom, broom
scoperto adj. disclosed, uncovered
scopo m. aim
scoppiare to explode, to burst (out)
scòrgere to notice (Group 10)
scorretto adj. incorrect
scorrèvole adj. smooth
scorso adj. past, last, previous
scorza f. peel, skin, rind
scottarsi to scald oneself
Scòzia f. Scotland
scozzese adj. Scottish; m. & f. Scot
scrìvere to write (Group 13)
scrittura f. writing
scrupolosamente scrupulously
scuola f. school
scuòtere to shake
scuro adj. dark
scusare, scusarsi to excuse
se if
sè oneself
sebbene although
seccare to annoy
seccatura f. nuisance
secco adj. dry
sècolo m. century
sede f. seat, headquarters
sedersi to sit (Group 27)
sedile m. seat
sedurre to seduce (Group 16)
seduta f. sitting, session
seduto adj. sitting, seated
sega f. saw
sègala f. rye
segno m. sign

segregazione f. segregation
segreto m. secret
seguire to follow
selezione f. selection
selva f. wood, forest
selvàggio adj. wild
semàforo m. traffic-lights
sembrare to seem
seme m. seed
seminare to seed, to sow
seminterrato m. basement
sèmplice adj. simple
sempre always; *per sempre* forever
seno m. bosom
sensato adj. sensible
sensìbile adj. sensitive
senso m. sense; meaning
sentenza f. sentence
sentiero m. path
sentire to feel, to hear, to smell, to taste
sentire la mancanza di to miss
senza without
senzatetto m. & f. homeless person
separare to separate
separatamente separately
seppellire to bury (Group 3)
sera or *serata* f. evening
sereno adj. clear
sèrie f. series
sèrio adj. serious, earnest
serratura f. lock
servire to serve, to be of use
servìzio m. service
servosterzo m. power-steering
sessantina f. about sixty
sesso m. sex

seta f. silk
sete f. thirst
setta f. sect
settantina f. about seventy
settecento m. eighteenth
  century
settembre m. September
settentrione m. north
settentrionale adj. northern
settimana f. week
settimanale m. weekly
  magazine
severo adj. strict
sezione f. section
sfacciato adj. cheeky
sfavorèvole adj. unfavourable
sfera f. sphere
sfida f. challenge
sfidùcia f. mistrust, distrust
sfilata f. parade
sfiorare to graze, to touch
  lightly
sfortuna f. bad luck
sforzarsi to endeavour
sfratto m. eviction
sfruttare to exploit
sfuggire to escape
sgelo m. thaw
sgobbare to swot
sgomb(e)rare to clear, to
  empty out
sgradito adj. unwelcome
sgridare to scold
sguardo m. look, glance
shampoo (pron. /shumpaw/)
  m. shampoo
si oneself, himself, herself,
  itself, themselves; each
  other, one another; one,

you, people; B (music)
sì yes; so (poetic)
sia . . . sia both , . . and
siccità f. drought
Sicìlia f. Sicily
sicurezza f. safety, security
sicuro adj. sure, certain;
  secure
sidro m. cider
sigaretta f. cigarette
sìgaro m. cigar
sigla f. initials
significato m. meaning
signora f. lady, madam, Mrs
signore m. gentleman, sir, Mr
signorina f. young or
  unmarried lady, Miss
silènzio m. silence
sìllaba f. syllable
simbòlico adj. symbolic
sìmbolo m. symbol
sìmile adj. similar, alike
simpatia f. liking, inclination
simpàtico adj. genial, nice,
  pleasant to talk to, to stay
  with, to look at
sincero adj. sincere
sindacalista m. & f. trade-
  unionist
sindacato m. trade union
sìndaco m. mayor; auditor
sinfonia f. symphony
sìngolo adj. single
sinistra f. left
sìntomo m. symptom
sipàrio m. drop-curtain
siringa f. syringe
sistema m. system;
  establishment

sistemarsi to settle down
sistemazione f. arrangement
situazione f. situation, plight
sleale adj. unfair
slitta f. sledge, sleigh, sled
slittare to slide, to skid
smarrire to lose (Group 3)
smĕttere to cease, to stop
  (Group 35)
smĕtterla to stop it
smŏrfia f. grimace
sobborgo m. suburb
soccorso m. aid;
  pronto soccorso first aid
società f. society
sŏcio m. member
soddisfacente adj. satisfactory
soddisfare to satisfy (Group
  5)
soddisfazione f. satisfaction
sodo adj. hard, solid, compact;
  uovo sodo m. hard-boiled
  egg
soffiare to blow
sŏffice adj. soft, gentle
soffitto m. ceiling
soffocare to choke, to
  suffocate
soffrire to suffer (Group 20)
soggetto m. subject
soggiornare to stay for a time
sŏgliola f. sole
sognare to dream (+ *di*)
sogno m. dream
soldato m. soldier
soldo m. coin, money, penny
sole m. sun
sŏlito adj. usual;
  di sŏlito usually

solo adj. only, alone
soltanto only
sonetto m. sonnet
sonno m. sleep
sopportare to bear
sopra on, upon
sopraccĭglio m. brow
soprano f. soprano
soprattutto above all
sopravvĭvere to survive
  (Group 38)
sordo adj. deaf
sorella f. sister
sorgente f. source
sorpassare to overtake; to
  exceed
sorprĕndere to take by
  surprise (Group 39)
sorpresa f. surprise
sorrĭdere to smile (Group 39)
sorriso m. smile
sorso m. sip, drop
sorta f. sort, kind
sosta f. pause
sostanza f. substance
sostenere to support (Group 6)
sostituire to replace (Group 3)
sostituto m. replacement
sotterrăneo adj. underground
sottile adj. thin; subtle
sotto under
sottolineare to underline
sottomĕttere to subdue
  (Group 35)
sottoporre to submit (Group 11)
sottosegretărio m. Minister of
  State, Undersecretary
sottrarre to subtract (Group 12)
sovrano m. sovereign

sovrapporre to place upon (Group 11)

spaccato adj. split; sharp

spaghetti m. pl. spaghetti

spago m. string

spalla. f. shoulder

spalliera f. back of chair

sparare to shoot

spàrgere to spread (Group 10)

sparire to disappear (Group 3)

spassàrsela to have a good time

spasso, *andare a spasso* to go for a stroll

spaventare to frighten

spavento m. scare, fright

spazzare to sweep

spècchio m. mirror

specialista m. & f. (medical) consultant

specialmente specially, especially

spedire to send

spègnere to extinguish (Group 10)

spèndere to spend (Group 39)

speranza f. hope

sperare to hope

spesa f. expense; shopping

spesso often; adj. thick

Spettàbile adj. Messrs, Dear (Sirs)

spettàcolo m. show

spettare to be someone's duty, turn, decision

spia m. & f. spy; f. red light

spiacente adj. sorry

spiacèvole adj. unpleasant

spìcchio m. orange segment, garlic clove

spìccioli m. pl. small money

spiegare to explain

spietato adj. cruel, pitiless

spillo m. pin

spìngere to push (Group 10)

spintone m. elbow-pushing

spìrito m. spirit, soul; wit

spiòvere to stop raining (Group 22)

spiritoso adj. witty

spogliarsi to undress

sporco adj. dirty

spòrgere to hold out (Group 10)

sport m. sport, game

sportello m. counter, window

sposarsi to get married

sposo m. bridegroom

spostare to shift

sprecare to waste

spugna f. sponge

sputare to spit

squadra f. team; square (drawing)

squillare to ring out

stàbile adj. stable, steady, firm; m. block of flats

staccare to detach; to draw (a cheque)

stagione f. season

stagno m. tin; pond; adj. tight

stampa f. print

stampo m. mould

stanchezza f. tiredness

stanco adj. tired

stanza f. room

stare to stay, to stand (Group 21)

starnutire to sneeze (Group 3)

stato m. state

stàtua f. statue

statura f. stature, (person's) height

statuto m. statute

stazione f. station;
stazione invernale f. skiing resort

stella f. star

stellato adj. starry

stèndere to stretch out (Group 39)

stenodattilògrafa f. shorthand-typist

stenògrafa f. shorthand-writer

stenografia f. shorthand

sterlina f. pound sterling

stesso adj. same, -self

stile m. style

stivale m. boot

stoffa f. cloth

stòmaco m. stomach

stòria f. history; nonsense

stòrico adj. historical; m. historian

storto adj. crooked

stovìglie f. pl. crockery, dishes

stràccio m. rag

strada f. road, route, way, street

stradale adj. road;
polizia stradale f. highway police

strage f. massacre, slaughter

straniero m. foreigner; adj. foreign

strano adj. strange

straordinàrio adj. extraordinary

strappare to wrench, to wring

stretto adj. narrow; m. straits

strìngere to hold tight (Group 10)

strìscia stripe, slip

strumento m. instrument, tool

struttura f. structure

studente m. student

studentessa f. female student

studiare to study

stupendo adj. splendid

stùpido adj. stupid

su on, upon

subire to undergo (Group 3)

sùbito at once, immediately, soon

succèdere to happen; to succeed (Group 34)

successivo adj. subsequent

successo m. success

succo m. juice

sud m. south

sudare to perspire, to sweat

sudore m. perspiration, sweat

suffràgio m. suffrage

suggerimento m. suggestion

suggerire to suggest (Group 3)

sugo m. juice, sauce

suicìdio m. suicide

suo adj. his, her, hers, your, yours

suonare to play; to sound; to ring

super super; f. high-octane petrol

superare to exceed

superficie f. surface

suppergiù about, approximately

supplemento m. supplement, surcharge

supporre to suppose (Group 11)

susina f. plum

sussidio m. subsidy

sussurrare to whisper

svantaggio m. disadvantage

sveglia f. alarm-clock; early call

svegliarsi to wake up

svendita f. sale, selling off

svenire to faint (Group 6)

svignarsela to steal away

sviluppo m. development

Svizzera f. Switzerland

svizzero adj. Swiss

svolgere to develop; to carry out (Group 10)

tabaccaio m. tobacconist

tabaccheria f. tobacconist's shop

tabacco m. tobacco

tabella f. chart, list, table

tabellone m. notice-board

tabù m. taboo

tacchino m. turkey

tacco m. heel

tacere to be silent (Group 4)

tacitare to silence

taglia f. size (of clothing)

tagliare to cut

taglio m. cut

tailleur m. tailored suit

tale adj. such; certain; m. a fellow; someone

talento m. talent, skill

talmente to such an extent

talora at times

taluno m. some; somebody

talvolta sometimes

Tamigi m. Thames

tamponamento m. hit from the back

tamponare to hit a car from the back

tampone m. pad; *tampone assorbente* m. sanitary pad

tana f. den

tanto adj. so much

tappa f. halt, stop, stage

tappare to block up

tapparella f. rolling window shutter

tappeto m. carpet

tappezzare to upholster

tappezzeria f. upholstery

tappezziere m. upholsterer

tappo m. bung, stopper, plug; podgy person

tara f. tare

tardare to be late

tardi late; *fare tardi* to be late

targa f. plate; number-plate

targare to affix a number-plate

tariffa f. price

tartufo m. truffle

tasca f. pocket

tascabile adj. and m. pocket

tassa f. tax

tassare to tax

tasso m. rate;
  tasso d'interesse rate of
  interest
tastiera f. keyboard
tasto m. key (musical
  instrument)
tatto m. touch
tatuare to tattoo
tàvola f. table;
  tàvola calda f. self-service
  restaurant
tavolino m. bar table
tàvolo m. table
tazza f. cup
tazzina f. little cup
te you, to you
tè or *the* m. tea
teatrale adj. theatrical,
  theatre
teatro m. theatre
tècnica f. technique; technics;
  technology
tècnico adj. technical; m.
  engineer, technician
tedesco adj. German
tegame m. saucepan
tègola f. tile
teiera f. tea-pot
tela f. cloth
telàio m. loom
telecàmera f. television
  camera
teleferica f. cableway
telefonare to telephone
telefonata f. telephone call
telefonista m. & f. operator;
  telephonist
telèfono m. telephone
telegramma m. telegram

teleobiettivo m. telephoto lens
teleromanzo m. telecast novel
telescrivente f. teleprinter
televisione f. television
televisivo adj. television
televisore m. television set
tema m. theme; composition
temperatura f. temperature
tempesta f. tempest
tempestoso adj. stormy
tèmpia f. temple (head)
tempo m. time; weather
temporale m. thunder-storm
temporalesco adj. stormy,
  thundery
temporàneo adj. temporary
tenàglia f. pincers, tongs
tenda f. tent; curtain
tendenza f. tendency;
  inclindation
tèndere to stretch out (Group
  39); to tend, to be inclined
tendina f. curtain
tenere to hold (Group 6)
tènero adj. tender
tenore m. tenor
tentare to try
tenuto adj. bound, obliged
teoria f. theory
teòrico adj. theoretic
teppista m. & f. hooligan
tergicristallo m. wind-screen
  wiper
terminare to end
termòmetro m. thermometer
terra f. earth, land;
  a terra flat
terraferma f. mainland
terrazza f. terrace, balcony

terremoto m. earthquake

terreno m. ground

terrìbile adj. terrible

terriero adj. landed

terrificante adj. terrifying

territoriale adj. territorial

territòrio m. territory

terrore m. terror

terrorista m. & f. terrorişt

terzina f. three-line stanza

tèschio m. skull

tesi f. thesis

tesoro m. treasure; honey

tèssile adj. textile

tessuto m. fabric, material

testa f. head

testimònio or *testimone* m. testimony, witness

testo m. text

testone m. blockhead

tetto m. roof

tièpido adj. lukewarm

tifo, m. *fare il tifo per* to be a fan of

tifoso m. fan

tìglio m. lime-tree

tigre f. tiger

timbro m. stamp

tìmido adj. shy

timone m. rudder

timore m. fear

tìngere to dye (Group 10)

tinta f. dye

tintarella f. suntan

tìpico adj. typical

tipo m. type; chap, fellow, bloke, guy

tipografia f. printing-house

tirare to pull

tìtolo m. title; capacity

tìzio m. chap, fellow, bloke

toast m. toasted slices of bread and ham

toccare to touch; to be someone's turn

tògliere to remove (Group 8)

tògliersi to take off

tollerare to tolerate

tomba f. tomb

tondo adj. round

tonnellata f. metric ton

tono m. tone

topo m. mouse

tornare to come back

toro m. bull

torre f. tower

torrente m. stream, torrent

torta f. cake, tart

torto m. wrong; *avere torto* to be wrong

Toscana f. Tuscany

toscano adj. Tuscan

tosse f. cough

tossire to cough (Group 3)

tostato adj. toasted

totocàlcio m. football pools

tovàglia f. table-cloth

tradimento m. treason

tradire to betray

traditore m. traitor

tradizionale adj. traditional

tradurre to translate (Group 16)

traduttore m. translator

traduzione f. translation

tràffico m. traffic

traforo m. tunnel

tragèdia f. tragedy

traghettare to ferry
traghetto m. ferry
tràgico adj. tragical
tram m. tramway
tramezzino m. sandwich
tramontare to set
tramonto m. sunset
tranquillo adj. quiet
trànsito m. transit
trapassato m. pluperfect
trarre to pull, to draw (Group 12)
trascòrrere to pass, to spend (Group 7)
trascurare to neglect
trasferimento m. transfer
trasferire to transfer (Group 3)
trasmèttere to transmit; to broadcast; to pass down on (Group 35)
trasportare to carry
trasporto m. transport
trattare to treat; to negotiate; to deal
trattarsi di to be a question of
trattativa f. negotiation
trattato m. treatise
trattenere to restrain, to hold, to check (Group 6)
trattenersi to stay, to stop
trattino m. dash, hyphen
tratto m. stretch;
   ad un tratto suddenly
trattore m. tractor
trattoria f. family restaurant
tràuma m. trauma, shock
tredicèsima f. Christmas

bonus, thirteenth monthly salary, pay
tremante adj. trembling, shivering
tremare to tremble, to shiver
treno m. train
trentina f. about thirty
tribunale m. court; tribunal
trimestrale adj. quarterly
trimestre m. term
Trinità f. Trinity
trionfare to triumph
triplo adj. triple, treble
triste adj. sad
tromba f. trumpet
troppo adj. too much
trovare to find; to see
truccarsi to make up
trucco m. trick; make up
truffa f. fraud, swindle
truffatore m. swindler
tu you
tubo m. pipe
tuffarsi to dive
tuffo m. dive
tumultuoso adj. tumultuous
tuo adj. your, yours
tuonare to thunder
tuono m. thunder
turismo m. tourism
turista m. & f. tourist
turno m. turn, shift
tuttavia but, nevertheless
tutto adj. all, whole
tuttora still

ubbidiente adj. obedient
ubriacarsi to get drunk
ubriachezza f. drunkenness

ubriaco adj. drunken
ubriacone m. drunkard
uccello m. bird
uccìdere to kill (Group 39)
uccisione f. killing
uccisore m. killer
udire to hear (Group 25)
udito m. hearing
ufficiale m. officer; adj.
  official
ufficio m. office
uguaglianza f. equality
uguale adj. equal
ùltimo adj. last, latest
ultra extremely, ultra
umano adj. human; humane
umidità f. dampness;
  moisture; humidity
ùmido adj. damp, moist,
  humid
ùmile adj. humble
umiliante adj. humiliating
umorismo m. humour
umorìstico adj. humorous,
  funny
ùnico adj. only; unique
unificare to unify
uniforme adj. uniform; f.
  uniform
unire to unite (Group 3)
unità f. unity
università f. university
universitàrio adj. university;
  m. university student
universo m. universe
uomo m., pl. *uòmini*, man
uovo m., pl. *uova* f., egg;
  uovo à la coq poached
  egg;

uovo all'òcchio di bue fried
  egg;
uovo strapazzato scrambled
  egg;
uovo in camìcia boiled
  egg
urlare to shout, to scream, to
  howl
urlo shout, scream, howl
urtare to bump into, to hit
urto m. bump, collision
usanza f. custom
usare to use, to employ, to
  handle
usato adj. used, second-hand
uscire to go out (Group 24)
uscita f. exit, way out;
  lìbera uscita (soldiers) off
  duty
usignolo m. nightingale
uso m. use
usura f. wear and tear; usury
utensile m. tool
utente m. user, consumer

vacante adj. vacant
vacanza f. holiday;
  in vacanza on holiday
vagabondo m. wanderer
vàglia m. money-order
vago adj. vague
vagone m. waggon, railway-
  car
valdese adj. Waldensian
valere to be worth
vàlico m. frontier crossing
vàlido adj. valid
valìgia f. suitcase
valle f. valley;

Valle d'Aosta Aosta Valley
valore m. value; valour
valoroso adj. valiant, brave
valuta f. currency
valutare to value, to estimate
valutàrio adj. monetary
vàlvola f. valve
vanga f. spade
Vangelo m. Gospel
vantàggio m. advantage
vantaggioso adj.
   advantageous
vantarsi (di) to boast
variàbile adj. variable
varietà f. variety
vario adj. various; varied
vasca f. basin, bath-tub
vaso m. vase
vastità f. vastness
vasto adj. vast
ve you, to you; there
vecchiàia f. old age
vècchio adj. old
vedere to see (Group 32)
vèdova f. widow
vèdovo m. widower
veduta f. view
veìcolo m. vehicle
vela f. sail
velare to veil
veleno m. venom, poison
velina f. carbon-copy
velluto m. velvet
velo m. veil
veloce adj. fast, quick, speedy
velocità f. speed
vena f. vein
vendèmmia f. vintage, grape-
   harvest

vèndere to sell
vendetta f. revenge
vèndita f. sale
venditore m. seller
venerdì m. Friday
Vènere f. Venus
venire to come; to cost
   (Group 6)
ventàglio m. fan
ventènnio m. twenty-year
   period; the Fascist regime
ventilatore m. ventilator, fan
ventina f. about twenty
vento m. wind
ventoso adj. windy
ventre m. stomach, belly
venturo adj. next
venuta f. coming
verace adj. truthful
verbale adj. verbal; m.
   minutes
verbo m. verb
verde adj. green
verdetto m. verdict
verdura f. greens, vegetables
vergogna f. shame;
   avere vergogna to be
   ashamed
vergognarsi to be ashamed
verìfica f. check
verità f. truth
vernice f. paint, varnish
verniciare to paint, to polish
vero adj. true
versare to pour out; to spill
versione f. version
verso m. verse, line of verse
vertenza f. controversy,
   dispute;

vertenza sindacale industrial dispute

vèrtice m. top, summit

vertìgine f. dizziness

verso towards

vèscovo m. bishop

vestiàrio m. clothing

vestirsi to dress oneself, to get dressed

vestito m. dress

vetrina f. shop window

vetro m. glass

vetta f. top, peak, summit

vi you, to you; there, here

via f. street; away, off; via; way

viaggiare to travel

viàggio m. journey, trip, voyage

viale m. avenue

vialetto m. path

viavai m. coming-and-going

vibrare to vibrate

vicedirettore m. deputy manager

viceversa vice versa

vicinanza f. closeness, proximity

vìcolo m. alley, lane

vietato adj. forbidden

vigente adj. in force

vigilare to look after; to invigilate

vìgile del fuoco m. fireman

vìgile urbano m. town policeman; traffic warden

vigìlia f. eve

vigliacco adj. coward

vigneto m. vineyard

vignetta f. vignette, illustration

villa f. villa

villàggio m. village

villano adj. rude, rough

villeggiatura f. holiday

vìncere to win (Group 17)

vìncita f. win, winnings

vincitore m. winner

vincolato adj. tied

vino m. wine

viola violet; f. violet

violare to violate

violentare to rape, to outrage

violenza f. violence

violinista m. & f. violinist

violino m. violin

vìpera f. viper

Virgìlio m. Virgil

vìrgola f. comma; *punto e vìrgola* semi-colon

virtù f. virtue

visìbile adj. visible

vìsita f. visit; medical examination

visitare to visit

visitatore m. visitor, caller

visivo adj. visual

viso m. face

visone m. mink

vista f. sight; view

vistare to visa

visto m. visa

vita f. life; waist

vite f. screw; vine

vitello m. calf; veal

viticoltore m. vine-grower

vìttima f. victim

vitto m. food

vittoria f. victory
vittorioso adj. victorious
viva long live
vivace adj. lively
vivente adj. living
vivere to live (Group 13)
vivo adj. living, alive;
 dal vivo live
viziare to spoil
vizio m. vice
vizioso adj. vicious,
 debauched
vocabolàrio m. vocabulary
vocàbolo m. word, item in
 the vocabulary
vocazione f. vocation
voce f. voice; item
vòglia f. wish, desire,
 willingness
voi you
volante adj. flying; m.
 steering-wheel
volare to fly
volentieri willingly, with
 pleasure, gladly
volere to want (Group 30);
 volere bene to be fond of
volerci to take (time), to
 require
volgare adj. vulgar
volo m. flight
volontà f. will
volontàrio adj. voluntary
volpe f. fox
volta f. time; turn; vault

voltarsi to turn round, over
volume m. volume
vostro adj. your, yours
votare to vote
voto m. vote
vulcano m. volcano
vuotare to empty
vuoto adj. empty

w (read *viva*) long live! Hail!

zaino m. rucksack
zerbino m. mat, door-mat
zero m. zero, nought, zero
 degree centigrade
zia f. aunt
zio m. uncle
zitto adj. silent, muted;
 stare zitto to be silent
zolfo m. sulphur
zona f. area, district, quarter,
 zone
zoo or *giardino zoològico* m.
 zoo
zoppo adj. lame
zucca f. pumpkin; blockhead
zuccherato adj. sugared
zuccheriera f. sugar-basin
zucchero m. sugar
zucchina f. or *zucchino* m.
 marrow, courgette
zuppa f. soup
zuppa inglese f. trifle
zuppiera f. soup tureen